Oilpatch Jeopardy:

Torn

In The

USA

EXPLOITS OF A CANADIAN PETROLEUM ENGINEER
IN THE UNITED STATES OIL AND GAS INDUSTRY

NEIL VERNON LEESON, P. ENG.

RIP BOOKS

RESULTS In Publishing
Calgary, Alberta, Canada

To: Harvey
The "other" "oilpatch"!
Neil
Calgary
April 2001

Canadian Cataloguing in Publication Data
Lesson, Neil Vernon, 1949-
   Oilpatch jeopardy

Includes bibliographical references and index.
ISBN 0-9681117-0-X

1. Leeson, Neil Vernon, 1949- 2. Petroleum engineers--
Canada--Biography. 3. Canadians--United States--Biography.
4. Petroleum industry and trade--United States. 5. Petroleum
engineering--United States. I. Title.
HD9570.L43A3 1996   338.7'6223382'092   C96-910558-4

Published by: RIP BOOKS
                 Results In Publishing
                 P.O. Box 75028
                 Westhills R.P.O.
                 Calgary, Alberta, Canada
                 T3H 3M1

First Printing 1997

Author's Portrait by: Photo Visions by Colin, Calgary

Cover Design by: Doyle R. Buehler -
                        Aces High Graphics & Design, Calgary

Book Design by: Sage Creek Books, Calgary

Printed and Bound in Canada by: Friesens Corporation,
Altona, Manitoba, Canada

TABLE OF CONTENTS

ABOUT THE AUTHOR

Neil Leeson is a Petroleum Engineer and a member of the Association of Professional Engineers, Geologists and Geophysicists of Alberta (APEGGA) and the Society of Petroleum Engineers (SPE). Neil's career in Petroleum Engineering began in 1976. His credentials include reservoir modelling, drilling/production operations, reserves determination, gas marketing, acquisition and disposition evaluation. Besides Western Canada and the Canadian Arctic, his experience comprises lengthy assignments in thirteen U.S. states.

The author's hobbies of aviation and military history have remained close to his heart. He has been a licensed pilot since 1967 and maintains interest through regular air show attendance and recreational flying. He experimented with skydiving while an Aeronautical Engineering student at the Southern Alberta Institute of Technology in the late 1960s. During the 1970s Neil was an aircraft owner/operator, a Lieutenant in the Canadian Armed Forces Air Reserves, and an Air Cadet Instructor. In hopes of passing on this tradition, his son is named after two valued friends who are brothers, Captains with competing Western Canadian-based airlines, and cousins to one of Canada's astronauts.

The author plans to continue a writing career with an account of consulting mayhem in the Canadian oilpatch. TORN IN THE USA sequels are also a possibility.

Neil is married and resides in Calgary. He consults to the oil industry, primarily in asset evaluation and acquisition.

PREFACE

You will find this book unique; otherwise return it for a full refund or a free copy of my sequel, no questions asked.

My goal was to make most of the text entertaining and appealing to the general public as well as the Oil Industry. Harmonizing technical and non-fiction documentary was challenging, so a detailed Glossary will assist you through any unfamiliar terms.

The objectives were to share my most memorable adventures in the United States oil and gas industry and to avoid litigation. As a Canadian Petroleum Engineer, fifteen years were spent *exclusively* assigned to, or participating in, U.S. drilling and production operations. Like most of my colleagues, my employers were Canadian and my home base was Calgary. There the similarities ended abruptly.

Let there be no mistake, this was a story of pain; but for me to suffer is for you to enjoy. You will be entertained with stories that you may not want to believe. To assure you that it all happened, great pains have been taken to corroborate my exploits with associate or third party accounts (quotations in *reduced italics* and spaced apart from main text). A background as extensive as mine obviously involved a great many colleagues. Some have chosen to decline recognition to protect privacy and avoid association. I have no problem relating to this decision, having threatened to write this book many times over the past decade but reneging for the same reasons. In 1994, however, my final adventure stripped away my remaining faith and hope, opening the door to disclosure without fear.

Out of the ashes surfaced a fire of pleasure in my life. To this day it remains a source of great satisfaction, a treasure almost overlooked. Very early into my involvement south of the border, a coincidence occurred that lacked significance. Nearly a decade later a related coincidence granted me a second chance of pursuit. It will remain a priority interest to my dying day. Rather than disclose it, you, the readers, are encouraged to solve this puzzle by reading the book. The message was not obvious to me at first either. Little clues in life often solve the biggest mysteries.

Not everyone gets a second chance at discovery. If not for my prolonged exposure to oil and gas operations in the United States, my second coincidence would have eluded me. There might still be bitterness for all my frustration and inability to control events. The pattern of disaster became so predictable, it was like watching crime movie reruns. When you are always playing the victim, it is time to re-examine the script.

The final years were more frightening because they were avoidable. Withdrawal was an option in 1989 and again in 1992 when fate provided escapes. In my mind, however, this second focus in the later years contributed greatly to the understanding and healing process. So as not to distract your attention from the prime focus - U.S. oil and gas operations through the eyes of a Canadian Petroleum Engineer - we will bury this aspect in the book for your enjoyment too. Now on with the main show.

While growing up in Nova Scotia in the 1960's, television was still a fairly new fad. It greatly contributed to my perception of the world beyond my limited territory. In many ways it shaped my aspirations and ambitions. Other than Hockey Night in Canada, the content was almost entirely American.

One of my favourite shows featured "normal situation" life in New York City and was called THE NAKED CITY. Possibly it was before colour television was popular. The closing monologue was " There are a million stories in the Naked City. This has been one of them." At the time, as a teenager, I lived only hours by air from New York. Yet the lives and characters portrayed were so fascinating, compared to my serene and humble surroundings, it could have been on another planet.

My career predictions did not anticipate future events that would cast me in roles assumed to be showbiz fabrications. My first hand exploits reminded me of Dynasty and Dallas scripts, modern day oilpatch clones of my favourite 1960's show.

As you may recall, Middle East conflicts and politics triggered several North American oil price shocks in the 1970s. Recognizing a myriad of opportunity, in 1976 my career intentions in the aerospace industry were left behind. The oil industry was beginning to boom and hiring was at a level we only dream of today. My opportunities were researched carefully and a position with one of Canada's large multi-national oil companies was successfully pursued. Its strength and appeal was the calibre and quantity of training it offered. Events proved it was a wise and profitable choice.

After five years of reservoir engineering and gas contracting experience, a new challenge in field operations was accepted. 'Why' was not so much an issue with me as 'Where'. As of October 1980, the United States theatre of operations was my new battleground.

Many of my associates viewed my choice with jealousy or scepticism. It may have been wishful thinking, but it seemed tailored for me - action aplenty and success would surely follow.

Western Canada, the Mackenzie Delta, and the Canadian Arctic had kept most Canadian energy companies too busy to entertain "foreign" fields of battle.

Politics changed all that. The National Energy Program was introduced by the Trudeau Liberal Government in the fall of 1980. New discriminating energy taxes and regulations penalized the oil industry while exempting coal, hydroelectric, and nuclear power. A Windfall Profits Tax had the effect of standing previously successful management teams in front of shareholders' firing squads. To survive for another day, a herd of Canadian oil firms elected to vote with their feet and escape to friendlier territory. The most logical and convenient choice was the United States. As this book will portray, all too frequently this exodus transpired without adequate planning or strategy. Unfortunately all would pay a price. For a majority, it was a price too high.

If you have ever wondered what distinguishes Canada from the United States, this book will solve the puzzle. Let me emphasize the comparison is oil industry to oil industry, not individual to individual. My network of friends, family, and associates in the United States is extensive and no one is considered expendable. I will be the last person to confuse the attitude of the United States oil industry, whether accidental or deliberate, with the attitude of the United States of America. This admission is backed up with a brief digression.

Since old enough to read, my admiration for American technology, particularly in aeronautics and space, has been real. It transferred me into an ardent student of American military history. So much so that I often daydreamed of participating in one of the celebrated quiz shows and my topic for the grand prize was U.S. military history.

Occasionally the presence of my American professional counterparts has been intimidating. As a Canadian Professional Engineer, however, countless stories evolved from my fifteen years of United States oil and gas joint venture exploits. The two adages painfully realized from exposure to this industry have been: (1) **expect the unexpected**; and (2) **verify, verify, and verify**.

To future Canadian investors and players in the U.S. oilpatch, the message is not to abandon your goals, it is to revisit your strategy. Spare no effort to understand "the script and the actors". If my work benefits one unsuspecting compatriot, tourist, or visitor, this book will be considered an accomplishment.

Now come join me. This book is for your reading entertainment.

Neil Vernon Leeson

9

ACKNOWLEDGEMENTS

The author extends his gratitude to:

Ed Beaman,
Bonnie Cooke,
Ray Hodgkinson,
Elaine Little, and
Nona Stitt

who read the manuscript of this book and offered many helpful suggestions. When approached for this assistance, their commitment was spontaneous and genuine. Such qualities define real friends and true friendships.

FOR:

my mother, Ada Catherine Leeson of Dartmouth, Nova Scotia.

While my life was spent fretting over recompletion results in Ohio and fuming over litigation tribulations in Texas or Utah, Mom's life was confined to a bedroom. During the fifteen years covered by my memoirs, she was totally bedridden and in great pain, suffering from arthritis. Thinking my career responsibilities were invaluable, I prided myself, with misguided candor, about keeping her informed with post cards and photos. After a March 1995 stroke left her blind, the concept of this book was borne. I longed to sit by her bedside, reading every page of my exploits, in hope that these revelations would render her last days more tolerable.

She passed away January 15, 1996 while this book was in progress.

Important - Disclaimer

EPISODE 1: BEFORE THE BEGINNING

I
(Heaven In Houston)

It all started for me on the third of July 1978. Unknowingly, I was about to enter a world of *subterfuge*. My perseverance to keep searching for ethics and values in people and circumstances, where few existed, led to the tearing apart of my moral beliefs and trust.

Like nineteen other Shell U.S. and Shell Canada technical representatives from various North American offices, Houston's Bellaire Research and Petroleum Training Centre was to be my home for the next nine weeks. In the first hour of classes several of the Instructors introduced themselves and the Phase One Reservoir Engineering curriculum. We all had been invited to this first of three advanced programs conducted each year in Houston for selected Shell employees. It was a privilege; this was my idea of Heaven and my excitement and enthusiasm was genuine.

The first morning recess was my opportunity to break the ice and meet my comrades, being one of two representatives from the Reservoir Business Group of Calgary, Alberta. The second was Geoff Freeman, a Mining Engineer and a fellow Maritimer. We had worked together for about a year.

Anxious to find out the identity and origin of my other classmates, the moment was seized to begin introducing myself. With Geoff by my side, liberty was taken to include him in my greeting. Being limited to a fifteen minute intermission demanded efficiency.

There was time to spare after skilfully manoeuvring through most of the class. Two distinguished, quiet individuals stood off to the side. "Hi, I'm Neil Leeson and this is Geoff Freeman and we're from Shell Canada, Calgary." Pride in representing our home base was difficult to conceal.

"Hi, I'm Dave Layton and this is Glynn Webb and we're from Shell Canada, Calgary!"

The hall was filled with laughter, including my own. What else could one do? The embarrassment could not have been greater.

We were aware that Calgary had planned to send two representatives from another Department. Neglecting to learn their identity and befriend them in advance had orchestrated an ice breaker fit for a Hollywood comedy movie. It was obvious then and there that this was going to be a great summer.

II
(Trust Prevails)

Early in 1978 my name was listed for Phase One. Being a Shell Canada employee for just over a year, past attendees had acquainted me with many of their adventuresome stories.

My understanding of Shell's objective was to achieve a high level of competence and confidence throughout their North American organization, utilizing specialized internal technical courses of nine, six and three weeks. For simplicity they were defined as Phase One, Two, and Three respectively. The theme was unique for each Phase. At a time when the oil industry was extremely aggressive and buoyant, assignment to Houston was a reward to loyal employees and a competitive stimulant for Shell.

Much of my contribution leading up to Houston involved modelling reserves and deliverability for one of Shell's new gas discoveries in the Alberta Foothills. When the Division Manager, Ken MacGregor, nominated me for Phase One, it was gratifying that my efforts and dedication were recognized. Leading up to departure, I was on cloud nine. The experience of spending nine weeks on course in Houston and establishing contacts throughout the Shell network was a dream come true. At the eleventh hour, a nightmare intervened.

Whether by accident or internal politics, my name was deleted from the Phase One list only weeks before the scheduled departure. It was fortunate that my supervisor provided leadership in the face of this adversity. Ken MacGregor came through for me and assured my attendance at Phase One in 1978. My intense curiosity with the American oil industry and this book would not have evolved otherwise.

Oakwood Gardens from author's apartment, summer 1978

III
(Differences Emerge)

Being single, Geoff and I were intent on getting the most out of our nine weeks. Shell provided each of us very comfortable accommodation at Oakwood Garden Apartments in West Houston. Just off Westheimer thoroughfare, Oakwood was an oasis. This huge complex consisted of three story, multiple unit, furnished rental suites. Features included outdoor tennis courts, swimming pools, and Jacuzzis. Indoor facilities were available when the weather failed to co-operate. Best of all, it was air conditioned.

A Canadian's first exposure to Houston in the summer was just as painful as an American's first exposure to Yellowknife in the winter. Conditions of 100 degrees Fahrenheit and 100% humidity were common this July and August. We got astute at running from air conditioned apartment to air conditioned car to air conditioned classroom. Geoff recalls how the locals mastered the environment.

"Nobody seemed to walk in Houston. To get across the street, say Westheimer, you used your car. After driving out of the lot, you made a right to go west to the next set of lights, made a U-turn, then drove east on Westheimer."

We Canadians were like fish out of water. Dave Layton had his own tactics for survival.

"The heat and humidity of Houston was something else. I learned very quickly that you had to run out and start your car, similar to what we did during our coldest part of winter, only to let the air conditioner bring the car down to a liveable tolerance. You had to cover the metal portions of the safety belts with towels to avoid branding yourself while buckling up. Our cars never saw less than the maximum cool and the highest fan setting. Our apartments were like tombs to the natives of Houston."

Being forewarned of abundant fast crawling beasts called cockroaches in this tropical climate, we arranged for third (and highest) floor apartments. It was assumed height would be an impediment. That was until the sliding door to the balcony was opened for the first time and huge tree branches were observed leaning against the railing. The enemy was encountered while arranging my belongings the first night. Lots of the enemy; cockroaches do climb trees! It was time to negotiate with Geoff.

"Neil wanted to trade apartments right away. I did not know about his roaches, but my place was too unique to give up.

First, my living room had a natural gas fireplace with a wall switch for lighting. Even though it was always too warm to use, it reminded me of Alberta and was always a good conversation topic when I had guests over.

Secondly, my bedroom had a huge king size bed . I had no intention giving up this luxury, having been exposed to a single bed or less throughout university. Since I hated doing laundry, I devised a routine. I slept on one side for four or five days, then moved to the other for the next four or five. So I only had to strip the sheets off for washing three times a month.

To discourage Neil, I told him my place was crawling with roaches too. Truth is, I rarely saw any, despite keeping my apartment at normal room temperatures."

My classmates will recall how Canadian ingenuity solved this dilemma. The air conditioner in my unit remained on maximum for the summer. The lowest thermostat setting registered in the 40s Fahrenheit. It was so cold one could hardly stand it. Sleeping required extra blankets. Guests rarely stayed more than a few minutes. Dave Layton shared a common bond with me on this score.

"Growing up in Calgary and southern Saskatchewan did not prepare me for ground floor apartment dwelling in Houston. We were appalled at the multitude, size and speed of the cockroach community with which we were expected to share accommodation. In came the fumigators to our rescue. Uh huh!!

Five days later we realized that this was a way of life we would have to adjust to or else, because they were not moving out.

Daily routine was waking up in the morning and slamming kitchen cupboard doors to knock the roaches out from behind. Then the streaming (not spraying) of a giant size bug spray can to knock off the not-so-little devils that had moved in overnight."

Once every two weeks the Oakwood management would fumigate. By determining the schedule for my unit, the air conditioner was left off that day. This manoeuvre solved two problems. First, the roaches were deceived into coming out of hiding by the instant warming and thus immediately overwhelmed by an evil smelling, but deadly effective, insect spray. Second, my action prevented the sprayers from entering a frigid apartment and assuming the air conditioner was being abused or in need of urgent repair.

It was a great accomplishment that few roaches were confronted *in my apartment*, with one big exception the final week, during my stay that summer. Phase One had a large contingent from Shell Oil's New Orleans office. Many friendships developed with my Louisiana counterparts but we remained a world apart on our views of sleeping with the enemy. Apparently roaches were as common and as numerous in New Orleans as wheat fields were in Western Canada. As the cold deterred visits to my place, the multitude of free ranging creatures in theirs affected me. It was the first of many obvious differences between the 'Canucks' and 'Yanks'.

Another was the priority we placed on comfort and privacy, no matter what the cost. We Canadians had our own apartments and rental cars. However, as many as four of our classmates would share the same apartment and car. Saving on per diem allowances was not a sacrifice we were prepared to make. Geoff and I had a motto. If we were here to work hard, then we were also here to play hard. Take Geoff's experiences with rental cars, for example.

"Shell insisted we use their approved rental agency and lease a vehicle within a defined value. The first car I was assigned was an Aspen. It looked cheap, sounded like a tin can, and was a pea green colour. Not a car for a cool dude. I had to get rid of it.

After numerous phone calls to the agency, and two interviews, I finally negotiated an exchange. My replacement was a yellow, two door Cordoba with a brown vinyl roof. It was a cool car and drove like a dream. Because it was quiet, smooth as silk, and had a great stereo, we preferred it for our weekend excursions."

IV
(Time For Play)

Weekends were treasures. Dave and Glynn had wives to answer to, so our escapades were not all that appealing to them. Shell Canada permitted married spouses one Houston visit during Phase One. Dave and Glynn exercised good judgement by not jeopardizing their reputation in advance of their family reunions.

"We didn't hang out with the wild crowd as Neil points out, either by good management or good fortune, having seen their condition in the Monday morning lectures. But we did mix it up on occasion at the Sea Party, etc."

One of the few times the Canucks all got together was a Saturday sailing excursion out of Galveston. Dave's hobby was sailing, so he made all the arrangements and did most of the crew chores.

"I set up an outing for about twelve other classmates and myself to charter a sailboat and head out into the briny off Galveston.

The crew arrived at nine and we had a chock-talk on the operation of the boat and how we were going to depart safely into the sea. We then raided a nearby hotel for about ten pounds of ice from the ice machines. We threw the ice in the cooler along with the pop and other libations that engineers are weaned on.

We departed the marina, entered the Galveston Channel and set sail. We had been off the dock no more than half an hour, with the sun nowhere near the yardarms yet, when the first crew member said, 'Anyone for a beer?' He went below and exclaimed, 'The beers are warm. Where is the ice?' I went below, only to discover it was like a sauna. The chipped ice had all melted and run out the cooler drain.

The temperature was over a hundred, the humidity just under and the water temperature in the low nineties. Welcome to summer sailing in Galveston. That is why there were so many boats for charter.

Perhaps it was the warm beer that made Neil sick with heat stroke. We cooled him with towels dipped in the tepid water from the channel.

Fifteen minutes into the channel in minimal chop we shook out the reef, hoisted the foresail and had a pleasant sail into the channel. I guess this was the start of my career in chartering."

Geoff and I carried out a 'must do' weekend list that was the envy of our classmates:

- New Orleans, featuring a football game at the Superdome, a night (and morning) partying in the French Quarter, and superb restaurant dining;
- Dallas, where we attended a four band outdoor concert extravaganza featuring Fleetwood Mac, Little River Band, Bob Welch, and the Steve Miller Band with 50000+ fans in the Cotton Bowl;
- Mexico's Nuevo Laredo, with a border stop in Harlingen, Texas to visit the headquarters of the Confederate Airforce;
- Galveston Beach *several times*, including the World War II battleship 'Texas' floating museum;
- Corpus Christi, where there were as many offshore oil production platforms as Canadian Navy ships docked in Halifax harbour;
- the nearby Johnson Space Centre, one of my most favourite venues then and now; and
- San Antonio, one of my favourite U.S. cities, with its city-centre sunken, abundantly tree lined, river walk sprinkled with trendy restaurants and coffee shops.

San Antonio river walk

Alamo, San Antonio, summer 1978

Corpus Christi offshore production platforms, summer 1978 (courtesy of D. Layton)

Author and Mississippi River at New Orleans, Sept 1978

Superdome at New Orleans from Geoff's car, Sept 1978

Our Phase One Course included a two day field trip to the Brazeau area of Texas. Not surprisingly, since Dave's extracurricular travel itinerary was less hectic than ours, his recollections were more vivid.

"One of the most memorable moments was our field trip to the Brazeau River. We got on a bus and headed off to the interior of Texas. Along the highway we saw signs in the desert saying watch out for flash floods. We were all too aware that when it rained in Houston, almost like clockwork around five in the afternoon, the huge drainage ditches that had a trickle of water in the bottom would rapidly fill and rush in torrents through these street-wide ditches in the city.

When we arrived at the river site, there was this little trickle which we forded probably half a dozen times. Our instructors pointed out huge dinosaur prints, the recent sediments and the layering, folding and other petrophysical stuff in the 105 degree heat. Then we came across a big fluff ball on the bank and I questioned what it was. The instructor said, 'Haven't you ever seen that before?'

He picked up a stick and knocked off the wall what appeared to be a shimmering giant eight inch dandelion that had gone to seed. It fell to the ground and immediately came to life. There were a thousand daddy-long-leg spiders scrambling around our feet, up our legs and back on the wall. Amidst the hysteria and hopping around, within about two minutes the spiders were back in formation on the wall with their legs streaming out behind them.

Along came the next group of classmates asking, 'What is that?' Picking up the stick, I obliged them. The spiders do that to keep cool in the extreme heat.

Later that week we heard of the terrible floods on the Brazeau River and watched on TV the dramatic rescue of Miss America, a native of Texas, being plucked from the roof of the family home inundated with water. "

Brazeau Field trip, Aug 1978 (courtesy of D. Layton)

Brazeau Field trip, Aug 1978 - one week later 20 inches of rain created a river where my classmates are standing (courtesy of D. Layton)

Brazeau Field trip, Aug 1978 - "real" dinosaur prints (courtesy of D. Layton)

Geoff was usually successful in finding a couple of our class-mates to join us in our outings. It was during some of these trips that my exposure to U. S. oilpatch stories unfolded. Many States were represented in our Phase One and some episodes frankly seemed far fetched. In later years their authenticity was no longer questioned, except that they may have been underestimated. Geoff remembered the finer things.

"September Labour Day weekend was a blast. Five of us crammed into my Cordoba for a six hour, all freeway, drive to New Orleans. One of our classmates, Judy, hosted us at her condo and arranged "in stuff" activities like breakfast at Brennan's and Saturday afternoon at Preservation Jazz hall.

That night we partied in the French Quarter till the sun came up. I don't know who drove or how we were able to find our way back to Judy's, but when I woke up Sunday afternoon a Pat O' Brien's souvenir Hurricane glass was sitting on my car roof.

On the holiday Monday we went to the Saints - Green Bay Packers football game at the Superdome. This was my first live NFL game and the Saints' receiver caught the kick-off and ran it back for a 95 yard touchdown. You don't easily forget fun like that."

By the end of the summer we had just scratched the surface of the cheaper local restaurants. Again expense was a deterrent to our classmates joining us, so on occasion we treated. Cooking in our apartments was rarely considered seriously. Houston's climate suited us far more favourably for socializing than what awaited our return to Calgary beyond September.

One of our favourite eateries was nearby on Westheimer and called The Boston Sea Party. All the fresh seafood you can eat for something like $20. It was a traditional Shell Canada favourite and we loved it. Dreams of it lasted for months after. The sight of long, long tables of every conceivable seafood and salad is still vivid. It was a first choice visit in future years when business trips again made Houston my destination. Geoff remembered it for a different reason.

"Neil preferred buffet style restaurants like the Sea Party, otherwise he always seemed to be the last one served. I recall several times when we treated our classmates to pizza. Although everyone else got served, the waitresses kept losing or forgetting Neil's order. He was a good sport, but it happened so frequently that I figured he was jinxed. I was reluctant to sit near him."

Local bars remained open until the early morning hours. Several caught our fancy. It is not exaggerating to say there were a few mornings when we got home just in time to shower and change clothes before class.

Despite the impression this leaves, we had a perfect attendance record that summer. To my knowledge our performance reports, compiled by all the instructors for our Calgary supervisors, were very favourable. The course was intense and we prided ourselves in being able to budget our time and energies accordingly.

V
(Parting Reflection)

Phase One and Phase Two overlapped for two weeks near the end of August. One of my cohorts from Calgary, Hank Baird, dropped by for a visit and we were having a beer in my apartment. The packing of all my belongings, in preparation for shipment to Calgary in a few days, had just been completed.

No sooner had the air conditioner been switched off than somebody's pet roach crawled out of the vent over the bedroom doorway. It was as long and meaty as my middle finger. You would question throwing back a fish that size.

It was not my first encounter with this beast. Thankfully this time Hank was present as a witness.

"As Neil mentioned, Phase One and Two Classes overlapped for a few days. From the time of our arrival in Houston, we heard of Neil's roach wars at his apartment. Some of us knew that Neil was not one to embellish the facts, but we were still sceptical of the rumours.

On this particular occasion I was visiting with Neil at his apartment after class. Naturally I had my jacket on since Neil kept the air conditioner at maximum cool in hopes that the low temperature would deter the roaches from invading. I persuaded him to turn it off long enough to enjoy a cool beer together.

Neil was relating his story of a prolonged battle with one particularly large member of the roach species. I was only taking him partially serious. Suddenly out of the air conditioner vent crawled the biggest roach I had ever seen.

Neil immediately dived into the closet and emerged with a large economy size can of aerosol insecticide. As if it had been rehearsed, he promptly and accurately emptied the entire can on the unfortunate creature. I was shocked at how little effect this dousing had. Smothered in white foam, it still managed to crawl back into the vent.

Shortly thereafter the rest of the Calgary contingent arrived at the door, having just missed all the action. In our usual democratic fashion, we unanimously decided that this war story could be discussed better at a local bar on Westheimer. This decision was somewhat influenced by the fact that it was probably going to take considerable time for the air in Neil's apartment to clear. I never saw that creature again - but then I never went back to Neil's apartment either."

This tiny bug made me realize that we had only been guests all along. The true survivor and victor was the native roach. It tactically emerged to reclaim its territory when conditions were favourable. It was in its comfort zone all the time; I was temporarily out of mine. It was time to leave.

We were dead broke, as we had drawn down our advances throughout the summer to the maximum. In having such a good time we neglected to add up the cost overruns. In the coming months our lack of prudence cost us a good portion of our salaries. My recollection was that we had accumulated the worst debt of any Shell Canada Phase One, Two, or Three attendee up to that time. It was not to be my last time returning from the States with pocket change blues.

Our experiences were the kind of quality memories that last a lifetime, not to be missed for the world. Our exuberance never wavered, as evidenced by Geoff's recreation of our return flight to Calgary.

"On the Continental Airlines flight to Denver it was just like old times. The steak meal ran out when they got to Neil. I was sitting beside him, and missed out too. As compensation, we were issued meal vouchers for a restaurant at the Denver Airport and free booze for the remainder of the flight. It was fortunate since we were out of money. Neil started his collection of miniature liquor bottles after we had breezed through a dozen or so.

We didn't get our meal at the airport. The concourse was too far from the Western Airlines departure gate for Calgary and our arrival from Houston was behind schedule.

The meals also ran out on the Calgary flight, so we drank all the way back, courtesy of Western. After we told one of the stewardesses our story, she felt badly and gave us a bottle of champagne. When we landed in Calgary I had to muster every brain cell just to stand up and stumble through Customs. I remember thinking I'm so hammered they may not admit me without a fuss."

(**FOOTNOTE** : In mid 1996 this author travelled on a U.S. airline to the eastern United States. The first leg of two hours to Salt Lake City spanned lunch; peanuts were served. The second leg of four hours to Cincinnati spanned dinner; a *small* snack was served. The third leg of one and one half hours to Tri-Cities, Tennessee offered peanuts. At each airport hordes of hungry passengers swamped the limited food outlets. Any layover less than an hour precluded getting served in time to digest the food, unless it was carried on board. Canadians take note! Even our No Frill airlines offer more, so be prepared when travelling on U.S. carriers by *packing a lunch*. Apparently the meal shortages in 1978 have become meal illusions in the 1990s.)

In my critique of 1978-10-19 to the Petroleum Engineering Manager, the value of Phase One was summarized as it was perceived at the time. My opinions still hold true to this day.

> "1. The manuals issued during the course have proven excellent references. I expect to derive a great deal of assistance from them in the future.
>
> 2. Presentations were thorough and well conducted, strengthening my experience and improving my confidence, particularly in areas where I considered my background to be weak (ie. Geology, Petrophysics).
>
> 3. The instructors were competent and experienced in their fields and I had a lot of respect for their presentations. Use of personal experiences and examples were effective learning devices.
>
> 4. The Geological Field trips stand out as interesting, enjoyable, and entertaining.
>
> 5. The Reservoir Engineering portion of the Course was the most valuable and rewarding for me, and R.T. impressive.
>
> Summarizing; I relate to Phase One as one of the most, if not the most, enjoyable experiences I have ever had. The relationships with the program, the BRC Staff, and my American classmates were influential and satisfying. There was a team atmosphere prevalent which contributed to a healthy and congenial class attitude and I will remember Phase One as a great morale booster."

My conduct was more diligent and frugal in the future, but by then the circumstances were far more serious and deliberate. Roles were inherited in the U. S. oil and gas industry that were readily characterized as equivalent to The Naked City television series of my youth. Stay tuned!

French Quarter, New Orleans, Sept 1978 (left to right: author;D. Turnbull-Phase Two;Geoff Freeman;Hank Baird)

EPISODE 2: OHIO - INDOCTRINATION TO FAILURE

I
(Naked City Here I Come)

It was the sixth of October 1980.

It seemed like decades had passed since my Phase One exploits. Much had changed, including my career direction. Gas Contract negotiations and reserve evaluations now occupied most of my time. While the goal was to expand my expertise and broaden my knowledge, the progress was not particularly encouraging. Alternative employment was not actively sought, but the market was periodically tested.

Somewhere in the industry my comfort zone existed, but the ideal destination was not yet clear. At least that was the assessment until opening my letter from Tom Seaton, an Executive Recruiter with T.J. Seaton & Associates Ltd. His confirmation of my appointment to United States field operations was a dream come true. My spirits soared. A new era was about to begin for me without having the slightest idea of where it would lead.

My new employer, the oil and gas division of a large Canadian mining firm, had ventured far from home. Some six months previously, $15,000,000 U.S. had been invested to drill 105 wells in Ohio with a German partner.

Ohio! Any sizeable oil and gas reserves in Ohio was news to me. A need for a field representative developed when anticipated results failed to materialize after completing half the program. Tom mated his client's needs with my wants.

"In an earlier assignment I had recruited a Chief Geologist for this company. The senior management of the parent company were quite impressed with his credentials and performance. Within a few months he was promoted to the Presidency after the ageing incumbent retired.

When I was contacted to search for a United States Operations Analyst, my focus was on professionals with a strong base of experience in many aspects of petroleum engineering.

Neil was an early candidate because of his thorough training at Shell and subsequent varied industry experience. He had a decisive, yet congenial, style.

His determination to get the job done was a strength that made him an obvious fit for this position."

There were other U.S. assets and activities in Texas, Utah, and North Dakota, but Ohio was reaching a crises. Our 50% German partner, although actively involved in Canadian mining prospects, was participating in an oil and gas joint venture for the first time. Of course, the corporate intent was to develop an aggressively successful operation in Ohio that would encourage continued investment elsewhere in the U.S.

It was not uncommon in the Canadian oilpatch to rely extensively on drilling contractors and ancillary services to perform their duties and responsibilities as directed by documented authority. An Authority For Expenditure (AFE) acts like a project map by providing itemized work procedures and budget guidelines. Deviation without prior approval was rarely tolerated.

When the Ohio project commenced, Charlie Chinneck was a consulting engineer assigned the role of observing and reporting on progress. It was not long before alarm bells triggered Charlie's concerns to Head Office in Calgary.

"Although the Operator's personnel were always polite, it was very difficult to get any information out of them. The only way to really find out what was going on at the individual well locations was to go out and check them visually.

A Daily Drilling Report was non-existent, at least for me. Their attitude seemed to be supply the money, then get out of the way.

I was treated like a spy during the early part of my involvement. I had to have the Calgary office intervene before I was able to get a look at the well files or individual well production."

Two of the first five wells, drilled to between 3500 and 4000 feet in Devonian shale, encountered natural fractures and produced at encouraging rates of one hundred barrels of oil per day (BOPD). Unfortunately only one of the next fifty wells came anywhere close to budget or productivity expectations. The dilemma was what to do about the remaining approved fifty wells.

The first of many controversial issues that attracted scrutiny was financial. The experience governed my opinion to avoid the consequences wherever possible for the next fifteen yea s.

The promoted costs of $150,000 U.S. to drill, complete, and tie-in each well had been allocated in advance. This was known as a 'Turnkey Operation', little used in Canada but very popular in the United States oilpatch. Success depended on a bond of trust existing between the investor and the promoter/operator.

Inherent with this arrangement was an ominous danger flag that deserved caution. The promoter/operator accepted all risks for over-budget expensing but also retained any surplus. In the wrong hands, it encouraged cutting corners and substitution of less dependable parts and service to ensure a profit surplus. This danger flag will be revisited in later EPISODES.

In a way it reminded me of the per diem expense strategy exercised by some of my U.S. counterparts in Phase One. The risk then was the loss of room, board, and transportation independence. In turn, it strained relationships and competed with energy required for course studies and socializing. Geoff and I had learned in Houston that quality results came from investing, not saving, money. The rapid deterioration of the Ohio program had its origins with the Operator's abuse of Turnkey Operation funds.

Sensing a disaster in the making, Charlie appealed for additional manpower to co-ordinate and monitor field activities. The door was opened for my involvement.

Several initial strategy sessions with the Vice President of Production and Operations, whom we shall refer to as 'Weaver', helped my preparation. To accelerate my indoctrination, Weaver recalled Charlie for daily consultation. Despite all Weaver's labours, it was only after my first site visit, within weeks of my hiring, that an appreciation of what was unfolding was acquired.

Shortly thereafter, the American promoter who attracted my employer to Ohio, whom we shall refer to as 'Thirsty' because he was rarely caught without a can of cola, paid a visit to Calgary. Despite travelling all day from Greenwich, Connecticut, our meeting lasted well into the evening. Thirsty's enthusiasm was infectious.

A 'salesman extraordinaire' was an astute label. He was very personable and likeable despite his obvious ignorance of oil industry technicals. He never wavered from his conviction that he would earn notoriety for orchestrating a new oil boom in Ohio - with our financial help, of course!

Our attempts to address contentious issues were surgically avoided. His script was rehearsed and repetitious. After hearing

Thirsty's version of the program's progress, I was almost convinced we had a winner on our hands until realizing we had discussed the same three wells over and over.

Wells #2, #4, and #10 pr oduced initially at rates of 100 BOPD. After six months they still averaged 40 - 50 BOPD. *His* math converted these results to 100,000 barrels of recoverable oil reserves per well. Without a breather, except to inhale another cigarette, we were blessed with an unforgettable expression. **"You see what this means. If we drill the next hundred wells (second half of our program), we'll make** *millllyuns* **of barrels.........***millllyuns***."**

It was easy to be sceptical when fifty-two marginal or unsuccessful wells out of fifty-five completed, so far, were ignored. Likewise for the exaggerated reserve predictions based on three wells that had already experienced a decline rate of 50% in less than six months (five times the normal rate of decline). To that we add Thirsty's expectation that most of the remaining fifty wells would have to be historic discoveries.

Charlie had listened intently all evening but kept his views to himself. The next morning he shared his opinions and recollections of his field experience in private. He was less than optimistic for any further Ohio involvement.

"The Ohio Operator was eager to drill the wells but reluctant to perforate and stimulate them. This was not surprising since it was my understanding that the turnkey funds were released to their account after each well had been cased.

Lack of production after stimulation was common and had a negative effect on the proposed expansion of the program. The Operator fully expected funding for a second one hundred well program. The fact that they had a very poor success ratio did not discourage them in the least. A significant contributing factor to the failure rate was that most of the personnel had very little experience in the drilling and production of oil wells.

This prospect was probably the most frustrating of my forty year oil industry career."

The second controversial issue, technical in nature, was irreversible and a grave lesson for the development speed of future programs.

The choice of drilling locations had little to do with science. Seismic was not employed, let alone understood. Too few wells had been drilled to this depth in the area to offer any interpretative value.

Services such as logging, fracturing, and perforating were primitive by Canadian standards and undependable. The deficiency of modern equipment and highly trained personnel plagued this program for the duration (see Section III, Villain No. 3 as an example). It appeared that the U.S. oil industry experts had discounted the long term potential of the area.

Filling this void was our operator, 'GW', who licensed wells wherever a mineral holder was co-operative. Unlike Canada where at least 95% of the Mineral Rights are owned by the Crown (Government), in the U.S. the reverse is true for individual land owners or descendants of homesteaders.

Likewise, the system for identifying and locating wells was completely different. Canadian well names provide area, co-ordinates, and often Operator. For instance: POCO Chain 8-18-033-16 W4M is an abandoned well in Legal Sub Division (LSD) 8, Section 18, township 33, Range 16, West of the fourth Meridian. Location is the Chain area of east central Alberta and 'Poco Petroleum' was the Operator.

Ohio well names, however, usually recognized only the mineral owner's name and number of wells on the lease. Finding, or giving directions to, a well under this system presented a far greater challenge than the Canadian way. As an example, the two successes in our first five wells were Avis No. 1 and Vargo No. 1. To avoid map overcrowding, we assigned numerical designations. On the map at the end of this Section these two wells are 2002 and 2004. Subsequently the next one hundred wells were labelled 4000 to 4100. It escapes me to this day that we actually got one hundred and one wells based on this system but presumably were only Cash Called for one hundred wells.

A drilling program of one hundred wells at a time simply overwhelmed GW's logistical infrastructure. The long range plan was to initiate an additional hundred well program at the conclusion of the first hundred. Under the constant stress to perform, shortcuts that would be considered intolerable, and possibly even illegal, in the Canadian oilpatch became common practice in Ohio. It was not universal for casing to be cemented, multiple well batteries to have separate metering, logging operations complete before stimulation, pumping units adequately sized or installed, year round accessibility, etc.

At various stages throughout my three years in Ohio, wellsites were inspected at the top of steep hills (sometimes the only hill for

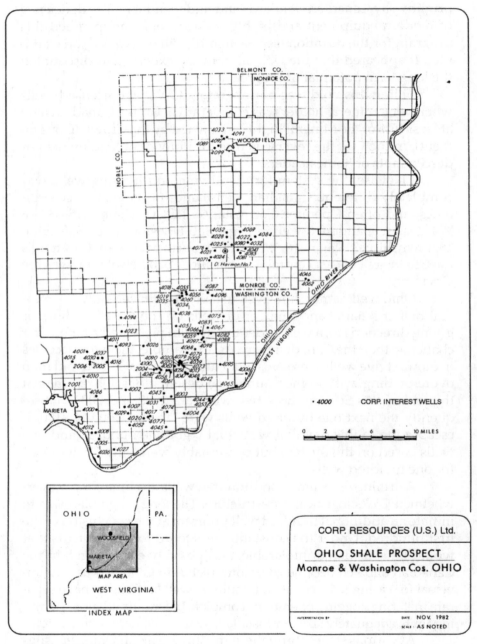

Map of Ohio well locations

quite a distance), in fields and woodlands totally remote from oil and gas gathering facilities or roads, and in many cases in the backyard of a residence. GW's agenda may have been honourable to the local land owners but it had quite questionable value for oil exploitation.

A further misconception was the expectation of recoverable reserves. Since drilling spacing units were limited to twenty acres, reservoir characteristics supported only an average of 13000 barrels of oil per well. Exceptional wells that encountered natural reservoir fracturing, of which we had three out of one hundred and five, were capable of twice that amount. After a year or more of history, our production decline analyses verified these potentials. In view of $150,000 well costs, 20% royalties, and suspiciously high operating costs, writing a happy ending for this script needed a magician and I was only an engineer.

II
(Getting Acquainted)

Just getting to the field was an adventure for a novice traveller like myself. My odyssey began with a taxi to the Calgary airport the twenty-fourth of October, 1980.

Base of operations was the southern Ohio city of Marietta, at the confluence of the Muskingum and Ohio rivers. Several bridges provided access to the south side of the river and the State of West Virginia. Once across the bridge it was approximately a 15 minute drive south to the regional airport, jointly serving the nearby West Virginia city of Parkersburg and Marietta.

Parkersburg had a population of 30,000, roughly twice that of Marietta. It was also more industrial based, with one hundred or so firms producing products such as chemicals, glass metals and plastics. Major contributors to the local economy were the resource based industries, which were making a comeback thanks to Canadian investment.

In my quest to learn more about the local history, it was discovered that West Virginia's first oil wells were drilled nearby in 1860, making Parkersburg the supply and shipping point for the "black gold" fields. Oil production was a major industry again for a short period in the early 1920s. An ominous sixty year cycle did not escape my attention. As a comparison the Alberta oil industry had been steady, with occasional booms triggered by government fiscal relaxation, for most of the 20th Century.

All my Ohio field assignments began and ended at the regional airport. Standard flight itinerary was Calgary to Chicago, Chicago to Pittsburgh, then small commuter aircraft (anywhere from eight to twenty passenger type) to Parkersburg. With stops, travel usually consumed the full day. My initial reaction on walking into this modest but modern terminal the first time was the surprisingly large number of Rental Car companies. Most of the majors were represented, as were several local firms unknown to me. Choice and availability rarely presented a problem. It was a wonder that this many survived with such a small market for so long.

It was here that Strategy No.1 was employed. An effort was made to spread my business around as much as possible, provided the rental rates were competitive. Dozens of trips were made to Marietta from 1980 - 1983, often staying many weeks or months at a time. Not befriending any particular establishment laid the ground work for general acceptance by most, if not all, the employees and owners. Over the duration of my involvement this relationship would pay many dividends.

To start with, it was an accurate source of intelligence for arrival and departure information on certain individuals. It was both a competitive and defensive edge.

Secondly, rarely did a local happening occur that failed to attract the attention of my 'airport intelligence' squad. There was never anything devious or unethical about my approach. It just seemed to make good business sense, after periodic retirements to Calgary, to get updated upon my arrival at the terminal. As a ready listener, in numerous circumstances it provided me a competitive edge for the tasks ahead. These informal 'debriefings' became so effective that it was often necessary to pretend ignorance of events when later discussing AFE or staff related issues.

Thirdly, no energy was wasted questioning directions or insuring dependable transportation awaited me. There were times when my flight was delayed by weather or missed connections, but I was always accommodated. Had it not been so, I dread to think how much worse some of my assignments may have developed and how my focus for the technical tasks at hand may have been jeopardized.

Looking back, the key to this harmony was being patient in nurturing relationships at the beginning. Rather than force my pace, theirs was accepted. After assimilating into the local environment, the comradeship expanded on its own. It is true these car rental agencies were physically remote from oilfield activity. This factor may have depreciated their strategic value in some eyes. The individuals who manned them, however, were far more intimate with what was going on than credit was given. It was to my benefit that this cooperation remained underestimated and ignored.

Marietta was the home of Marietta College, so accommodation was plentiful. My favourite motel was the Ramada on State Route 7. It was on the east end of town and near our production and administration office. Access to most of our wells in surrounding Monroe and Washington Counties was to the east. Several local restaurants were within walking distance.

Other motels were called 'home' for weeks at a time, including the Knights Inn which provided me with a kitchen equipped suite and had the additional bonus of an outdoor pool. Once in a while pace was changed to the Lafayette, a very old and historic motor hotel in the downtown core. Since it overlooked the Ohio River, dining in the Gun Room Restaurant was a special treat.

However the Ramada remained my comfort zone. The bar had nightly happy hours with ample free food. Each night a different culture was featured. It was as delicious and enjoyable as most restaurants and far more convenient after a long, frustrating day. It was not uncommon to have my supper there several times a week, downing a few beers with the money saved from my meal allowance.

On occasion there would be live entertainment, but mostly it was a disk jockey or cassette tapes. The dance floor was quite small and the clientele more oriented to overnight travellers. Attendance from the locals suffered because of this, but it suited me fine not to compete with the masses. I was in the minority as a non smoker and truly appreciated enjoying a few drinks without suffocating from lack of oxygen. Most of my business and social associates smoked, some very heavily. What suited me also was the softness of the music. Country was big in Marietta and it was a rare occasion to find a bar where you could actually carry on a conversation and see the person at the same time.

A prime example of the norm was the Holiday Inn directly across the highway. The bar was traditionally packed to capacity. Music was often live, always loud, and the dance floor swinging. Over the years, when I was either in the mood for action or considered it necessary for assimilating, it would be my destination. Only the occasional overnight stay was weathered there since the smoke and music were intense and permeated to the remotest rooms.

The word was the Holiday waitresses were the most attractive in town. During my first assignment, before being fully accustomed to single coloured U.S. currency, $10 was unknowingly tipped for a round of four draft beer instead of $1. I had service all night that would have embarrassed a celebrity. Next day, while commenting on this service, the truth was learned. My advice was that service would get a lot better if it happened again. My frugal side won out and that confusion was not repeated.

The Ramada's greatest advantage was the luxury of not having to drive or walk anywhere when overwhelmed by the urge to drown myself at the bar. One night in my second year the bartender was asked to surprise me with a drink hardy enough to eliminate my assignment frustrations for one night. His response was he had just the thing, a private, dust camouflaged, treasure. But by now my curiosity had become hardened to suspect all verbiage, in or out of the Ohio oilpatch. My patronage must have earned me some bonus points, for he did deliver. The drink was called Chartreuse and it is consumed straight, like a liqueur. Later it was verified as a French monk concoction, aged for ten years or more. His warning, that beyond two drinks more than my frustrations would be eliminated, was ignored. My last recollection was consuming a third three ounce shot. Morning greeted me on the floor by my table. The bar was silent, empty, and locked up.

The registration desk was just outside in the lobby, less than ten feet away. The day clerk was forewarned to expect some frantic banging on the door sometime during the morning. By now all the front desk shifts knew me. There was no way to avoid detection and still get to work. When the door was opened for me, I begged to keep it our secret and proceeded to my room with humility and a gruesome hangover. To my knowledge it has remained privileged gossip to this day.

Years later in Amarillo, Texas my Chartreuse experience won a strategic drinking victory over a wily litigation opponent. The following day, during a Deposition break, he proclaimed admiration and respect for having bettered him. He had victimized us for millions of dollars, yet it was the first and only time we witnessed his humble side. But that is another experience better told in EPISODE 9.

Leisure time was rare, as work responsibilities multiplied rather than subsided. When treating myself or special guests, it would be a Sunday evening visit to The Point Of View restaurant near Parkersburg. Perched high on a cliff beside the Ohio River, it offered a scenic and panoramic view of the surrounding country-side for many miles. The food and service were superb. It was always a must when our German partners were in town for meetings.

Marietta, as an old traditional city, was also very historic. It still had a flavour of its importance to river traffic of the 1800s. A replica sternwheeler, the Becky Thatcher, was utilized as a show-boat for cruises, live theatre or dining. Centre of attraction for me, however, was a fantastic old library. Many precious, quiet hours evolved there. Otherwise there was little else in the way of modern entertainment. Movies meant a drive to Parkersburg. The local Golf/Tennis Club was Private.

The rolling, forested hills and colourful farms (corn was predominant) with red clay topsoil reminded me of the Maritimes. The winter climate was similar but the summers were much hotter and included occasional tornadoes. Southern Ohio appealed to me as a tourist but it was never entirely comfortable living there. Whenever the focus was my assignment, the outcome rained on my parade.

III
(Rainy Days)

Rather than prioritize the problems and concerns, they will simply be addressed in order of my exposure. The adversities were so numerous that, in the end, the final outcome was not surprising.

The solutions, attempted or implemented, were in progress over my entire three year involvement. Most remedial action was the result of combining talents and efforts of many technical specialists and consultants. What was tried cannot be faulted. My view was that Mother Nature doomed our program, with a little human help, from the beginning. No amount of ingenuity could rescue it after the fact. You can be the judge.

VILLAIN NO. 1 : RIGHT COOKBOOK, WRONG RECIPES

Ohio Shale well completions demanded a unique approach. Inherent clays would swell when exposed to water, restricting and/ or preventing the movement of any reservoir fluids or gases. Conventional rotary rigs drill with water based mud, thus subjecting these temperamental clays to swelling damage in advance of completion. Lab tests on clay formation samples are recalled which reminded me of immersing hard dog food pellets in water for a few hours. Try it. In this case, as the saying goes, the picture is worth a thousand words.

Unless natural fractures were encountered during drilling, artificial fractures had to be induced hydraulically. That is, water injected under sufficient pressure to exceed reservoir pressure, some 3000 PSI for these well depths, and 'shatter' the rock. It was both the most inexpensive and convenient method. In most other reservoirs it provides any gases or fluids a path of least resistance to the wellbore through these fractures.

Usually sand is mixed with the water to help force open the rock and keep it 'propped' open against the forces of overburden pressure. Obviously this technique would not work in Ohio Shale reservoirs. Due to the overwhelming presence of inherent clays, swelling would nullify the benefits of inducing a proppant.

Because shale is so dense and tight, economic hydrocarbon recovery is impossible without natural or stimulated fractures. In the greatest irony of the Ohio program, two of the first five wells encountered naturally fractured oil shales. Quite respectable production rates, unencumbered by the costs and risks of artificial completion, created expectations within the Joint Venture that were difficult to overcome. In the next hundred wells, Nature and technology cooperated only once more. There were plenty of patients to cure.

REMEDIES

☑One solution was using inert nitrogen gas, compressed and injected at pressures exceeding reservoir pressure.

Credit for this innovative approach belonged to a recent Geology graduate of Marietta College. When applied to wells offsetting prolific producers, results were often encouraging. Unfortunately our twenty acre leases were too widely scattered to have an impact on our program. It did, however, earn this geologist solid employment with our Operator (who also drilled and operated wells for its own account as well as for other investors). Eventually led to an ownership position for him.

☑Another solution was to drill with compressed air as the circulation and lubrication median.

Compared to mud rigs, an air rig could drill these wells in half the time (about three days) without damaging the formation. Unfortunately this method prevented retrieval of cuttings for evaluation or detection of hydrocarbon shows.

An inherent risk was that encountering a fracture might result in an uncontrollable blowout. Several occurred during my tour, fortunately none were on our wells. A popular compromise was to drill down to the top of the Ohio Shale with a mud rig, then through the Shale with an air or cable tool rig.

☑Ohio was my only experience witnessing a cable tool rig in operation. By all accounts they were generally superseded in the industry by more efficient and safe rotary rigs in the 1930s and 1940s.

The concept was to 'chip' out a hole using a sharp chisel on the end of reinforced rods or bars. Most of the shallow Cow Run and Berea formation wells (1000 feet or less depth) drilled in Ohio earlier in the century used this method. The absence of drilling fluids was useful for recovery of undamaged rock samples and hydrocarbon detection.

☑Completion designs that were popular and successful in Canada were attempted, sometimes with last minute adjustments to conform with material deficiencies or substitutions.

'Foam fracs' referred to mixing water and energized gas to get deeper fracture penetration and accommodate the carrying of sand for propping. 'Reformate foam fracs' substituted lease crude for water but were highly volatile and flammable, requiring extreme caution and experienced personnel. Our *experiments* with these methods drew plenty of attraction in Ohio as they were relatively unknown locally.

POST MORTEM

⊠Nitrogen gas supplies were ample but expensive and inconvenient. The standard stimulation volume of 250,000 - 300,000 cubic feet required several pump trucks and in my view was grossly inadequate.

Proppant and gas are not mixable, thus fractures were prone to heal quickly and/or succumb to the deposit of formation fines or paraffin (wax). Our typical post workover rates averaged twenty bopd and fifty thousand cubic feet per day (mcfpd). It was not unusual to get only gas in the later well completions. Most declined to half these rates within a month or less.

⊠Performance was dependent on the well location, reservoir quality encountered, and the completion design strategy. The latter was governed by the economics of the program which, after the first five wells, deteriorated rapidly. The anticipated reserve recoveries did not materialize and therefore influenced additional investment. Much larger nitrogen fracs may have been an answer, but this vicious Catch-22 cycle prevailed.

The resulting synopsis was life threatening. Either : 1) reserves were too limited or absent or 2) the stimulation was too limited in design and available funds to facilitate adequate drainage of the reserves.

⊠Cable tool drilling, while unique, was too slow and expensive for maintenance and operation. Even utilizing it to drill through the shale only meant additional time and expense employing two rigs. The depth of our wells simply made it impractical.

⊠Air drilling, on the other hand, was responsible for most of our wells. Speed kept the Operator's costs to a minimum, however data retrieval suffered. Sample recovery and detection of hydrocarbon shows were both sacrificed to accommodate compressed air drilling. Consequently, it became much more difficult to determine if the well was a good completion candidate. Equally difficult was determining where to complete it.

☒All wells were automatically cased upon reaching total depth because it was included in the Turnkey cost. Significant savings could have been realized if this decision had been left up to the investor rather than the Operator.

Several of our cased wells were never completed. Without offset production history or technical encouragement from electric logs, the additional $30000 to $50000 for completing and equipping could not be justified. This problem involved many wells near the end of the program when the Operator had exhausted all Turnkey funds. It meant additional investment on our part. More about this issue in Villain No. 2.

☒Following on the heels of our casing disputes, it was also late in the program when we insisted on running a Cement Bond Log (CBL).

The CBL presents a picture of how effective the casing is 'bonded' to the formation with cement. Prior to stimulation at high pressures, it is imperative to ensure the annulus between the casing and the formation is sealed off well above and below the interval to be perforated. This confines, in this case, the pressurized nitrogen for maximum penetration. Otherwise the artificial fracturing will seek a path of least resistance, usually upwards in the annulus.

Examination of CBLs for the last remaining uncompleted wells revealed most to be suspect of reliability. It was never determined if inadequate cement volume, inappropriate cement formula, or lack of technical expertise was to blame. My suspicion was a combination of all three, since each would have contributed to saving Turnkey funds by the Operator.

In any event, the probability of a successful frac into the zone of interest was minimal. Completion costs could not be risked at this late stage in the program. Consequently several wells remained uncompleted and many potential recompletion candidates were shut-in.

☒Exotic completions were very expensive and relied on veteran contractors to avoid accidents and exercise experienced judgement. Many major service companies staffed offices in the area but more often than not it served as a training ground for new or local recruits. Here is an example.

In May 1982 we had scheduled Well No. 4092 near Woodsfield in Monroe County, for completion.

My arrival at the wellsite was co-ordinated with the service company. All their equipment had been prepared in advance for a nitrogen stimulation. The foreman was conducting the standard safety meeting prior to pressurizing to 3500 PSI. After verifying the program design, I stood back to observe.

At the extreme of the pressure envelope, there was a loud explosion. The wellhead had disintegrated and shrapnel was flying everywhere. My immediate reaction was to dive under the closest pumper truck. Metal debris could be heard peppering the fronts of various vehicles, all parked facing the wellhead about twenty-five to thirty feet back.

Although not hurt, my first recollection was looking up from my prone position to see the frac valve steel wheel (little larger than a hubcap) revolving out of sight into space. More amazing was the sight of several contract personnel running into the adjacent field. If the intent was to escape injury from falling debris, the safety procedures were in dire need of rewrite. Luckily there were only a few minor injuries like twisted ankles. The vehicles fared much worse and sustained substantial superficial damage.

Investigation revealed the casing bowl flange, that supports the wellhead with sturdy bolts, had been welded to the casing joint protruding above ground (acceptable procedure as long as it is accomplished and inspected by high pressure welders) instead of threaded and bolted. Unable to withstand 3500 PSI pressure, the weld failed and the wellhead was destroyed in the ensuing explosion.

Checking this flange prior to pressuring up was one of the safety steps. Accepting my responsibility, measures were taken to ensure this step was not left to assumption for later completions. It concerned me that the dangerous nature of our business was not being taken seriously.

Several weeks later the wellhead had been properly repaired and inspected. This same service company was managing the nitrogen frac and very reluctant to proceed with pressuring up. After several false starts, I placed myself with the most exposed operators to prove my confidence in the replacement equipment. The program then went ahead as planned and without mishap.

Well No. 4092, May 1982 (lease after explosion while pressuring up for nitrogen frac; remainder of casing collar flange on left side of pipe)

☒A further risk of applying 'state of the art' completion technology to these Ohio Shale wells was limited experience we or our competitors had with this formation. As the cutting edge, much of our efforts were more experimental than designed. No doubt we played a valuable role in demonstrating to our observers what application was not compatible. Our Foam frac candidates had the poorest results and reinforced fears of combining shale with water, no matter how limited in proportion.

Well No. 4092, May 1982 (second nitrogen frac in progress)

VILLAIN NO. 2 : WEATHER AND WHETHER

The countryside outside Marietta is studded with countless treed hollows and canyons, liberally served by paved, but mostly dirt, roads. In the fall, the colours paint an absolutely breathtaking panorama. In many cases, large, historic trees on either side of the road form an umbrella for miles.

The red clay tracts leading off to our wells were serene contrasts snaking their way to an isolated woodlot or hilltop amply populated with wildlife. I could not believe my good fortune at this bonus; that was until the first rainstorm.

When it rains in Ohio, it pours. Not that it does not rain in all oil-fields, but drilling most of our wells over the dry summer of 1980 created false security. Many lease roads were simply bulldozed through wooded areas, up steep hillsides, or ended at a stream or creek with a footbridge access for the pumper ('operator' or 'switcher' in our oilpatch).

When the rains finally came, lease roads washed out in front of our eyes. Streams and creeks became rivers. It was not uncommon for wells to be isolated for days.

There were several occasions where my isolation on hilltops lasted the better part of a day; heavy service vehicles were there for a lot longer. Despite using four wheel drive trucks, we often felt helpless when Mother Nature paid a visit. Naturally our operating costs suffered proportionately during fall and winter road maintenance, a further unexpected blow to our economic forecasts. Harsh reality heralds strong lessons. **Weather** and its consequences captured greater respect during the remainder of my tenure in the U.S.

The most serious economic uncertainty after 1980 was the direction of oil and gas pricing. Our Ohio program was predicated on receiving a tight gas incentive price for all one hundred and five wells due to the inherent tight reservoirs and low productivities. It was referred to as a CP107 Contract and netted about $3.00 per MCF at the wellhead during 1980. Oil prices were also peaking at $40 U.S. per barrel.

When world oil prices began their dramatic decline in 1981, we assumed our long term gas Contracts were secure. On the contrary, the major pipeline company that purchased our gas simply reneged. The unilateral compromise was about $1.00 per MCF **whether** the wells were already connected to sales pipelines or not.

Obviously there were immediate consequences for wells waiting on tie-in . Most were suspended indefinitely during the remainder of our involvement.

REMEDIES

☑**Weather** and **whether** combined to restrict maintenance on low productivity wells and exclude further completion and development of the remaining ones.

If a marginal well became a liability as a result of required road or pipeline repairs, it very often remained that way. An inventory exchange system using suspended wells was implemented to address equipment failures promptly and at minimal cost.

Eventually we identified a core of wells to maintain and thus reduced our field staff requirements accordingly. To conserve as many jobs as prudently possible, we assumed more lease and facility maintenance responsibilities, saving considerable third party contracting costs. One example is recalled involving cows and an angry farmer.

Our well was located on a small knob at the top of a hill in the middle of a cattle farm. One side was solid trees but steep; the other equally steep but with ideal grazing grass sloping down to a large field. The access road crossed the farm's perimeter and therefore was equipped with a gate to contain a large herd of cows.

Several times the farmer complained that his cows had wandered up the hill to the well. He insisted on having the lease fenced before a cow was injured or poisoned. Presumably they were attracted by the oil and grease that is common around most pumping units (particularly ours which were of dubious quality).

Since we considered the hillside too steep, and actually had not seen any cows or signs of cows near the well, we stalled on correcting the problem. The amount of fencing and the difficult terrain suggested a two or three man crew for at least a day. Contractor estimates were $3000+, further reason for hoping the problem would go away.

Then one day a cow got sick and required a vet. We refunded the fees even though it could not be proved that our well was the culprit. Isolating the wellsite, however, was no longer an issue. That Saturday the field foreman and I requisitioned metal posts (the angular type with wire hooks) and barbed wire from a local supplier and sweated off a few pounds working through till dark.

Doing this chore ourselves had many advantages. Weekends were set aside for just such emergencies. A cash purchase of the material cost much less than half the quotes of the contractors. The job was accomplished immediately. Design accommodated cost efficiency, safety and convenience of the pumper, and minimum waste of grazing land.

The farmer was most satisfied. The positive public relations was welcomed and we felt a personal accomplishment by saving several thousands of dollars.

☑The drastically reduced gas prices meant we had to strictly enforce free gas supplies off the wellhead to the lease owner. While agreeing to one hook-up was considered part of doing business, it was often abused to include homes of relatives or friends also within the lease boundary.

This lean and mean attitude was obviously not a big hit for public relations but it was long overdue as a business decision. Considering the average Ohio residence used only twenty to twenty-five MCF per winter month, it drove home the lesson of how precarious the program economics had become.

POST MORTEM

☒In my opinion we were betrayed by our Operator when it came to well locations. Far too many of our leases were bordering on inaccessibility and remoteness to market. While we shared responsibilities for the drilling program, local familiarity with weather conditions and pipelining challenges should have enticed the Operator to display leadership in this matter. After the fact experience was costly and irreparable. Diligence demanded a close working relationship with the Operator no matter how trivial the issue *appeared*. It was another lesson carried forward to other ventures.

☒The abandonment of contracted gas prices may have improved the profit margin of our gas Purchaser, but it meant certain death for our program.

Few experts predicted the free fall of world oil prices after 1981. Our economics allowed for some downward movement, albeit not near the magnitude of $40 U.S. to $15 U.S. per barrel. No participant in our Ohio program could be faulted for this lack of vision. Fifteen years later, it was still bouncing around in the lower extremities and confusing a lot of experts.

The gas pricing debacle does have a culprit.

A major gas transmission company enticed our involvement in Ohio with promises of long term gas prices of $3.00 per MCF *or better*. It is logical to assume this Purchaser relied on internal studies and forecasts to model marketplace swings. No doubt both Producer and Purchaser benefited from these Contracts in the beginning.

Consumers were paying a premium, but at the time there was very limited production in the eastern U.S. States. Resource exploration provided increased supply security as well as contributing meaningfully to local employment. The $3.00 per MCF price drew criticism, but it promptly engineered a Supply and Demand equilibrium.

It is interesting to note that the U.S. interstate reference (NYMEX) gas price has ranged from $2.50 - $3.50 per MCF most of the winter of 1995/96. The current world oil price average of $20.00 per barrel apparently has little influence compared to the early 1980s. The governing factor for U.S. east coast gas pricing was still the same , however, as it was in our Ohio era. Local *economic* reserves and productivity are limited unless favourable pricing restores the balance.

The Ohio Shale wells were low pressure, low rate, but long life at the right price.

Operating a well involves fixed costs such as electrical power or propane fuel, well and lease maintenance, gas chart integration, vehicle costs, road and pipeline repairs. Once the gas Purchaser reneged on a Contract, production had to be suspended to avoid losses. As a result, our program production and cash flow declined until we reached the level of a caretaker operation.

In the end, the investors who took all the financial risks were the recipients of the pain. The gas Purchaser, although deserving of some accountability, simply passed the buck.

My praise for the use of lawyers in this book is rare. The reasons will become obvious as you read on. If we had used a credible one back then, however, the ending of this EPISODE would have been much different.

Well No. 4046

Lease road to Well No. 4054

Well No. 4054

Well No. 4004

Service Rig at Well No. 4048

VILLAIN NO. 3 : MUSICAL CHAIRS

The AFE system of procurement was alluded to earlier. As equipment costs were based on new pricing formats, it was *assumed* our cash calls would be used to acquire new equipment. Subjecting wellbore casing and tubing to high fracture pressures demanded quality equipment to avoid premature failure. Likewise surface

Lease road traffic jam

facilities had to withstand the natural elements and the rigors of daily operation. Sounds good in theory but it did not turn out that way.

Often our wells were equipped with used pumping units of unknown origin or quality. Monthly operating costs soared from frequent motor and bearing replacement. More often than not, removal of the bottom hole pump and rods revealed either one or both were living on borrowed time and had contributed to premature failure.

Likewise many of the wellheads were substandard versions, previously used, or had questionable safety margins due to improper storage. Valves were notorious and it was frustrating to spend so much good money after bad.

Production storage tanks and treaters for gas and water separation were the most obvious abuses. Again many were used and deteriorated. Turnkey costs included surface facilities for each lease, but

Battery in the wilderness

Well No. 2004 flaring gas, Sept 1982 (one of three profitable wells in 105 well program)

when wells were close together it was not uncommon to see them piped into a central battery. There was nothing wrong with this. In fact it was cost and operationally efficient. Surplus savings, however, failed to find their way back to our account.

The same was true of gas meter runs and above ground flowlines. The multitude of leaks was a clear and costly indicator of the pipe quality.

REMEDIES

☑There were not a lot of solutions, other than to exchange bad equipment from a good well for good equipment from a bad well. Monitoring all wells, specifically the remote ones, reduced inventory disappearance. An interesting story about conducting a detailed field inventory comes to mind.

Our German partners insisted on sending representatives from a large New York accounting firm to oversee the inspections. We shall refer to them as 'Steve' and 'John'. Both were in their mid twenties and were very personable. Observing field operations and conducting a hands on audit was a rarity for them. We had allotted about ten days, as the wells were very spread out. They enjoyed small town life compared to the big city.

Snakes were a major problem in our operations. Some wells were near swamps or deep in the bush. Black snakes and water moccasins were two types that we considered most threatening. In the steaming summer sun, they often found their way into our treater houses or under pumping unit bases. We were well versed in avoidance precautions.

Our pumpers often carried handguns for their protection on the more dangerous leases. Our auditors thought this was normal, coming from New York City. They incorrectly assumed being armed was a reaction to human danger. Seizing the opportunity to brag about trials and tribulations of life in the big city, we were treated to numerous exploits fit for Hollywood.

Their role was to record and photograph the description, quantity, serial number, and condition of all inventory on each lease. They performed this job diligently until one day, on opening a treater house door.....a huge sleeping snake (particular kind escapes my memory since snakes of all kinds were very numerous in these parts) made its presence known after they had entered. It was coiled and ready to strike.

There was a retreat to the truck at lightening speed! From that point on, they leaned out the window for a visual inspection and waited to hear the serial number called out to them. The quality of lease photographs deteriorated.

John, the Italian connection, introduced me to the art of 'Cow Tipping'. Apparently it was a popular sport where he went to college in upstate New York. According to his story, they would sneak out of their dormitories late at night on a dare. Farms and cattle operations were nearby. Once a field of cows was found unguarded, all would be pushed over. John claimed they were unable to get up on their own and would just lay there. Presumably in the morning the owner's first impression was that his/her herd had all died a mysterious death. It was a fate probably wished on John and his cohorts. No doubt it was a lot tougher pushing cows *up* than *down*.

As a fan of hockey, the National Hockey League scores are religiously checked in the newspaper each day during the season. A namesake of John's plays for one of the American teams. Whenever he is listed in the scoring statistics, my memory recounts Cow Tipping. It was not determined in my mind if it was for real or a story of distraction.

☑Faulty wellhead equipment was a serious and most dangerous problem. We established a routine of visually checking for leakage periodically, particularly suspended wells. Field hands carried thirty-six inch pipe wrenches and extension handles as standard equipment to continually tighten couplings and flange bolts. These precautions prolonged the life of the wells in many cases and our lives in others.

More than once we had to deal with a conservation mess after a leak sprayed a fine oil mist on the tree bordered lease. The oil was very light and high gravity (45 to 50 degrees API). In the hot summer sun the glittering shiny leaves could be seen for quite a distance. It was less noticeable after a few weeks when they began to die and turn brown.

One assignment involved a stopover in New York City for meetings between our management, the program promoter, an evaluation 'specialist' invited by the promoter, and our German partner. Now there are some real stories worth telling here, but the similarities with flashbacks of the NAKED CITY series prompted me to exercise prudence. It will suffice to give one example where Weaver tempted fate.

It was around 10 PM when the meetings ended the first night. Our Manhattan hotel was only a few blocks away, so we decided to walk for exercise. Charlie Chinneck, myself, and our President, 'Ron', called it a night as it was near 11 PM and we had another early agenda. Weaver was more adventuresome and checked out a nearby club for a nightcap. The next morning we read in the newspaper where a shoot-out just after midnight killed five patrons.

Following several days of discussion, all of us, less our German partner, returned to Marietta to see some of the problems firsthand.

To avoid the tedious and complex travel arrangements to get from New York City to Parkersburg, the promoter hired a private jet. By my recollection it was a six or seven passenger turboprop and was waiting for us at the airport as our cabs screeched onto the tarmac a few minutes late. Although my experience flying in small aircraft was considerable, it was not comforting for all of us. The ride was not the smoothest and some of our party were far happier after touching the ground.

A well that was very near the city limits had been nitrogen fractured recently and it was thought to be a good place to start our field tour.

Ron and I were walking up to the wellhead when we heard a loud hissing sound. The casing gauge had several thousand pounds of pressure registered, suggesting either a heck of a well or the formation had failed to accept the nitrogen frac.

On inspection, we found the main casing coupling cracked and leaking. It worsened as we observed, so we beat a hasty retreat. We later bled the pressure down, killed the well with water, and replaced the defective hardware. To my knowledge, that well never did produce economically.

Then it was the turn of the 'Scientist' to steal the show.

His claim to fame was an invention, represented by a sealed black box the size of a carton of cigarettes, which was to be lowered into the wellbore by wireline. The theory was that it could detect, quantify, and record the location of any hydrocarbons. Considering this feat had to be achieved despite the influence of steel casing and cement bond, it was even more astounding since no electrical impulse was required to activate this 'magic box' as we called it.

Other than Thirsty, none of us took this character seriously. How could we? When we got off the aeroplane, he stuck a pipe in his mouth, grabbed his suit bag by one hand, and twirled himself around like a windmill all the way to the terminal. Just where Thirsty found him we were not sure, but we heard it was through an ad in some science magazine. Hence the label 'Scientist' and no disrespect was intended for any professional scientists who may read this book.

The Scientist was always vague about how his invention worked, not that we considered it possible. He had no previous oil industry experience and avoided providing references. Weaver put the whole issue of this hoax in perspective. He asked the Scientist if his hydrocarbon detection invention worked on the same theory as reverse osmosis. Without hesitation he responded in the affirmative, declining elaboration when pressed by Weaver.

To us it was just another story of the Ohio oilpatch to add to our collection. Not only did we totally discount the probability of potential, we vigorously encouraged Thirsty to ignore it also.

Thirsty, however, was convinced of a breakthrough that would earn him the title of oil baron of the eastern U.S.

So he used his services on a couple of his own wells. The resulting expenditures on consulting fees to the Scientist and completion costs on the candidates were totally wasted. By the time it was determined that no success whatsoever had been realized, the Scientist was long gone.

☑The local solution for avoiding pumping unit capital and maintenance cost was to install a Plunger Lift System, also known as a "Rabbit". It was cheap by comparison and maintenance free.

Operators were infatuated with them without really having an understanding of their use. "Rabbits" represented a major saving for Turnkey cost programs and required minimal supervision.

The concept involved installing a close tolerance steel mandrel in the tubing. While sitting on fluid at the bottom of the hole, gas pressure would build up sufficiently to drive the "Rabbit" uphole. Fluid, water and/or oil, would be pushed and siphoned to surface over a period of time. Depending on gas and fluid influx rates, this could take hours or days.

The wellhead was configured to accommodate the "Rabbit" in a catcher until most of the gas and liquids were bypassed to the Separator. As the gas pressure was relieved, the mandrel slowly returned to the bottom of the well.

My problem with this system was our low pressure, low productivity wells. In most cases, there was not sufficient energy to drive the mandrel all the way to surface. In addition, where the Sales Inlet pressure exceeded wellbore pressure, the "Rabbit" could not discharge adequate gas volumes to repeat the cycle.

The Ohio oilpatch was rich with rumours of "Rabbit" success. Many times I learned the hard way that it was not uncommon to 'invent' successful results. By educating myself with all the Technical Papers and texts available on the Plunger Lift System, my judgement convinced me it was a futile exercise for these types of wells. Commitment of funds could not be justified.

Apparently the "Rabbit" supplier concluded that if we could be brought on side, then his marketplace would explode. When he offered to install a couple of systems free on a monthly trial basis, consent was given.

Both of us monitored operations with great interest. After several months and extensive equipment alterations, my scepticism was verified. As soon as our arrangement was cancelled, rumours flooded back to me - ' those Canadians are too ignorant and incompetent to know a good thing when they see it '.

☑Flow lines, believe it or not, were bright orange plastic and installed above ground. When a road or stream had to be crossed, trees were used. Every fall, come hunting season, we were kept busy for weeks repairing holes. They were used to sight in the guns.

This 'hobby' impacted home with dramatic effect one day. Leaning over a line rupture, assisting the pumper with repairs, the remote silence was broken by high powered rifle discharges. In no time my body was pressed flat on the ground, hoping to hide behind the two inch line. A hundred feet up the hill, where our orange plastic snaked beside a mud track, the earth erupted from several impacts during the next few minutes. The pumper did not move, but kept tightening the bolt on the clamp. He explained calmly that there was no danger. We were out of the line of sight and as soon as the shooter had adjusted his sights, represented by a line hit, he would move on. Apparently that is what happened, but my knees were weak as we walked up to fix this new leak.

Since the lease owners got free gas for their residence, they had an incentive to patrol and maintain these lines for us. Gradually most of the trouble areas were replaced with steel pipe. Economics of the remaining tied-in wells had become so poor with falling gas pricing after 1981 that ruptures were not addressed.

☑Although AFE budgets allocated funds for protecting our facilities with paint, it was not long before the elements prevailed and rust flourished. Most of our tanks and treaters remained a primer reddish orange. An amusing story sums up this section.

Over a several day period in the fall of 1981, most of our lease equipment within sight of a main township road received a coat of taupe/ green paint.

It came as a surprise, albeit a pleasant and most welcomed surprise. Any other wells owned or operated by GW in these areas also were freshly painted.

As the local story goes, a bus load of New York City investors were paraded through the field under the guise that all their wells were identified by their chosen colour. You guessed it, taupe/green. My schedule prevented me from meeting any of these investors to verify this. A bus was seen touring, but it was days before this story made the rounds. Little significance was attached to the forest of taupe/green facilities.

It would have added a touch of realism to paint some black patches on the sides to resemble oil. Many of the wells had never produced or produced very little. These tanks looked good as new for a very long time.

POST MORTEM

☒All the project funds were advanced in good faith but without adequate supervision.

☒The program was too large to properly monitor in the early stages, when it might have made a difference.

☒We spent like we were there for a long time, when the locals knew from history it would be temporary.

☒The concept of Turnkey Operations failed in Ohio.

IN SUMMARY, THERE WERE NO SHORTAGES OF EXCEPTIONAL DISAPPOINTMENTS. HIGHLIGHTS OF SUCCESS WERE PRECIOUS AND FEW. THE CANADIAN OILPATCH VALUES OF TRUST AND ETHICAL CONDUCT WERE PAINFULLY ABUSED.

WHEN WE DEPARTED OHIO, WE LEFT EVERYTHING BEHIND. AN INTERNAL EVALUATION OF 30 SEPTEMBER 1982 ESTIMATED THE 15% PRESENT WORTH VALUE OF THE OHIO ASSETS AT $1,488,000. LESS THAN A YEAR LATER, WITH A MORE REALISTIC ASSESSMENT OF WHAT WE HAD, WE WERE

NEGOTIATING TO DISPOSE OF EVERYTHING. IN
DESPERATION WE ACCEPTED LESS THAN OUR ENGINEERING
VALUE, BUT THAT IS BETTER DESCRIBED IN EPISODE 4.

YOU COULD SAY WE CAME FULLY CLOTHED AND LEFT
NEARLY STARK NAKED. IT ADEQUATELY DESCRIBES MY FEEL-
INGS ABOUT BOTH THE MAGNITUDE OF OUR INVESTMENT
LOSSES AND THE FAILURE OF OUR LONG RANGE BUSINESS
POLICY. THERE ARE A LOT OF SURPRISES YET TO COME ON
THIS LATTER ISSUE, SO STAY TUNED FOR EPISODE 3.

IN THE INTERIM THERE WERE FLEETING MOMENTS OF
GLORY. I WOULD BE REMISS TO IGNORE THEM JUST TO
DRAMATIZE THE IMPRESSION OF TOTAL DOOM AND GLOOM.
THERE WAS A PERSONABLE SIDE TO OHIO AND THESE EXPE-
RIENCES ARE STILL CHERISHED. LET'S VISIT A FEW.

IV
(Juice and Destinations)

As mentioned earlier, the complexity and magnitude of our
field problems, particularly the technical ones, justified the urgency
for assistance. Qualified Ohio operational specialists from Canton,
reserve evaluation consultants from Tulsa, and completion design
experts from Calgary all saw duty in our program. It had been decided that 1981 would be the year of decision. A second hundred
well program was to be cancelled unless answers and production
performance were forthcoming.

It was typical for the participants to put in ten to twelve hour
days, seven days a week, trying to co-ordinate and manage multiple testing, completion, and recompletion programs to satisfy the
unknowns and uncertainties of the program. Whenever my tour exceeded six or eight weeks, fatigue became an impediment.

This problem was solved by occasionally taking the entire
weekend off and leaving that world behind. Not unlike the outings
during my nine week Phase One course in Houston, the benefits

were inspirational and immediate. Both my professional and personal life reacted positively to these escapes. This concept was incorporated into all my U.S. assignments as Strategy No. 2.

Appealing to my keen interest in aviation and history, I ventured to nearby cities or adjacent States. My reward was just the kind of release and satisfaction that books are written about. Given all the pain and frustration of the Ohio program, each escape was my juice to deal with the next ordeal. My most memorable journey led indirectly, many years later, to a hobby still enthusiastically pursued to this day.

WASHINGTON, D.C. OR BUST(ED)

Spring of 1982 - knee deep in mud and up to our necks in workover programs - it was time for an escape. I had the perfect destination and expected there would be no problem convincing our resident consultant at the time, Art Williamson from Williamson and Delves Consulting Ltd. of Calgary, into joining me.

Art had been in Ohio several months by this time. His firm specialized in completions. Under contract to my employer, as well as several junior oil companies from Calgary also active in the Ohio / West Virginia area, Art brought much needed experience that was lacking in my background. The workload justified his opening of a local office and the transfer of key employees from the Calgary office.

Art and I had a common bond in our keenness for aviation. We were both licensed and experienced pilots. At one time we both owned our own aircraft. The 'blood' had been there a long time for both of us. Once airborne for the first time, the soul never forgets the sensation. Regardless of health, age, occupation, wealth, or stressful environment, a pilot always goes back to his roots in spirit or body. Aviation enthusiasts will associate with this healthy addiction.

Washington, D.C. was a Mecca of American history and aviation. From Marietta it was 335 miles or about six hours driving. Half of the distance is on Interstate divided highway. My enthusiasm convinced Art that by leaving very early Saturday morning, we could be in Washington by early afternoon.

Our intentions were to spend the remainder of Saturday afternoon at the Smithsonian Institution, of which much had been read in magazines. In the evening we could sample a restaurant or bar. That would leave Sunday morning for any other sights of interest before heading back to Marietta after lunch.

Now let me tell you what really happened.

If you have ever driven through West Virginia and Maryland, you know how scenic it is. Rubber-necking and driving 60 mph do not mix, so we lost some time being tourists. Weekends are also notorious in this area for roadside or front yard flea markets. We lost a little more time. Navigating through Washington, D.C. is not the same as driving across town in Marietta. Once we got to the city centre late Saturday afternoon, we discovered other 'must see' attractions.

By the time we had driven up to, or by, The White House, the Washington Monument, the Jefferson Memorial, the Lincoln Memorial, and Arlington National Cemetery, it was dark and well into the evening.

First order of business was to find a reasonably priced and safe motel not too far out of city centre. We were directed to the southeast of D.C. proper and had no trouble finding suitable accommodation. We were so near exhaustion and hungry that it felt like we had just put in a normal field day.

Our map indicated that Andrews Air Force Base was nearby. Actually we could hear occasional military jet traffic. Not that we had not seen an air base before, but this one was often referred to in aviation articles or military history. (Certainly the American hostages from Iran remember it fondly.) It was special to me, considered it worth seeing, and argued my case to reach inward for a little more energy.

Art, on the other hand, was hungry. He also had a bigger frame to consume his energy. We already had a long, eventful day. Food, followed by sleep, was his choice.

What a dilemma! You might ask why we just did not go our separate ways and reunite at the motel. Then you would be asked if you had ever been to Washington, D.C. at night, as a first time tourist, and alone. Case closed; we stayed together.

We solved this dispute the logical way, with a coin toss. Victor chooses, Loser - no hard feelings.

The name of the restaurant and the kind of meal escapes me. It was close to the motel, but even at that it must have been near midnight before we got to bed.

Sunday morning, after some breakfast (Art was having no more of my fasting to save time and money), we headed directly for the

National Air and Space Museum at the Smithsonian. You have heard the expression 'like kids let loose in a candy store'. Believe me it applied here.

Entire hangar-size rooms were devoted to themes such as:

1) **AIR RACING:** symbolized, for example, by the suspended original Hughes H-1, designed and flown by Howard Hughes to a new world record of 567 km/h (352.322 mph) on 13 September 1935;

2) **WORLD WAR II:** symbolized, for example, by the suspended original Supermarine Spitfire S/N EN474, representing the premier Royal Air Force fighter from the Battle of Britain era;

3) **THE JET AGE:** symbolized, for example, by a suspended original North American X-15, the first aircraft to fly four, five, and six times the speed of sound and enabling it to bridge the gap between manned flight within the atmosphere and manned flight beyond the atmosphere into space;

4) **THE SPACE AGE :** symbolized by a full-size mock-up of a Lunar Module, identical to those landed on the moon in the Apollo missions.

Films were shown on a continuous basis in most theme rooms, such as the last landing during the Apollo 17 mission or black and white aerial combat documentaries. There was not a minute to lose trying to take in as much as possible.

When it closed at 6 PM, we were still there. We tried all our negotiating ploys with security to stay longer. They would have none of it and forced us out the door shortly after. While it seemed like we had been inside a week, we wished we had another week at our disposal. It was overwhelming. It was absolutely a must see for aviation buffs. One cannot say enough about it and do it proper justice. We were just glad the opportunity was seized to see it. We had barely scratched the surface; the Smithsonian encompassed fifteen other museums and galleries.

Here we were in the centre of the city again at night, six to seven hours steady driving from Marietta, and we were **both starved**. Decision time. We felt so good about the excitement of the day, we got a motel room and pigged out at a buffet. Plan B seemed logical; get up real early and scoot back to Marietta before noon when we had a workover rig scheduled for a recompletion.

The fact that we did not get going next morning as early as we wanted did not phase me. My plan was to make up time by speeding half of the way on Interstate 70. My assumption was that everyone would be hurrying *into* Washington on a Monday morning, clearing our speedy departure without fear of traffic jams or radar traps.

The plan worked to a 75 mph perfection until just beyond Hagerstown, Maryland, 75 miles north of Washington. Breezing to the top of a big hill with a panoramic view of eight to ten miles of flat, isolated freeway below and beyond, I remarked to Art that it was an obvious location for a radar trap. The next thing we noticed was the red flashing light in my rear view mirror.

Our sole concern that day was getting back to the workover by noon. While inwardly steaming about what this ticket would cost me in U.S. dollars, Art was reassured that my punishment would be accepted without argument and we would be on our way in minutes. To assist the process, I jumped out of the car and ran back to the Highway Patrol cruiser with my license and rental car registration.

The trooper had already finished his radio check to ensure the car was clean.

*"I suppose you're one of those hotshot politicians who thinks you can hotrod through my County. I've heard all the stories before how important you politicians are, and it has **never** prevented me from writing up the ticket. That's why I only got two stripes. I used to have three but some Washington bigwig took offence and had me busted down a rank. Like I said, forget the stories cause you're gettin a ticket anyway."*

Being dumbfounded is why his conversation has remained so vivid over the years. Glancing at my watch, my guilt was readily admitted and the consequences accepted. My ticket was requested politely, thinking how angry Art was getting.

" Just where are ya from , anyway", he asked?

He was told promptly that we had been visiting Washington all weekend. It had been so fascinating that we lost track of time and were late for a Monday appointment in Marietta, Ohio.

" So what do you do in Marietta? I see you have a rental car."

What was sure to sound foreign to him was briefly summarized, explaining that we were in the oil industry out of Canada and were drilling a bunch of wells near Marietta. Because we were really interested in aviation and military history, we just had to see Washington, D.C.

Boy, did that open a can of worms. He insisted on my company in the patrol car. During the next forty-five minutes, without so much as an opportunity for me to interrupt, he told me of his interest in the American Civil War. One of the national magazines (it may have been Time) had recently published a story on his discovery of a battleground previously unrecognized by historians.

The Northern and Southern armies had clashed in a major battle some fifteen miles south. (Weeks later, to satisfy my curiosity, the history books in the Marietta library were checked. My knowledge of the U.S. Civil War was nil. Sure enough there was a National Battlefield called Antietam. This story was related several times over the years until someone corrected my pronunciation of 'Anti - tam' to 'Ann - tee - tam'.)

After years of research and metal detector investigation, he verified his theory of additional clashes by unearthing a plentiful inventory of spent and live ammunition, belt buckles, buttons, coins, and medals. He was very proud of proving the historians wrong and being recognized for it.

All this time Art was sitting serenely in our car, twenty feet or so ahead, not having any idea what was causing a delay which was reaching a crises for our travel plans.

With diplomacy and courteous dialogue, my ticket was accepted and I extricated myself from a conversation that really did not interest me. My legs bolted back to our car after promising to keep my speed down.

Now we were worried about 'how' late we were going to be, not 'if'. My decision was to let some time pass before throwing myself at Art's mercy. My first priority was to get out of range of the Trooper so speeding could make up some time.

Within a few minutes our silence was broken with my gasp " there's another flashing light behind us, **but honest we weren't speeding**".

It was only a few minutes delay, but each minute was costly for our timetable. Our Civil War celebrity had forgotten to give me back my license. This time *he* ran up to our car. In a way it was my reward for listening to him for so long. A far greater reward was to follow, but that would take until the end of the decade and many EPISODES later in this book.

When we got to Marietta early in the afternoon we went straight to the field. Luckily for us the workover was behind schedule. Life went on as before. Then the unexpected happened.

My ticket was $75 (talk about a string of 75s) and due in two weeks. Payment was mailed promptly, using a chequing account maintained in Marietta since my initial arrival for just such an emergency. What followed contributed to my first of two adages for U.S. operations and appears in later EPISODES as '**Expect the Unexpected**'.

In Calgary a few months later a summons was issued for my arrest. My cheque had bounced and a second notice had been ignored. This notice had been sent to the Marietta motel address whose letterhead had been used when payment was mailed. Unfortunately, as was my habit, motels had been changed in the interim. Big trouble could be expected at the airport unless this mess got straightened out quickly. And my presence was due back in Marietta without delay.

Knowing sufficient funds had been deposited back in 1980 and had not been withdrawn, my first call was to the Manager of the Marietta bank. To my surprise, he informed me that $5 was deducted each month in which no transactions occurred. Since it is usually my nature to be cautious about incurring these kind of burdens, further investigation revealed the bank had treated my lowly few hundred dollar deposit like an 'all privileges' account. No statement had been issued to warn me of the deteriorating balance or the peculiar fees (at that time, although common now). Naturally my mood was testy.

An apologetic letter from the bank and a reissued cheque to the Maryland Highway Patrol removed me from the 'most wanted speeder' list in time for my next Ohio assignment. It has often been considered looking up that Trooper to assure him the whole incident was a misunderstanding. My fear was that the reputation of Canadian oilmen (and oilwomen) had been characterized in the same script as the politicians he disdained. No doubt my bad cheque was coffee talk at the station.

DAYTON ON MY MIND

One of my more memorable solo excursions had been a must since the early days, but it was the first Sunday in October 1981 before it could be worked in.

Dayton was 190 miles northwest of Marietta, so only a three and one-half hour drive. It was fortunate that the following year of my tour was so busy, otherwise I probably would have argued with myself every weekend to return. It is the home of Wright-Patterson Air Force Base and the Air Force Museum. More recently it hosted the Bosnian peace talks and subsequent Peace Accord late in 1995.

Dayton was the birthplace of aviation. It was home to the Wright brothers and Orville's historic five minute and four second flight of November 09, 1904. The stories of the brothers' early years, their bicycle shop, their printing press business and their early aviation efforts were in evidence throughout the greater Dayton area.

Wright-Patterson was one of the largest and most important bases in the United States Air Force. Included in this 8174-acre military complex were dozens of logistics and systems headquarters responsible for American security throughout the world. Specialists in planning, project engineering and management, weapons testing, and weapons systems acquisition were among the jobs of 24000 employed there in 1981.

This base was famous before my birth. During World War II, captured enemy aircraft were brought here for assessment and testing. Many of the new generation, post World War II jets had their 'bugs' ironed out here. Likewise many of America's most famous Test Pilots, such as Chuck Yeager, drew assignments to Wright-Patterson. The Air Launched Cruise Missile, the F-15, the A-10, and the F-16 were among the major programs in progress at the time of my visit.

The Air Force Museum was dedicated September 03, 1971 by President Richard Nixon. Over 160 indoor and outdoor static exhibits of military aircraft and missiles were on display. Numerous countries were represented, as was nearly a Century of flying history. From the World War I Spad VIII to the XB-70, it was the oldest and largest military museum in the world. Of those visited on several continents, it remains the best. If you are determined to see one aviation museum in your lifetime, see this one. My trip was uneventful and very pleasant, prompting a return one year later.

The second time a friend accompanied me. 'Renee' worked for a water hauling contractor we used during workovers. To my satisfaction, her two teenage daughters and teenage son were encouraged to come along. No small feat considering there was not a blood vessel in their collective bodies interested in aviation.

My salesman talents must have been good back then. They took a genuine interest in the displays and their historical significance. It was enjoyable being a tour guide and sharing my knowledge. It was gratifying to witness their willingness, in the end, to actually enjoy 'an adult thing'. They were rewarded with their favourite meal, pizza (what else for teenagers), on the way back that evening.

They grew up with this oasis in their own backyard without awareness. A foreigner had travelled thousands of miles and made it a priority to see. The realization that followed is a common weakness in most of us. We tend to take our heritage and surroundings for granted until an outsider attaches significance.

A personal example is Kananaskis Country, a Provincial Park 45 minutes west of Calgary. It offers plenty of cross-country and downhill skiing venues for winter recreation. Very rarely have we used the camping and golfing facilities. Until Father's Day 1996, any other value was overlooked or taken for granted.

In our first venture testing picnic facilities, we checked in at the Barrier Lake Visitor's Centre and discovered The Colonel's Cabin Picnic Area.

A one hour nature walk exhibited and identified many of Alberta's popular trees and flowers. Several rest stops offered commanding, elevated views of the surrounding protected forest and lake area.

The remains of a World War II prisoner of war camp, which held up to 700 German officers, was revealed in a 20 minute self-guided walking tour. Many artifacs, paintings, and photos were on display in the restored Commandant's Cabin.

It was all interesting, informative, and *free*. The picnic grounds were our private domain this day. We had unknowingly driven by the entrance, to crowded destinations elsewhere in the Park, for years. Based on the privacy we experienced that Sunday, apparently most other visitors did also.

FAIR'S FAIR

During the summer of 1982, there was a class event in a city that had always been on my list to visit. Distance was a deterrent at 475 miles each way. Plenty of unused vacation days remained. The opportunity might not have come again, so it was off to Knoxville, Tennessee in August 1982 to visit The 1982 World's Fair.

The attraction for me was the theme "Energy Turns The World". It was not that long ago when the 1970s doom-and-gloom projection catch phrase, the "Energy Crisis", had cast the world into an uncertain future. The intent of this World's Fair was to demonstrate that tomorrow would bring new answers and a new quality of life by focusing on the energy question and the creative energy of mankind. When you consider the subsequent strides in more efficient production methods and wiser uses, leading to increased supply and lower cost, they may have had a point.

Given the energy theme, Knoxville was an appropriate site. NASA had a large exhibit, so it was automatically my first and priority destination.

Knoxville was the home of the Tennessee Valley Authority, the nation's largest public utility; the Oak Ridge National Laboratory; and the University of Tennessee, which conducts extensive energy research.

These institutions, along with the U.S. Department of Energy and a number of leading national corporations, joined forces with the Fair. By sponsoring an international energy symposia, the ultimate goal was to spawn new solutions to the world's energy problems. It was obvious no symposia could help our Ohio problems, so my determination was to enjoy the outing.

What is most remembered about this three day excursion was the scenic drive through West Virginia, along the eastern border of Kentucky, across the south-western tip of Virginia, and eastern Tennessee. Again abundant front yard flea markets interrupted my timetable more than a few times.

The weather co-operated the entire time, but the stifling heat of Knoxville that August was imprinted on my mind. Although the rolling countryside was scenic and stunning, the city's size and isolation reminded me of Regina.

It seemed like an improbable venue for a World's Fair. That was until the Great Smoky Mountains National Park was discovered, less than an hour's drive southeast. The park is open all year and offers 238 miles of paved and 146 miles of gravel roads.

The Great Smoky Mountains are old and worn. Millions of years ago, the continents of Africa and North America collided, bending and folding the bedrock. The resulting mountain peaks rose to 20,000 feet above sea level.

The forces of erosion - wind, water, and ice - almost reduced the Smokies to a level plain. This plain was then lifted high into the sky once again. Time and the elements eroded this elevated plateau down also. Again the worn land was uplifted. This plateau, represented by the mountains we see today, is still being carved away.

The name came from blue, smoke-like haze that almost always hangs over the mountain peaks. Several days is hardly sufficient to witness the breathtaking scenery throughout this fifty-three mile long, eighteen mile wide treasure of 520,000 acres.

It boasts some of the highest mountains in eastern North America and one of the oldest land areas on Earth. Sixteen summits rise more than 6000 feet, and the main ridge drive remains above 5000 feet for thirty-six miles. There were more vehicle turnouts per mile than any other park in my travels.

Fontana Dam, the tallest dam east of the Rockies, was built during World war II to provide power for Oak Ridge National Laboratory. Behind the dam is Fontana lake, the centrepiece of the Fontana area.

Few protected areas in the U.S. support more varied vegetation or rival the more than one hundred native species of trees. In the 1996/97 American Forestry Association's National Registry of Big Trees the Park is listed as home for seventeen champion or co-champion trees. Included are some of the largest tracts of old-growth forests remaining in the east, estimated at 100,000 to 120,000 acres.

Since establishment in 1934, it has become one of the most visited parks in America. The 469 mile scenic Blue Ridge Parkway originates here and snakes north through the Appalachian Mountains to Shenandoah National Park in northern Virginia.

Complementing the scenery was the congenial attitude of the people of Knoxville. Kindness and genuine hospitality made me feel comfortable. The Fair's layout and design easily accommodated the huge mass of visitors without inconvenience. Pavilions were colourful and innovative.

Pigeon Forge, Tennessee (gateway to Great Smoky Mountains National Park)

Author, Knoxville World's Fair, Aug 1982

The exception was the Canadian exhibit. Our handout brochure featured the Maple Leaf flag superimposed over the province of Ontario. The impression, on those less knowledgeable about

Canada, implied Toronto was the capitol city in the centre of the country, with Thunder Bay on the west coast and Ottawa on the east. While it may have seemed harmless, using the Fair's exposure was unfairly opportunistic.

Knowing that all provinces had contributed to Canada's Pavilion, this did not seem fair. My feelings were expressed to the staff (college students from Ontario), who showed little sympathy. Clearly, the organizers should have known better.

BUSINESS WITH PLEASURE

By spring 1982, we had given up almost all hope of salvaging the Ohio project. Our German partner, however, kept insisting we explore all potential solutions.

Since Pittsburgh was one of my stops on the way to Marietta, a two day layover May 16-18 allowed me to attend a technical convention. It was hosted by the Society of Petroleum Engineers and the theme was oil and gas recoveries from unconventional tight reservoirs (certainly applicable to Ohio). The list of speakers was distinguished and some technical papers caught my attention. Unfortunately it was too little, too late.

What was accomplished was an appreciation for Pittsburgh as a very scenic and friendly city. Relying on more rumour than fact, a bland, dirty, crowded, coal and steel town was expected. Nothing could have been further from the truth.

Pittsburgh was very green and clean. At night, after the seminars, I strolled the downtown Point State Park, along the river, without worry of safety. Actually three rivers met at the apex of the city core. Just across one of them was the Three Rivers baseball Stadium, appropriately named.

Post cards carried the caption " Pittsburgh at night is one of the most beautiful cities in all the world". Rainbow night lighting, with reflections off the waters, reminded me of my first visit to New York City. It was not wise to venture any more comparisons.

This uneventful exploit was mentioned because my memory was still vivid on experiencing the opposite of what was expected. Anyone passing through Pittsburgh should arrange a stopover, even if it is just for the day.

Maybe it was just being in the vacinity of, but still distant from, the oilfields that made it seem so medicinal. In any event, it helped to maintain my sanity a little while longer. The events of EPISODE 3 would tax my faculties in a far greater capacity than my experiences in Ohio. In a rude way, Canada's version of The Naked City villain was discovered.

Pittsburgh, May 1982 (apex of three rivers)

Panoramic view of Pittsburgh, Three Rivers Stadium on left

EPISODE 3: ....AND HUNG OUT TO DRY

I
(Shoot The Messengers)

Oil and gas prices had declined considerably between 1980 and 1983. Exploration and development costs had increased with inflation. The National Energy Policy had devastated the balance sheets of most Canadian oil and gas companies. The exchange rate between the Canadian and U.S. currencies had turned decidedly in favour of the Americans. Timing could not have been worse for the long range energy investment policy of our parent mining employer (Corporation).

Many of the Corporation's United States ventures were marginally economic or failures. The decision to participate in a high risk wildcat venture in the Canadian Arctic was also unfavourable for an energy company our size.

The consensus of the Calgary staff for some time had been to consolidate and retrench in Alberta, where we knew the ground rules and our limitations. However the Corporation set policy, sometimes rolled the dice, and we carried out instructions.

It was not comforting to be blamed for Ohio, but it came with the territory. My conscience was clear, knowing I had given everything I had. Having spent half my years of employment *on the road*, my personal and professional commitment carried a price tag money could not solve.

Marriage intentions and family relations were relegated to second place. Hobbies of real estate and stock market investing were too difficult to monitor from afar. Prolonged absences resulted in some serious losses; not all were retrievable. An enviable network of Canadian contacts faded. The stigma of the Ohio fiasco became my excess baggage; a resume discredit.

My risks in these outcomes were adsorbed with humility. No accountability was expected from the Corporation other than what was agreed to under the terms of employment. That was the Canadian way, or so it was thought.

Failure in Ohio terminated future Joint Venture oil and gas operations with our German partner. No doubt this was a business embarrassment. In years to follow I was apprised of the Corporation's efforts to minimize Ohio's financial impact on our partner's investment. If anything, this only prolonged the agony rather than swallowing a bitter pill and getting on. As for the oil and gas employees, however, the reaction was swift and unforgiving.

The oil and gas division was actively marketed by our parent during the first half of 1983. A new junior capital pool emerged as a potential suitor. It would have been preferable to weather the storm together, rather than being cast adrift in a lifeboat of unknown construction.

The following extraction from my records suggested to me that rather than learn from our Ohio experiences, we copied them. The actions of our parent were all the more provocative when considering their profitable mining operations.

The summer of 1983 was one for the archives. Pains were taken to share it, despite being off topic. The Americans don't deserve all the credit for this book.

PLOT # 1:
In April 1983 the Corporation's President advised Petroleum Division staff that a sale of part of the assets was imminent. The goal was to transfer premises and staff to the Purchaser as a going concern with the same people but under new management.

Contrary to the uncertainty to which the staff had been subjected, disposition promised to be the best option for all concerned. Everyone was encouraged to carry out their role in the affairs of the Division diligently and with a positive attitude. In return, we would be kept advised.

• Even to an untrained eye, there was something wrong with this picture. Reference to part of the petroleum properties referred to many of the marginal and/or contentious assets. Valuable Saskatchewan and Alberta properties were retained by our parent. Of course, as employees, we knew that and were concerned that the limited cash flow and development potential of the offering would not sustain either the premises or staff for long.
• The Purchaser's initial stock offering price of $2.55 eventually declined to the equivalent of $0.20. In 1992 the Purchaser was acquired by a large Canadian oil and gas corporation.

- The employees performed all that was asked of them. Rather than take advantage of other industry opportunities, as some of us were fortunate to have, we put allegiance ahead of survival. We ensured the acquisition went smoothly. Less than a year later, only three of the Division's original fifteen employees were still on the payroll of the Purchaser.
- Despite the pledge to keep us informed of material changes, we learned at the eleventh hour that there were **no** provisions for including staff seniority, title or benefits in the transfer and **no** offer of severance for termination.

II
("You Will All Forget About It")

In late June 1983 we received written terms of employment from the Purchaser. The offer was non-negotiable and open for acceptance until 30 June 1983, the effective sale date. On 29 June 1983, five senior staff convened a meeting to discuss our concerns with the Corporation's General Manager and senior negotiator (GMN).

The meeting lasted ninety minutes and here is a flavour from the notes taken. Participants included Operations Vice President (OVP); Exploration Vice President (EVP); Controller (CON); Senior Reservoir Analyst (SRA); and myself (NVL).

PLOT # 2:
(EVP) You claimed salary and benefits would remain the same over the transfer. My benefits are decreased by about $10,000 ..... that isn't equitable.
(OVP) My situation is similar, the Purchaser gave us letters of employment only five to seven days ago.
(GMN) As of January 10, 1983 the salary and benefits of individuals were to remain the same, until the transfer date. If you are unhappy with the terms now, quit, or try to negotiate as individuals. I'm concerned that you are resisting going over to the Purchaser.
(EVP) But the Purchaser is not going to negotiate. They gave us letters and said there was no room to negotiate.
(GMN) Then you must accept that.
(SRA) Everyone who has been dealing with the Purchaser has found their people do not know the situation or terms of employment.

(OVP) I'm actually getting a decrease of 20% of total benefits
(GMN) Some of you are still fortunate to still have your jobs. Keep that in mind.
(NVL) But the Purchaser should be offering the same benefit package.
(GMN) If you believe that, negotiate with the Purchaser.
(EVP) At the April 13 meeting I asked you to talk to the staff, and you assured all of us the salary and benefits would be on comparable terms. I assumed the Purchaser would be offering comparable benefits and as a result kept a positive attitude.
(GMN) Benefits will be explained to you by the V.P. of Administration.
(NVL) Can we get a two week extension to decide on the employment letter?
(GMN) You must make your decision by 09:30 June 30 or they won't offer it again.
(EVP) You represented to us to 'keep a positive attitude' and that we would be getting the same or equivalent salary and benefits.
(GMN) If you put in the effort, you will be rewarded accordingly. I have no comment on misrepresented items.
(NVL) We don't want to throw away our experience. Would you work there?
(GMN) If the Purchaser was in Vancouver, I would. I have a good feeling about their management team. They intend to have 1/2 billion $ in assets in five years. They will negotiate for drilling funds in Germany. We feel strongly about them.
(SRA) If you don't sign the Purchaser's offer, what happens?
*(GMN) We would likely terminate people that didn't go over there. No transition is easy, but **after time you will all forget about it**.*
(EVP) Why didn't you tell us when you were sure the deal would go through? In take-overs, companies often offer all employees a bonus to stay on during the transition and for some period after this. I'm talking from $5,000 to $50,000 per employee depending on length of service and position.

Our mood of confusion was pretty clear and it has been belaboured enough. In the end the Corporation got their bucks, in excess of $25 million. The choice properties contributing much of the cash flow were retained. Most General and Administrative expenses were eliminated. The jury is still out on what we got.

The 'forget with time' theory did not quite pass the test. Possibly it might have something to do with inequities. The Corporation hardly missed a beat since 1983.

III
(The Oilpatch...is a small world)

During my Ohio field tenure it was shocking to experience or observe constant abuse of goodwill and trust. Prophetically it now appears this was timely training. It still remains puzzling that a powerful and wealthy corporation, my employer, would renege on a contract.

Rather than dispense with a simple matter of earned compensation, the Corporation resorted to insults. A logical excuse or agenda for their behaviour escapes me to this day.

My duties had been performed and dues paid. The Corporation's mistake was thinking it was just about money.

PLOT # 3:

To the Corporation's senior negotiator (GMN), my request of June 30, 1983 was submitted in accordance with instructions from the Vice President of Administration:

"Substantial overtime was accumulated during 1982 as the result of extended Ohio field assignments. The interoffice memo of March 3, 1982 (copy attached) authorizes special time off or pay as compensation.

The Corporation, as the result of property and asset sales to the Purchaser effective June 30, 1983, has terminated my employment with the Oil and Gas Division. Therefore, I am hereby requesting remuneration under terms of my employment.

The overtime for which I am entitled totals 47 1/2 days. Since there have been no salary adjustments since October 1981, my average daily rate in 1982 or 1983 will apply. Summaries of applicable periods are attached. All times listed are supported by expense account statements maintained by the Corporation's Accounting Department. Copies from my personnel file can also be supplied if desired. "

The Corporation reacted promptly, as per the President's July 5, 1983 response:

" I received your letter dated June 30, 1983 and it will be dealt with appropriately. I must say that it has been interesting to see the varied reaction from staff members to our approach to the recession, which was to keep the staff intact and to find them the opportunity of a new home along with the sale of our oil and gas properties, rather than invoke massive layoffs a year earlier as so many other companies did."

You would have thought my request included one of their Mines. It surprised me that senior management dealt with such trivia. According to the Financial Times of January 10, 1983, the Corporation's 1978 - 1981 profits were (in millions of dollars) 4.5, 22.7, 31.8, and 11.9.

The reaction reminded me of my initial conflicts in Ohio. Our Operator would aggressively resort to offence when faced with defending an action contrary to contractual or AFE responsibility. Our Ohio adversaries were very skilled at distracting attention from the original crises. It was a tactic recognized early on.

When resolving an Operator issue became too complex, time consuming, and energy inefficient to justify the means, fair judgement prevailed for the benefit of our program. It was not as important to win as it was to maintain integrity and purpose. These qualities bond co-operation and working relationships for future commitment. The oilpatch, Canadian or American, is a small world.

IV
(Not About Money)

The similarities between Ohio and the Corporation were hard to ignore. Either my side of the story was distorted, or needed clarification to avoid confrontation.

Unofficially my advice was '*I was entitled to nothing and I would get nothing*'. After consideration, my July 11, 1983 response to the President clarified my position.

PLOT # 4:
" *Thank you for replying to my letter of June 30, 1983 to Mr. 'GMN'.*

Firstly; during a staff meeting April 13, 1983, Mr. 'GMN' assured all staff who chose to remain with the Oil and Gas Division through the transition, and assume a new role and challenge at the Purchaser, would do so with a compensation package equal to what was currently in place at that time. With few exceptions, most employees realized a 20% reduction in salary due to the loss of so many benefits. However, this became evident only when the Purchaser's offer was presented — a short time before the Corporation's official termination notice on June 30, 1983. Although approached, neither party was willing to negotiate this matter. I remain to be convinced that assurances given in bad faith are tolerated in either Mining or Petroleum industries.

Secondly; a meeting was held this June 29th with Mr. GMN to voice our concerns about conflicting statements on our benefit package. It quickly became evident to all of us that neither our rights nor aspirations had been considered during Corporation - Purchaser negotiations. Time and effort to demonstrate legitimate concerns or issues at the very least deserves reply.

Thirdly; my "reaction" is based on Corporate Policy which directly affects me, recession or not, and thus would be imprudent to ignore. This reaction was discussed with the Vice President, Administration on June 29, when it was agreed that if presented in proper written format, it would be assessed and actioned in a timely manner in accordance with the Policy guidelines. We are discussing overtime pay which was earned and thus entitled under the terms of employee termination."

Integrity was on trial and values were at stake, not money.

V
('June 30 Is A Full Work Day')

One might have wondered who was minding the fort back at the Mines, with such a barrage of correspondence. Each succeeding reply introduced more complex, time consuming, and energy inefficient rationale for avoiding the issue. It sounded distressingly familiar.

The Vice President, Administration sent a July 19, 1983 Letter Agreement. After a three page exhaustive exoneration of their rigid stance, the Corporation blinked.

"However in the interest of a satisfactory settlement and in line with the concerned policy that we have followed in Calgary we are prepared to recompense you for 10 days. If you agree to this settlement please return a copy of this letter duly signed."

The Corporation may have been large, successful, and wealthy but they were morally lacking when it came to distinguishing between rocks and people. Although many of the staff investigated legal action, most were convinced otherwise, either by the potential expense or by persuasion.

In my reasoning, both my career and persona would suffer by succumbing to a retreat from principles. Preference was to have the Courts judge the Corporation's record. Settlement was not a motive or priority.

As the Plaintiff, a Statement of Claim was filed before July ended. Examination for Discovery commenced in December 1983. The Corporation incurred travel and accommodation costs for their Officers to attend.

On January 30, 1985 the Corporation, through their attorney, offered a settlement for the overtime that had been claimed. It did not include compensation for legal expenses, which were considerable. The point of no return had been passed and it was rejected.

My Counsel was blunt.

"We would emphasize our advice to you that the effect of a Rule 169 Offer of Judgement is that should you go to Court and get less than 'the offer', the Court will order you to pay the legal fees for the Defendant for proceeding to Trial in this matter, and you will forfeit your right to legal fees as against the Defendant. As you are aware from our previous opinion letter, we have advised you that it is likely that the award at Judgement may be less than 'the offer'."

Court of Queen's Bench Action No. 8301 proceeded to Trial in Calgary in February 1985. VPO and VPE were called to testify on my behalf. The Corporation bore the inconvenience and expense of relocating two of their senior Officers to Calgary for a three day period.

Judgement was rendered February 15, 1985. The outcome was favourable since the Corporation had failed to honour the Contract between us. Opposing Counsel sparred for six more weeks before it was resolved that the Judgement award, in all its complexities, exceeded the pre-trial 'offer'. In the end a four figure cheque was collected, $500 less than my legal fees.

What transpired was not an act of revenge, stubbornness, or pride. It was a rare opportunity to stand up for principle, to show one's true values. My values were not for sale. Most people may have taken the easier route, but the choice was mine alone and it was taken without regret.

To sum it up in one line, it would be the June 28, 1983 memo from 'GMN' to All Staff: *"I would just like to remind everyone that Thursday, June 30, is a full work day for the Corporation"*. It was a connotation that reveals more between the lines with each reading.

EPISODE 4: OHIO - NEW BLOOD, OLD WOUNDS

I
(Terminally Ill)

The Ohio assets became the property of 'Tripoli Resources' (Tripoli) in July 1983. Although a new company, it was adequately staffed. Their recent acquisition included several major U.S. properties and a position was offered to me as the result of my U.S. experience. The corporate long range focus, however, was the expansion and development of the Canadian assets.

My first priority was to provide an updated U.S. property status to the Vice President of Production, Tom Gorkoff. Elaboration was provided for Ohio and North Dakota, where an extensive performance evaluation had been prepared recently.

As for immediate attention, Ohio was the most critical. Our Operator, 'GW', had filed for Chapter 11 bankruptcy protection early in 1982. Our past Promoter was the replacement. If you guessed the Greenwich chain smoker, 'Thirsty', you're right.

To sum up my impressions of the project's future, a Summary Memorandum prepared August 17, 1982 was reproduced. Here are selective extracts.

"RE: Cumulative Gas and Oil Sales - Ohio Program
Gas and oil sales, derived from Weekly Status Reports, are provided below on a weekly basis. It should be noted that neither flared nor vented gas volumes were measured and thus were not recorded. This amount can be considered substantial, however, during the early history of the Program when lack of gas line tie-ins would have otherwise impaired oil production. Subsequently the GOR calculations lack accuracy.

Week Ending	Gas Production (mcf)	Oil Production (bbl)	Cum. Gas Production (mmcf)	Cum. Oil Production (mbbl)	Weekly GOR (mcf/bbl)
1980-08-08	770	747	0.770	7.664	1.031
1981-05-01	3930	962	139.222	56.013	4.082
1981-05-29(a)	341	1239	150.755	60.538	0.275
1981-12-11(b)	2022	492	214.881	82.312	4.110
1982-08-06	1039	346	267.270	98.111	3.003

NOTES: a) the Gas Purchaser curtailed deliveries and decreased price in half
b) Operator 'GW' filed for Bankruptcy and was replaced by 'Thirsty'

Further representation of production history is provided in the attached graphs for ready reference.

We can summarize from Graph I that the peak daily oil production rate was reached in December 1980 and never again challenged. Unless completion techniques are improved or the problems associated with pumping the wells are solved, then cumulative production is estimated to be in the range of 115000 barrels by December 1984. This represents an increase of only 17000 barrels over the next 29 months.

Similarly in Graph II gas production peaked in February 1981 and, due to 'the Purchaser's' cutback of June 1981, remained on a steep decline slope. Forecast of the cumulative gas production by December 1984 is estimated at 332 mmcf, or approximately an additional 65 mmcf assuming the current dismal market conditions prevail.

From Graph III it is apparent that oil and gas production rates tracked each other closely through the history of the program. The replacement of GW as operator in December 1981 arrested the sharp production decline temporarily; however the long term projection is still constant decline unless considerable expenditures for recompletions are committed. Likewise the failure of artificial lift on most wells must be addressed and resolved - also at considerable cost.

Conclusions:
Since only fifteen to twenty wells represent the bulk of current production, the more feasible and economic approach to the Program would be to contract daily operations out to a local and inexpensive group at the going rate of $200 to $300 per well per month. Allowing for minimum remedial overhead, the project should average 400 to 500 barrels of oil per week and generate some cash flow. Once the

gas marketing situation has been resolved sometime in 1983 or 1984, and after extensive research has been conducted to determine how to complete/recomplete those zones in wells suspected of severe cement invasion, an opportunity may exist to once again attempt to rectify GW's mistakes."

Although these forecasts were now one year old, little had changed. The interpretations were still applicable in mid-1983. Production decline was exactly as predicted. The gas marketing curtailment and weak pricing was unresolved. Operating costs had escalated under Thirsty's guidance, mainly from inexperience. It was not for lack of faith or effort.

Thirsty believed in Ohio just as strongly as when he promoted Canadian firms into the area back in 1980. He raised considerable funds from family, friends, and investors to drill and operate his own program. This involved possibly as many as ten new wells.

The weak link in his plan was a common mistake with all participants. Rushing ahead so as not to miss out, adequate evaluation and preparation suffered.

Ohio lacked a mature oilfield environment. Most contract services and equipment suppliers were relatively new and inexperienced for tackling the risky technical challenges.

Certainly there were recoverable oil and gas reserves in southern Ohio. Thorough evaluation on an individual well basis, however, revealed most were not economical unless capital costs, overhead, and administration were minimized and controlled.

When an investment strategy lacks comprehensive technical and financial budgeting, the result is all too often similar to what developed in Ohio. Instead of basing operational decisions on theory and practise, reliance was placed on local hearsay and rumour.

Needless to say, Thirsty fared no better than us Canucks. To my knowledge, he lost everything and filed for bankruptcy several years later. In Ohio, no quarter was given, regardless of nationality.

Thus the stage was set for Tripoli's indoctrination. Ohio was not a pretty sight in the summer of 1983.

Total program production averaged 50 BOPD and 100 MCFPD, of which Tripoli's share was 47 1/2 percent. Estimated remaining recoverable reserves were insignificant. Plug and abandonment liability for one hundred and six wellbores, however, was not.

My preference was to sell these assets without delay. Tripoli was of the same opinion, but wanted to get a current and accurate accounting of the balance sheet first. This urgency was predicated on a sizeable and unexpected invoice from our German partner's New York office. It supposedly represented previously unpaid operational bills to Thirsty. Tripoli's Controller, Rod Mitton, asked me to brief him. It was news to both of us, and a new relationship was born.

In August 1983, I met Mac Bender for the first time. He was an independent oil and gas accountant, specializing in auditing. Rod contracted him to 'covertly' scout Ohio's pulse. Part of his two week assignment was spent at our German partner's New York office, the rest checking out field operations with Thirsty in Marietta.

Upon return, Mac's report confirmed our worst fears. Thirsty's operational skills left a lot to be desired. Our German partner's project management ability was equally suspect.

"I was contacted while I was just finishing another assignment at Dome Petroleum. Rod's call caught me at home at 7 AM on a Friday. Knowing I was working an audit, he was anxious to know when I could be ready to go to New York. Fortunately I had planned to wind up my work that day, so we agreed to confer at noon.

I met Rod and Bob Cox, Tripoli's Land Consultant, for lunch. Rod seemed troubled by his recent phone call with Tripoli's German partner's New York Office Manager, GB. His request for $40,000 - $50,000 U.S. to cover past expenses had raised Rod's suspicions. Rod asked for copies of the accounting records and was told there weren't any. I was retained to go down to New York and reconstruct a set of books for the partnership's verification.

Rod explained that responsibility for technical management of the Ohio project would be Tripoli's; financial accounting had been entrusted to the German partner. Since Tripoli had decided to sell these assets off, it was imperative to minimize costs before going to market.

I met with Neil for the first time that afternoon. Time was of the essence, as I was scheduled to leave for New York on Sunday. Neil summarized the history of the Ohio program and counselled me on the background of the main characters.

As I recall, the highlights were as follows:

>The original drilling and operating company, GW, had gone bankrupt at the end of 1981. It had a passive business relationship with the promoter, Thirsty.

>As Thirsty had a limited technical and administrative infrastructure for managing his own Ohio wells, he was the logical and most convenient replacement for GW.

>Thirsty became Operator of Record for the partnership, responsible for well operations. He established a field office in an old abandoned house on State Route 7, just east of Marietta. According to Neil, there was practically no furniture except a mattress on the floor of one of the upstairs bedrooms. Thirsty often slept

there to avoid motel expenses. Thirsty's headquarters were in Greenwich, Connecticut where accounting and invoicing were supposedly performed. At first we found this confusing, as it had been assumed that GB was keeping the accounting records.

>Thirsty's Office Manager, CG, had been a local used car salesman. His Assistant Accountant, HB, had been a college dropout and most recently a truck driver. As the quality of technical support was suspect, Tripoli monitored and scrutinized all proposals before approval.

>The German partner's New York office managed accounts Payable and Receivable, as received from Thirsty, on behalf of the partnership. Until Rod's invoice surprise from GB, all was assumed in control.

You must realize that hearing this all for the first time did not arouse my suspicions of any wrongdoing, although it did seem quite unorthodox. I looked forward to meeting the principles and hearing the other side of the story. If there is one thing consistent with auditing, its that there are always two sides to every story. I must admit though that the story Neil painted for me seemed like something out of a television script. I left Calgary open minded and enthusiastic for adventure. It was no secret that the Canadian oil industry was considered dull in comparison to American operations.

When I arrived at the New York office, GB, who had been forewarned of my intentions, provided me with a one page printout. Although I readily recognized it as a summary of bank transactions, I was stunned to learn it was "the accounting" for the project. GB agreed it would be a good idea for me to prepare a proper set of books for the partnership. He admitted having limited accounting experience. We agreed he would supply me with everything I needed.

My first priority was to categorize and document all bank statements, agreements, and bankruptcy correspondence. Standard filing practises had been ignored, resulting in "paperwork shambles". It was clear the New York office had little or no appreciation of the true status of Ohio operations from a financial management standpoint.

The deeper I researched, the more obvious the inconsistency of data and reporting. By the end of the first week I had decided to get myself to Marietta without further delay. I had two objectives: 1) audit the records at Thirsty's field office; and 2) confront GW's Bankruptcy Receiver.

On the latter, I was most prepared to do battle. The Court appointed Receiver (Trustee) had retained all revenues for more than a year from all wells previously operated by GW. I did not dispute that the Creditors were entitled to the spoils of GW's assets. The partnership's wells, however, did not fall into this category but GB had never ventured to challenge the Receiver. As a matter of fact, the partnership was also a major Creditor, which made the Receiver's actions even more bizarre. In my view, allowing these funds to remain suspended was inexcusable.

On Monday, GB met with the Trustee in Pittsburgh and relayed my instructions for promptly releasing the suspended revenues. I needed an extra day to finalize my New York audit. I needed to verify that the only invoicing managed by GB were those pertaining to Thirsty's operating expenses. Once these costs were arranged in a methodical monthly format, they were inexplicably disproportionate to the services rendered. I was determined to get to the bottom of it so I met GB in Marietta on Tuesday.

After dinner at a steak house next to the Ramada, GB invited me across the street to the Holiday Inn to meet "the guys". Throughout the evening I proceeded to meet all the office staff, field personnel, and what seemed like most of the oilfield suppliers and entrepreneurs in Marietta. Everyone seemed to know GB and CG quite well and were more than happy to join us for a drink. GB produced his credit card to the waitress when we entered and there were few bar patrons who were left without reward this evening.

My first stop, the next day, was Thirsty's field office. I prepared a list of all the documents I could think of that I would need as backup for my bookkeeping report. I relied on Thirsty's office staff to compile it by day's end.

Secondly, I visited the West Virginia office where GW's operations were managed. The former Vice President of Finance was the Office Manager, reporting to the Trustee. According to Thirsty, he was responsible for all past and present production records, a service provided by the Trustee for all GW's Creditors.

I drove east from Marietta along Route 7 about twenty miles before crossing a bridge over the Ohio River into the town of St. Marys, West Virginia. It was a quaint, scenic little town with a population of a thousand or so. The main employer was the Pennzoil refinery.

After GW's departure in late 1981, his operations were relocated to the second floor of a small women's clothing store on Main Street. A railway line ran down the middle of this main artery. It was quite different from GW's old office, which had been on a remote gravel/dirt road, about eight miles southeast of the town. It was on top of a high hill with an impressive view of the rolling countryside for miles around. GW had called it Spindletop, after the site of the initial prolific Texas oil discovery at the turn of the Century.

I minded my manners, as the Office Manager was about 6' 3" tall and weighed close to 300 pounds. On this, our first and only encounter, he entered the office wearing cowboy boots and coveralls; no shirt. He pointed out that all the records were in a room across the hall, stored in black garbage bags. To his credit, he knew which bags contained good printouts and which were "garbage".

As we sorted through a mountain of paper, the stories started flying. He informed me that Thirsty's Accounting Assistant, HB, had worked for GW in the same capacity. Apparently HB regretted his employment change as he was no longer able to sit at his desk in GW's old office and shoot gophers out the window. I listened and reacted with poise. I knew the more congenial our relationship, the more likely I was to secure the data I needed.

Including the records from New York and Marietta, I now had several boxes of backup. I wasted no time getting back to Calgary so I could begin assembling the books.

Interpreting these records was not as difficult as I had imagined. Most of the cheques issued by the New York office were advances to Thirsty for operations. I thought this odd as the production and sales reports continued to be generated by GW's Office Manager at the Trustee's expense. Whether Thirsty provided compensation for this service was never determined.

My observations of Thirsty's Marietta office revealed his two office staff contributed very little. At most, vehicle and wellsite repairs were co-ordinated. By my standard, the salaries were quite generous.

In analyzing the statements from Thirsty, I concluded the partnership's funds were being seriously mismanaged. The evidence suggested one or both ominous warnings; intentional fraud or incompetent financial management. The costs were simply way out of line for the services provided. Lack of, or inconsistency in, operational and payroll records drew additional suspicion. Based on my auditing experience, I had no other choice but to report this assessment."

Mac was a natural for U.S. operations. His solid, wrestler-like appearance was a deterrent to intimidation. He was a tenacious advocate for getting to the 'bottom line'. His knowledge of accounting and auditing procedures was equally thorough for the United States as it was for Canada.

You will meet Mac again in later EPISODES. His dedication and perseverance was admirable. I still secretly refer to him as Bull Dog Bender. He earned this title in Utah, much like a soldier earns a medal for bravery on the field of battle.

Late in September 1983, our German partner sent a representative from Germany to Calgary for discussions on Ohio's future.

We had met several times in Marietta during 1981 and 1982 field assignments. At the time, both of us were studying and writing exams to upgrade our skills. In his case, it was the German equivalent of our PhD. in Engineering, so he will be referred to as 'Dr. M'.

Dr. M impressed me with his quick ability to 'recognize burning trees through a smoking forest'. Despite my advantage of considerable field experience, it is my belief that we shared a common opinion of Ohio's fate from the program's beginning.

Our Calgary meeting stressed examples of apparent financial mismanagement and operational disarray. In our opinion, Ohio was a terminally ill patient. As support, Mac provided a first hand account of his recent fact finding trips to New York and Marietta.

"Rod informed me that my report had been forwarded to Germany, where it had caused considerable consternation. A technical specialist was designated to

meet with Tripoli and myself to review the findings. Dr. M's assessment would determine the fate of continued operations.

Dr. M arrived in Calgary after flying overnight and came directly to Tripoli's office. Besides Neil and myself, Rod, Bob Cox, and Tom Gorkoff attended from Tripoli.

I reviewed what I had uncovered and outlined my suspicions. It was unanimously decided that I would audit Thirsty's financial records in Greenwich as soon as possible. So I was off again to New York before month end."

We had decided that disposition, if possible, was the only solution to otherwise long term pain. Our ultimate goal was to depart with a shirt still on our back. We offered to represent our partner's share in any negotiations. Dr. M listened intently but said little.

At the end of the day, Dr. M caught a flight back to Germany. Months later we learned that the Office Manager of their New York office had been relieved of his job.

II
(*Millllyuns* of Dollars.....Wasted)

In late September Mac was off to Greenwich with a new agenda. A three week audit of Thirsty's books was intended to determine what, if any, sale value we could expect. Mac uncovered plenty of secrets.

"I was in Greenwich a total of three weeks. Thirsty's wife acted as Office manager and Accountant. In all, she was quite helpful providing the records I needed. During the first week and a half Thirsty was out of town; I presumed in Marietta. On his return both he and his wife went on a week's vacation.

The most blatant abuse I uncovered was a 40% to 50% payroll burden charged to the joint account above the actual salaries. Also a 10% overhead fee was levied on every charge, including Payroll and Employee burdens. Not only was this excessive, but it was insupportable for two reasons: 1) third party invoices were processed and accommodated by monthly advances from GB; and 2) contractual arrangements between the partnership and Thirsty disqualified percentage commissions in favour of fixed, lump sum payments for services.

Standard auditing procedures dictated events for months afterwards. Our query was followed by their response which was followed by our rebuttal; then additional responses and rebuttals. A claim was eventually submitted by Tripoli *on behalf of the partnership, seeking about $100,000 U.S. in erroneous invoices and charges.*

Before year end the audit results were provided to Tripoli's German partner. Although we avoided reference to collusion and mismanagement, the implication was obvious from the path painted by the facts. Tripoli was satisfied to have an accurate balance sheet to facilitate property disposal. By now sale negotiations were well underway. Retribution for the financial state of affairs was left up to the discretion of the Germans.

This adventure began with Neil relating a story about finally finding an "isolated" wellsite location. The lease road was blocked with felled trees and a primitive fence. After hiking a distance over a hill, he found the well. Beside it was a truck riddled with bullet holes——and a crude distillery being run off wellhead gas. He decided it was one for the books and left well enough alone. It all seemed too implausible until I began the audit.

It had been quite an experience for me. Eventually I had plenty of my own stories to relate."

In a way, Mac's findings were ironic. Thirsty, having lead us into the Ohio ambush and having witnessed the carnage, followed the same route to the same dead end canyon.

The audit results indicated he had been slaughtered financially also. Along the way, however, he had invented some new mistakes. The North American oilpatch was in the middle of a recession in 1983 and was unforgiving.

This was the last sight or sound of Thirsty. Our paths diverged but I have often thought about him. We enjoyed his likeable personality and sympathized with his misfortune. In the end, though, the U.S. oilpatch was no place for gamblers unless you were born with a gift for rolling seven or eleven at the craps table.

III
(Finale, At Last)

In the fall of 1983 I teamed up with Tripoli's Land Manager, Bob Cox, to solve our Ohio predicament. The U.S. field of operations was new to Bob, but he quickly assessed the reality of the situation. He actively advertised that our interests were for sale. Months went by without any serious action. Any and all enquiries were treated with composure. No, optimistic desperation is the truthful description.

It was doubtful we could sell these assets at any price. If our German partner had blinked, my recommendation would have been to quit claim our interests to them. It is to Bob's credit that we persevered and held out for a credible withdrawal.

We received an unsolicited offer of $2,500,000 U.S. for all one hundred and five wells from a Marietta independent in November 1983. At first it seemed too good to be true. After several weeks of long distance negotiations, Bob and I flew to Marietta. It was our intention and understanding that after a field inspection, the deal would be finalized and a security cheque deposited.

Our first stop was at the airport rental car booths to introduce Bob to my 'intelligence agency'. After getting caught up with all the rumours and gossip, we checked in at the Ramada. My 'agents' joined us later that evening at the Holiday Inn. They were celebrating one of their birthdays, and buying a few drinks was the least one could do for all their help in the past. (At 'Macie's' cake cutting she must have blown out all the candles and got her wish. Months later one of the commuter airlines hired her as an air hostess for the Parkersburg - Pittsburgh route. It was probably a good move on her part. Finalizing our disposition closed the chapter on Canuck investment in the local oilpatch. The rental car business was bound to suffer with our departure.)

Next morning we met our potential purchaser for the first time. 'Wally' was an elderly, certainly retirement-aged, seasoned industry veteran. He was particularly fond of his close friend, JD. Every day he downed several glasses, usually straight, of Jack Daniels whiskey to lubricate his motor.

While Bob worked on some last minute technical changes to the agreement, my schedule for several days was touring the field with Wally. His wife was his business partner and accompanied us.

Wet weather had rendered some of our lease roads impassable, even to Wally's four wheel drive truck. We all climbed up a steep grass hill to inspect one pumping unit he was particularly interested in. A barbed wire fence presented the last gasping hurdle before gaining access to the wellsite. While straddling this barrier, Wally collapsed and rolled part way down the hillside.

He had suffered a mild heart attack, but refused hospitalization. When we got him home, shaken, JD came to the rescue and helped his 'motor' to recover. It was not my choice of medicine, however his business partner was more intimate with his needs.

This was also a turning point in our negotiations.

Perhaps Wally's business partner had more input over the next day or two. What was supposed to be a " Deal " was not a deal at all when converted to print. Bob had drafted an agreement in Calgary with anticipation of minor cosmetic changes.

Wally's new version of purchasing our assets was definitely a deal breaker. Instead of paying for the wells, he just planned to rent them and compensate us from revenues. Bob terminated the negotiations and we returned to Calgary dejected.

" In the summer of 1983, as a Land Consultant, I had a short term contract with Tripoli to clear up some deficiencies from their recent major transaction. Initially I concentrated on the Canadian assets but the U.S. properties increasingly became more complex than had been anticipated. In the fall of 1983, I accepted a position as Tripoli's Land Manager. Neil and I joined up shortly after to divest Ohio as a priority assignment.

As Neil indicated, our negotiations with Wally were not very productive as he was unable to raise the necessary funds. Before we left Marietta, he introduced me to a North Carolina investor, 'Dave', who was keen to salvage Wally's deal.

Following several weeks of discussions, Neil and I flew to Marietta in mid- December for meetings with Dave and his associate, a young Houston businessman. They proposed a restructured deal of $1,100,000 U.S., with a $250,000 U.S. deposit, for a reduced number of 80 wells. Many of these required substantial capital for tie-in or recompletion costs, so we were agreeable to accommodating almost any reasonable change.

These negotiations were more intense than the ones I had the previous month with Wally. The Houston connection was obviously the main financial contributor. He struck me as a very energetic, but stressed, investor who was not totally comfortable with the deal. Despite several potential 'deal breakers', I eventually received the security deposit. By year end the balance of the purchase price was also secured.

Wally remained invisible during these negotiations, but we suspected his presence in the background somewhere. I do not know how this venture turned out as we had no further contact with these individuals after the deal Closed."

My intent had been to introduce Bob to Thirsty's Office Manager, CG. The 'Cheese', as he was known, was a real Naked City character and Bob was anxious to meet him.

He had a special table reserved at the Holiday Inn bar, elevated above all others. Most, if not all, nights he could be found there. Only unsuspecting transients would dare sit there without being 'summoned' by the Cheese. When he was in need of information, fact or rumour, he would send a messenger into the bar to summon the source. In return for co-operation, drinks and smokes would be liberally distributed, presumably on an expense account. Locals who participated were naturally honoured.

The Cheese was always more informed than anyone else in Marietta. His notoriety ensured the supply of informants always exceeded demand for information. His 'assistance' was relied on many times to solve my queries. It was my most amazing recollection of Ohio. If my experience had been in producing movies, the Cheese would have been hired and a script designed around him. He was fascinating and it was heartbreaking that Bob was not able to witness this spectacle in action.

The Ohio assets had now been reduced to the first five well program and twenty of the one hundred well follow-up group. We considered most to be nearing the end of their economic life.

The first five wells contained some of the best producers in the total program. Ironically, these benefited from optimum completion designs and quality equipment, critical ingredients missing on the next one hundred wells. Continuing to advertise the 'leftovers' in Ohio newspapers and networking paid off early in 1984. Bob was instrumental in disposing of this group for a premium value compared to what we expected.

> "During the final months of 1983, I had lengthy sale discussions with the New York manager for our German partner, GB.
>
> He had been approached by a syndicate offering to purchase this five well group only. I did my best to have the remaining unsold wells included, but relented to their final offer of $135,000 U.S. Most of our interest had been assigned to the German partner as compensation by the previous owner. I believe our ownership was only five or ten percent.
>
> Our Ohio holdings had now been reduced to just twenty wells. Administration and divestiture efforts were scaled down, however I continued to be vigilant for opportunities."

During the spring of 1984, a Columbus group, with other interests in the Marietta area, picked up where Wally left off.

Their representative 'Kendell' travelled to Calgary for negotiations. It was a sign of serious intent. My involvement was brief, addressing some of Kendell's technical queries. Kendell seemed satisfied to conduct his own field inspection, so my offer to accompany him to Marietta was withheld and he did not ask. Most of the negotiations were handled by Bob.

"The negotiations with Kendell's group moved very quickly. Tripoli was most interested and agreeable to a deal. Contrary to delicate discussions over value in the past, their offer of $135,000 U.S. satisfied our aspirations.

Selling these final 20 wells was received with relief and commendation by Tripoli. All the Ohio assets had been assigned relatively little value in the acquisition. Disposal had come at a time when my attention was required elsewhere, particularly Utah."

Some months later, while I was embroiled in a new horror story in Utah, Bob Closed Ohio permanently. Tripoli netted approximately $600,000 U.S., which far exceeded our expectations. The bonus was the removal of a substantial daily administration cost and long term environmental liability. Focus was now elsewhere in the U.S. and everyone's energy was vital.

AFTER FOUR YEARS OUR ORIGINAL $7,500,000. INVESTMENT HAD VANISHED FOR THE EQUIVALENT OF ONE YEAR'S INTEREST. EVEN THOUGH IT WAS NOT MY MONEY, YOU CANNOT IMAGINE WHAT A NAKED FEELING THIS WAS. IT WAS SUCH A RELIEF THAT THIS EPISODE IN MY CAREER WAS FINALLY OVER. SURELY THE WORST WAS BEHIND ME.

Typical services rig used in Ohio, pole mounted, at well No. 4091 in 1983

Service rig removing tubing and seized bottom hole pump at well No. 4098, 1983

EPISODE 5: UTAH - TEMPLE OF DOOM

I
(Circle The Wagons)

In July 1983 an old friend, Dennis Olson, called for a favour. Although it involved mutual U.S. assets, it sounded innocent and no urgency or significance was attached.

Dennis and two of my Shell alumni, including Ken MacGregor, had acquired a publicly traded junior oil company, Warren Explorations, in 1982. Included in the mixture of assets were oil and gas wells in Texas and Utah. Warren's new owners, all of whom I had previously worked for or with, directed their focus to divesting the U.S. properties and reorganizing the Canadian assets. To satisfy my curiosity, a brief visit with Dennis clarified their intentions for me.

Having concentrated my energies on Ohio and North Dakota since 1980, I was unaware that Warren was Tripoli's partner in most of a ten well Utah program. Their request to compare our Utah joint venture technical files did not immediately arouse any concern. My co-operation was provided to support their endeavors.

Tripoli's Utah ownership resulted from their recent major acquisition. All wells had been previously purchased or drilled between 1979 and 1981 in Duchesne County of northeast Utah. The targets were various lenticular sands in the Wasatch Formation, ranging in depth from 7,500 feet to 13,700 feet. Six were producing a total of 250 BOPD, two were marginal and shut-in periodically, and two were listed in our records as "Temporarily Suspended Due To Royalty Dispute With Land Owners".

Drilling and Production operations were managed by a Salt Lake City contractor, herein referred to as " Operator ". Leases had been secured on Indian Tribal lands by the Operator in the Altamont Field of the Uinta Basin (Basin). Since the initial 1000 BOPD discovery well by Shell Oil in 1972, the Basin had expanded to forty miles in length and hundreds of prolific wells.

Our Operator maintained a field office, supply yard, drilling and workover rigs, and a multi-service trrucking company in the town of Duchesne, 125 road miles east of Salt Lake City. These integrated capabilities enabled the Operator to perform a major role in the Basin.

When Warren alluded to serious concerns with the Operatorship, I cautiously listened and prayed in silence that it would not turn into another Ohio. Dennis convinced me otherwise.

At Warren's prompting and guidance, we readily agreed to a joint venture (JV) property meeting involving the other four small Canadian independents. There were no U.S. partners.

The two suspended wells, 1-27 and 1-28, had been Cash Called for $3,500,000. U.S. to Drill, Complete, and Equip. Each Duchesne County well held 640 acres in Sections 27 and 28.

Based on analogy with local producers, recoverable reserves of at least 117,000 Stock Tank Barrels (STB) were assigned each well. Tripoli had the major share at forty percent, Warren was next at twenty percent. Rather than a temporary royalty dispute as inferred by the Operator, it now appeared the JV would have to plug and abandon both wellbores.

Warren discovered that neither had been fully drilled, logged, tested, or completed. This information was not supplied voluntarily. Ken and Dennis patiently attempted several times to meet with the Operator. It was this intransigence that alerted them to other potential shortcomings in their Utah assets.

The Operator had commenced drilling late in the Primary Term of the Lease. Contract provisions between the Operator and the Lease Owner required drilling each well to total depth and production testing to prove economic reserves prior to an agreed date. When this agreement was violated by our Operator, the leases were terminated by the Tribal Nation.

All operations were suspended to avoid confiscation of the drilling equipment. The penalty to recover both leases was a major financial burden, rendering both wells uneconomic.

Based on the limited reporting by the Operator, we had assumed up to this time that both wells had also been technical failures. If not for Warren's diligence, they may have remained that way. As in 1978, Ken's perseverance had influenced my future again. From this lesson was coined my first of two axioms for Canadians conducting U.S. oil and gas operations: **Verify, Verify, and Verify**.

We collectively pooled our talents and energies to investigate the entire Utah program. With delicacy, my time was juggled between Ohio, Utah, and U.S. assets in four other States.

In follow-up JV meetings, the regularity of suspicious or questionable operating procedures and costs reached panic proportions. Tripoli, recognizing the gravity of concern, delegated their Senior Landman, Tim Malo, to co-ordinate future meetings and develop a remedial strategy. Tim had good reason for thoroughness; these assets were carried on the Books for $6,605,000 U.S. at a 15% Present Value.

Like Tripoli, most of the other JV owners were not aware of how out of control Utah had deteriorated. Our long distance energy investments obviously deserved far more attention and monitoring than we originally allocated. The average monthly operating costs of $11,000 per well had been an ongoing JV cause for concern. Until Warren's initiative, the complaints were mainly internal. This atmosphere prevailed despite a JV sponsored audit in 1982. The U.S. consultant's report was extremely critical of the Operator's performance. After verifying a few issues, the consequences of this ominous warning were ignored.

By the fall of 1983 the magnitude of the dispute was serious and growing daily. Tim proposed the JV fund an auditor's fact finding visit to the Operator's Salt Lake City office. Fear had produced volumes of conjecture and we had no way of knowing how much was unfounded.

Tim's plan was to stress the auditor's unofficial nature to ensure the Operator's co-operation. Otherwise, we would have been bound by accounting protocol to request specific audit dates. From experience, we knew an audit could be delayed up to a year.

Mac Bender was fully committed elsewhere. Fortunately we were able to secure the services of another, equally capable, independent auditor.

Rick Nixon, of Phaeton Resources, was known to several of the JV participants. He came recommended for this specific assignment. Rick arranged a three day 'visit' to the Operator's Salt Lake City office in November, a prudent investment by the JV. Rick's report was startling.

" I recall reviewing the land contract and lease files at Tripoli's office and finding them to be incomplete. More importantly, the joint venture billings indicated that more activity was taking place with respect to the leases than the production revenue received by Tripoli would support. I summarized all of the information required to complete title to Tripoli's interest and requested same from the Operator.

As luck would have it, the Operator had just hired a new land manager who claimed not to be familiar with any of the properties in which Tripoli had an interest. I offered to obtain the information myself if granted access to the files. The Operator agreed and I attended at their offices.

Lucky twice. The senior management was away at the time of my visit and the new manager granted me unrestricted access to any file I needed, including the financial records. My review indicated that Tripoli was possibly being over billed as many of the costs included in the joint venture billings did not represent the status of the assets. I made copies of the missing land documents and the relevant accounting and financial information, returning home with same for greater scrutiny by Tripoli's staff. "

My second of two axioms for Canadians conducting U.S. oil and gas operations was born out of Rick's findings; **Expect The Unexpected.**

It was assumed in the early years of the Utah program that everything was 'fine and dandy' as long as the Operator was silent. In Canadian operations, we had been accustomed to open communication whenever an operator needed assistance. It was rare to have surprises. Repetitious ones usually spelled a change of operators.

As in most complex occupations, the oilpatch depends on teamwork for its success. Individuals are not expected to be expert in everything, although some profess to be.

The solution for the Canadian investors in U.S. oil and gas operations was simple. Assign a field observer for the duration of all major, and periodically to all routine, operations. Establish an authority and reporting level between this representative and the operator. Share the pain and declare the gain. Unfortunately for Utah, this advice was too late.

During the next several months we continued to convene JV meetings regularly. All known and suspected controversies were documented and supported with backup. Various scenarios were theorized for resolving our differences and going forward with the program.

In April 1984 Tripoli sent myself and three senior officers to Salt Lake City to discuss our concerns and negotiate potential remedies. Our mandate from the JV was to return with a settlement or mobilize for war.

II
(War It Is)

The economics of our wells were painfully burdened by Lessor Royalties and Gross Overrides (percentage of gross revenue and exempt from capital and operating costs) considered excessive by Canadian industry standards.

The former averaged thirty percent of gross production, roughly twice the average. The latter, as applied to Tripoli's interests, averaged twenty-five percent after payout of well and operating costs. In Canadian operations, this was unconscionable. Naturally there was no room for adjustment here as these terms had been accepted prior to drilling. It demanded, however, strict scrutiny and control of other expenses to compensate.

It was this urgency to limit operational costs that spearheaded our meeting with the Operator. The more sensitive issue of dealing with the two uncompleted wells on expired leases was in our back pocket, pending progress on the pressing operational debates.

The Operator's Salt Lake City office was compact and staffed with about a dozen employees. The owner was the President and his wife the Office Manager. His oldest son, in his late twenties, was the Corporate Counsel. The youngest son, in his early twenties, was the Vice President of Operations.

The mood was congenial on arrival. A large conference room had been reserved. After introductory formalities, we got right down to business. Months of investigations had influenced our opinions and we wanted to dispel or verify them without delay.

My elaboration on the major components of our presentation required more than two hours. After ninety minutes, the President advised me to shut up; he had heard enough. Stressing that we had come a long way to deliver the entire message, we insisted on continuing. Before long he stood up, told me to shut up in no uncertain terms, then left the room.

One could sympathize with his frustrations as we were questioning the integrity of family. It was just as unpleasant for us.

In any event, the trenches had been dug.

What delivery, between two mature corporate entities, deserved such a reaction?

As we retraced the events of each issue, it was impossible to ignore the common denominator. Whether they or we liked it, the personnel and business practises of the Operator were responsible for inappropriate conduct. The fact that it continued for years without being addressed did not help matters.

When the Operator refused to accept accountability, the only alternative for protecting our interests was conflict.

Anticipating litigation as one of the solutions, we had prepared detailed documented examples of each dispute for later reference. It will suffice to revisit only a few briefly to generalize the trend:

1. Average monthly operating costs of $11,000 U.S. per well were supportable with entries but not invoices.

2. The Operator provided affiliated roustabout labour, well servicing, water hauling and chemical supplies. The timing and inappropriateness of some of these services/charges were not logical. Requests for selective backup were ignored.

3. Discrepancies between oil production and oil sales could not be quantified.

4. Equipment purchased under AFE New Classification often turned out to be recycled, substandard inventory requiring additional repairs or replacement.

5. Drilling/Service Rig rates charged did not conform to Contract.

6. Contract Pumper and Administrative Overhead rates did not conform to Contract.

7. Technical integrity was suspect in a series of unsuccessful and over budget workovers.

8. The two suspended wellbores, partially drilled in 1981, violated Lease Terms and Conditions. No refunds had been offered for the substantial portion of the unused Cash Calls.

Complicating the situation and poisoning the atmosphere was the knowledge that the Operator drilled and produced its' own wells in the same Township. This conflict of interest did more to destroy our comfort zone with the Utah program than any other issue.

As our meeting was prematurely concluded, we retired to our hotel for much deserved and needed alcoholic refreshments. This was not a convenient agenda in 1984 Salt Lake City.

We had to register as a Club Member of the hotel and buy a Membership card at minimal cost. Taking this card to a sales booth in the lobby, we bought our choice of liquor in miniature, airline-type bottles. Then we took our treasure to a lobby lounge some distance away, where we had to order and purchase mix separately.

In visiting Utah today, you will find these laws and customs relaxed considerably.

The stress and disappointment of this particular day were more palatable after a few stiff drinks. My memory recalled how "Ohio Wally" had coveted his JD ration so lovingly after his battle with his ticker several months earlier (EPISODE 4). With a law suit threatening, my fears were shared with JD also.

We now knew how Foreign Ambassadors felt when peace talks broke down between belligerent countries. Operational disputes were rarely settled by the Courts in Canada; Regulatory jurisdiction was more common.

Ohio had been a training ground for operator receivership, Chapter 11 protection, and investor rights. Preparing for potential legal action was a new experience, and a most unsettling one. Our plan was to schedule a JV audit as a pre-emptive strike, declare the results privately with the Operator, negotiate a settlement, and accept the Operator's resignation.

On such naive desires and hopes, this Canadian Engineer got a rude awakening to U.S. reality. Law suits, lawyers, and the Courts are standard components of doing business in the U.S. oilpatch. They are not feared, they are built into the Business Plan. This phenomena was experienced repeatedly during my fifteen years of U.S. oilpatch involvement.

Before you complete this book, you may have the impression that my litigation exposure and experience surpassed my engineering expertise and involvement. You may be right.

Our hotel, Little America, should not be ignored. Conveniently located downtown, it had superb accommodation and was reasonably priced. I stayed there many times over the years and always felt comfortable. Its' restaurants offered excellent variety and quality, also at reasonable price. My loyalty was genuine, as you will discover later.

III
(The Only Way To Fly)

Tripoli's Executive Vice President, Dr. Richard Bowens, was also a pilot. Better still, he had the use of the Corporate all weather, oxygen equipped, turbo charged Mooney 231B.

My recollection is vague on who suggested flying privately to Salt Lake City for the Operator's meeting. I will confess to being strongly in favour and influencing Richard's decision.

The importance Tripoli assigned to this meeting was demonstrated by the contingent of representatives. If all four of us elected to go by the 'Tripoli Mooney express', aviation guidelines and Company safety policy would have prevented it. As it turned out, our associates Bob Cox and Tom Gorkoff were strictly fair weather flyers. They were flyers only when absolutely necessary.

We could have taken a third person. Both considered confinement to a four place, single engine aeroplane for five hours, mostly over mountains in unpredictable April weather. They declined in a nanosecond and went commercial on Western Airlines.

It had been four years since I had been flying at the controls, but the thrill never wore off. Given my rusty skills, assistance was offered to Richard as he felt comfortable employing it. Richard was the best kind of pilot - cautious and experienced.

We planned the flight for 17000 feet to safely clear the rocks. Our route was south across Montana to Butte, continuing straight south through Idaho to Pocatello, then south again to Salt Lake City. It was my first time in a Mooney. The journey was uneventful and delightful.

In no time, or so it seemed, we were circling Salt Lake City. Being non- commercial, our landing clearance was fourth priority behind the airlines, military, and business jets. It was a busy airport and we had time to kill waiting our turn.

The scenery, flying slowly at mountain top height over the Great Salt Lake, surpasses that of any other city in my view. It was a delicate balance of flying skills to absorb the sights and diligently follow traffic. Two pilots are a convenience, if not a necessity, for busy airspace. Richard did most of the work.

Our commercial travelling associates had a stopover in Denver. We timed our departure from Springbank Airport (satellite of Calgary International) to coincide our arrivals.

Fate intervened when mechanical problems delayed the Western flight out of Denver by several hours. Learning this, it was hard to control our ego. The 'Tripoli express' had landed within minutes of our estimated time of arrival.

It was first class reliability (on the return flight, our record proved awesome).

Eventually we all rendezvoused at the Little America Hotel. Richard and I had extra time to clean up and relax over a drink first. When we convened, we dispensed with the airline complaints of our associates, then went out for a welcomed meal.

That evening we rehearsed the major issues for the Operator's meeting. Our lengthy list was a reminder of how dysfunctional the Utah program had become. Need for onsite representatives to monitor operations had never been more obvious. Due to the absence of this precaution, our working relationship with the Operator had deteriorated to embarrassment.

Between the four of us, we had extensive Canadian and international industry experience. Still, the scope of the next day's meeting was precedent setting. The operating infractions were so blatant, we struggled to find compromise.

We were thousands of miles west of Ohio, yet the script seemed familiar. Our Ohio operator also had in-house counsel. When his actions had brought everyone else to the eve of destruction, bankruptcy allowed him to escape accountability - opportunity counselling, perhaps!

As we discussed previously, the Operator's meeting ended in a storm. The following day we were greeted by Mother Nature's storm; heavy rain and low ceiling with fog. We delayed our departure until noon, when most of the weather had moved on to the southeast.

The commercial airlines had dozen of flights grounded due to the fog. When flying resumed, the take-off delay was in hours.

As for us, we were one of the first departures. Private and executive aircraft shared the east half of the field with the military. Other than the Mooney, our side of the field was inactive. Except for anticipated icing at flight altitude, we were comfortable that the weather briefing was favourable to our itinerary.

Richard activated the flight plan after one last weather check and mutual assurance with the conditions. It was fortunate we capitalized on being tourists on the way down. The return was mostly above or in overcast.

Our Mooney was equipped with weather radar and sophisticated avionics for navigation. We also had leading edge wing and carburetor de-icing, which we activated frequently.

Carburetor icing was readily detectable by decreasing RPM at a constant speed. We took turns watching the instruments intently. At the first sign of trouble, carburetor heat was applied. As this icing problem persisted, we reckoned wing icing was a distinct danger. We busied ourselves verifying our navigation and mapping alternate airports along the route in the event of an emergency. Richard asked Air Traffic Control for permission to descend from our 18000 foot altitude to warmer air. Once cleared, the flight was routine.

We arrived back at Springbank in the early evening. Next day, we discovered we had beaten our associates back by hours. Their Salt Lake delay had resulted in a missed connection in Denver. The flying conditions most of the way were not to their liking either, adding to their misery.

The enjoyment of flying privately to Salt Lake provided a happy ending to an otherwise unfruitful assignment. With war on the horizon, pleasantries would be few and far between.

IV
(Bull Dog Returns)

Upon our return from Salt Lake City, the first order of business was to select a U.S. attorney to represent the JV. We did not know where or how to start the process. In this crucial first step, an investment in counselling would have returned handsome dividends.

One of the JV participants recommended a small Denver law firm specializing in oil and gas litigation. At a time when none of us were experienced in U.S. law, we were quick to seize any shortcut. Rather than screening candidates, caution was forfeited for expediency.

'Chuck' became our lead counsel out of Denver. Because the disputed properties and the potential Defendant were in Utah, we also had to hire a Salt Lake City law firm as local counsel. We failed to realize how inefficient and costly this could be and it was never brought to our attention in time to rectify it.

We did not relish the use of our energies and finances to fund a lawsuit. History, however, would prove that litigation was the one device in the U.S. oil and gas industry that captured your opponent's immediate attention. In fact, reaction was so swift and spontaneous, one assumed it was a corporate faculty.

As years and adventures passed, most of my unpleasantness originated with industry partners employing in-house counsel. As soon as an issue became adversarial, it immediately became litigious. Naturally, the side retaining counsel throughout was better prepared, utilizing offence for defence.

Attorneys serving strictly in a Land Management function are invaluable. The inclusion of a litigation lawyer in the structure of a small to medium resource independent, however, should be viewed as a "Red Flag" and worthy of avoidance. It is a position obviously occupied for good reason.

The spring and summer of 1984 produced a multitude of meetings between the JV partners and the lawyers. We continued to advance our optimism of a quick settlement. Before disclosing our litigation intentions, the Operator was approached for a three to four week audit booking. With the utmost diplomacy, and the threat of withholding payment of JV billings, we reconciled on two weeks in early July.

While Chuck supported the audit strategy, he warned us to expect at least one additional year preparation time and expense for Trial. His schedule included preliminary Defendant depositions in the fall, with critical ones of Officers and Field Supervisors in the spring of 1985. Audit results would provide the basis for who we would depose and why. In addition, these results would establish the amount of damages the JV would be seeking.

As the completion of the audit would signal the beginning of legal hostilities, our JV partners pleaded for promptness. Several had limited resources to sustain a prolonged battle. In the first few months the escalation of costs did not escape anyone's attention. Law suits, by their nature, epitomize the art of delay, detour, and dilution of precious funds. Tim had his hands full co-ordinating meetings, audits, JV concerns and counsel enquiries.

Our urgency for auditing was to verify the questionable circumstances raised in our April Operator's meeting. In our view, if the properties were being operated as we suspected, every day without an operator change was a costly delay.

Some of these concerns could be addressed through a field inspection. Under the terms of our operating agreement, we were entitled to visit our JV properties at any reasonable time, provided we notified and cleared it with the Operator first.

The JV agreed to contract Mac Bender to accompany my pre-arranged late May tour. Mac's involvement was key at this early stage. Unless logic prevailed and a peaceful settlement ensued, his talents would be needed over a prolonged period. The more intimate he was with the issues, the more reliable his testimony would prove.

First stop was the Operator's Salt Lake City office. After an introductory half day meeting to discuss accounting inquiries with the Controller, 'Luke', Mac and I headed east to the field.

"The additional purpose of my involvement in the half day meeting with Luke was to bring up the outstanding queries from the audit conducted in 1982 by a U.S. auditor for the JV. We had hoped to resolve some of these and finalize a schedule for the audit I would be doing.

We had informed Luke that I would be along to discuss this previous audit (so he could be prepared). Unfortunately his attitude was that the audit was totally out of order and he wasn't prepared to reply to anything, let alone try to resolve any queries. We did get some of the minor items resolved (because they didn't amount to anything financially). Basically he just laughed at, or passed the buck, on the major issues. I was successful, however, in setting up my audit for July 1 as they were moving offices in May and June.

What caught my eye during our meeting was a musket loading rifle displayed on the wall behind Luke's desk. Apparently he was a gun enthusiast and used it regularly at competitions and hunting. He also had a quart sealer half full of yellow oil (the colour comes from the wax that is inherent with most Wasatch formation oil in the Uinta basin.) He turned the jar upside down to show the viscosity of this oil at room temperature; something like dried molasses."

The drive through this portion of the Wasatch Mountains was spectacular. Liberally dispersed formation outcrops can be fatal if a Geologist is behind the wheel. Just less than half way was the picturesque town of Heber, a short drive from visible world famous ski slopes. Plenty of restaurants and motels, even a small private airfield. Keep it in mind for the 2002 Winter Olympics.

There is practically no commercial development beyond Heber until reaching the town of Duchesne, at the western edge of the Altamont Field. Mac and I stayed there two nights, trying each of the town's two motels. One backs on to a railway track. We assumed it was out of service. We were wrong on that one.

"Neil neglected to mention that the other motel in Duchesne was on a service road that paralleled the main highway and was the only straight stretch of road around. To our misfortune, it was used as a drag strip after midnight by the locals."

In essence, an unofficial field audit was conducted. We comprehensively inventoried and photographed all our leases and equipment. We also talked to any local contractors and pumpers who were so inclined. Mac was polished at interrogating without raising suspicion. He extracted some interesting gossip, and valuable clues, this way.

Concentrating on the producing wells, we were greeted with a myriad of ills and pain. The gate entrance to one of the first wells had a five or six foot dead rattlesnake hung over the wire fence. It was held up for Mac to take my picture. The caption will be left to imagination.

"The 10 wells in the JV Program were divided into two sections by the Strawberry Reservoir which was dammed where the main highway crossed over on its way into Duchesne, which was on the east side. We visited 3 or 4 wells on our way into town.

Most of the wells were on a plateau that was very flat and barren (almost desert). The locations were all very large and bare (no rocks, weeds or anything) with lots of room for service rigs and tanker trucks to manoeuvre. We took lots of pictures for our records as preparation for Court. We also detailed a diary describing each photo and recording wellhead pressures at each well.

One well, 1-28, had had a workover go haywire and was flowing at least 100 barrels of oil out of the casing. Both tubing strings that were part of the Triplex pumping system were sitting on the ground. Apparently the Operator had tried to kill the well to rerun the tubing but were unsuccessful. This may have been fortunate as this well was carrying the field financially.

The only employee we saw was at the north end 1-24 well where the pumper was asleep in his truck beside a stream that passed by the location. We didn't wake him but Neil walked up and took his picture."

It was difficult not to recognize the complacency in our operations. Several wells were shut down when they should not have been. Some lease roads and wellsites were devoid of tire prints or any other sign of human intrusion.

Operator's field inventory yard

Operator's field inventory yard

Typical wellhead conditions

Blacktail Ridge, facing north (note gas sales line traversing lease at road entrance)

Most leases were environmental nightmares. Oil and chemical spills were common and unattended. While the batteries were neatly laid out, the leases were very messy around wellheads and oil truck loading areas. Much of the equipment was in disrepair. Disconnected surface lines were unplugged and torn insulation strewn about. Some lease roads were impassable from spring run-off erosion.

During this entire day, with one exception as alluded to by Mac, we had not seen any of our field operators. The snakes made up for it. Although it was only May, it was already very hot. Rattlesnakes prefer shade and took up residence in several of our treater houses. Their announced presence was sufficient to deter our entry. Mac wondered if our pumpers were expert at stealth in performing their daily duties.

"On about the 3rd or 4th location we came across our first live rattlesnake. He was inside the housing at the front of the Treater, stretched out on red hot gravel. Here's where Neil showed his uncanny ability to hit things with rocks. The first rock hit the snake on the head, which woke him up in a hurry. The second rock hit him again and this seemed to make him mad. Fortunately for us his nest was under the cement pad that the Treater sat on and he decided to head there and not in our direction. I think Neil got in 3 or 4 more hits before this guy got away."

Inspecting the two 'suspended' wells was a major undertaking. They were perched on top of what is known as Blacktail Ridge, a crowning plateau several thousand feet above the basin floor. A winding, narrow, little used, and poorly maintained track led us to the summit.

It took us more than an hour to manoeuvre our way to the top. Since we had only a mid-sized rental car, we were fortunate to make it at all. Several times we discussed turning back, but there was no place to turn around. It was ideal for sightseeing; it was the periphery of the ridge most of the way up. Mac had his doubts our little rental car would make it.

"We talked with a Shell pumper who said we would never get up the lease road without a high centred 4 X 4 vehicle. This road leading up to our well had a switchback every 300 to 400 feet and was very narrow and rough. It was full of 12 to 15 inch deep cuts made by the spring runoffs. By driving back and forth across the road, at right angles to these fissures, we were able to get up the road. There was hardly enough room for a truck to turn around.

At the top of the bluff were two abandoned, uncompleted wellbores. It was here we had our second encounter with snakes this day. The first was built at the edge of the bluff. Standing on the edge of the pit you could see straight out probably 20 miles and straight down 2000 to 3000 feet to the plateau.

As we were walking beside the pit we came across a 6 to 7 foot rattler. Neil promptly hit it with a rock. Again, fortunately for us, the snake decided to go downhill instead of at us. Moving with incredible speed, it stopped about 15 to 20 feet downhill from us. Neil proceeded to hit him with progressively larger boulders. Each time one of these 20 pounders hit the snake, it would jump straight up about 2 feet off the ground. Fortunately these snakes only came out one at a time."

On top it resembled a flat oasis. Plenty of small trees, scrubs, and wildlife. At 1-28 the drilling and mud pits were left unclaimed. During the spring they had filled with water and became graves for several deer whose carcasses floated with other debris and black oil. The latter had indicated a hydrocarbon zone had been penetrated. There was no way of knowing how many dead animals lay at the bottom of these eight to ten foot deep pits. No doubt, over the past three years, drilling mud chemicals had been deadly to many un-suspecting wildlife. There were places where all the snow still had not melted, giving some measure to depth at the height of winter.

The wellhead consisted of a joint of 10 3/4 inch casing which we knew was landed to 1950 feet. A large gate valve was chained in place, preventing us from determining if any pressure existed. The projected depth was 9795 feet, but we had no way of knowing what depth had been reached. No other equipment was on site. A menacing, live rattlesnake was guarding another pit containing garbage, scrap iron, and wellhead parts. We wanted to explore the contents, so we drove the snake away after hitting it several times with boulders.

At 1-27, it was much the same conditions. The wellhead, how-ever, was open to atmosphere and did not appear to have any pres-sure. We dropped stones down the 10 3/4 inch casing and thought we could hear splashes. The projected depth for this well was 9650 feet.

Other than occasional four wheel drive tracks, probably hunt-ers, the plateau was deserted. Even if these wells had been success-ful, we could not imagine how an operator would access them in winter or how crude oil would be trucked out economically. We were in awe at the impairments the Operator had overcome to transport drilling rigs and supplies to these locations. We discovered from the audit that most of the equipment and rig parts were airlifted by helicopter, at great expense.

Although we had a panoramic view for twenty or thirty miles, Mac had seen enough and encouraged our departure while it was still daylight. It was obvious his mind was already on the audit the following month.

"To this day I don't know why the Operator didn't avoid the plateau by locating the wellheads at the bottom of the bluff and doing a 300 to 400 foot whipstock. Millions of dollars could have been saved and the wells completed on time."

V
(Showdown)

Once Mac and I had briefed the JV and our legal team on our findings, there was no turning back. Discussions aimed at securing the Operator's immediate resignation peacefully were terminated. We had not been taken seriously. Emphasis now shifted to Mac's role in the two week audit scheduled for late July.

Chuck assigned an associate from his law firm, 'Shirley', to accompany Mac to Salt Lake. Besides being an attorney, Shirley was also a CPA. Given the time constraints, her accounting assistance was imperative, although costly. Mac had his hands full trying to deal with an uncooperative and hostile Operator.

"In their new offices, the Operator had the entire top floor of the building, probably tripling their old office space. Shirley and I were put up in an inside hallway alcove on the far side of the floor from where the Operator's staff worked. We were provided with one small table and two chairs to work at. After a couple of days Luke brought in a small card table from home so we would each have our own 'work space'.

This remote location (which was beside a whole outer wall of unoccupied offices that were filled with furniture) was intended to keep us segregated and provide for difficult working conditions. Fortunately it also provided us the privacy of being able to discuss things without being overheard or having to leave the premises to discuss things as we came across them.

Knowing that we would probably be going to Court on these issues, Shirley was most helpful because she had a much better idea of what the Courts would want.

As mentioned, the company was run by the family. Dad was President, Mom (who went by her maiden name in the payroll records) was Office Manager, and the two boys. Mom ran the office with an iron fist (Shirley was especially helpful in being able to deal with Mom). I still have an impression of her marching around the office with her 'granny glasses' attached to a string around her neck. With a perpetual cigarette hanging out of the corner of her mouth, dropping ashes on to her dress, she barked orders at all the staff.

I think in some cases the staff were naive about auditing because they provided us with documents we didn't expect to get; e.g. entire payroll journals for the complete two year period for everyone in the company.

We focused mainly on the issues brought up by Neil from his many 'desk audits' (Neil had identified pretty well all his 'trouble spots'). While Shirley was documenting and copying all pertinent data relative to Neil's concerns, I did an audit review of current operating expenses.

Other than the physical location of our 'audit room', and being ignored by the Operator's staff, we were reasonably well treated. If we asked for specific invoices or backup, we were supplied with it promptly. If we were fishing for additional information or ideas why things were done a certain way, we were stonewalled.

The Operator, overall, were carrying on the operations the same as they did the drilling. The expenses selfishly favoured the Operator over the investors who put up the money to make it all work. The Operator had a very small Working Interest in the wells, so any direct costs were charged mainly to the other owners. With the escalation clause in the Overhead, the joint account was being hit for $1100 to $1200 per well per month. Costly workovers using the Operator's rigs appeared to be at inflated prices. Everything but the production of oil seemed to be maximized to return profits to the Operator."

Despite the impediments, Mac was able to meet his objectives. His audit results were convincing and clearly disclosed the Operator's true intentions.

Early in August, our lawyers finalized and filed a Statement of Claim.

Immediately thereafter Chuck petitioned the Court to grant an injunction forcing the Operator to disclose all records. Chuck contracted the internationally recognized accounting firm, KPMG, to join forces with Mac on a follow up audit.

The Operator, through its in-house counsel, continued to refuse all co-operation until threatened with Contempt of Court by the Judge.

In mid-August Mac returned to Salt Lake City. This time, he was forced to rent office space and copying equipment. He also hired a clerk to reproduce and catalogued all data. The KPMG employees, half dozen strong, contributed to a frantic, war-like atmosphere. Mac won the battle and retrieved the results we anticipated.

"KPMG's Denver office was retained to conduct the 'litigation audit' as they had a special group of people well trained in this area of oil and gas operations.

They were the principal auditors, I was assisting them because I had done the preliminary audits they were 'following up' on. There were 4 or 5 CPA s from KPMG, and myself, because of the nature of the audit (being conducted under Court order).

The audit itself was very strange. We rented a room in the same office tower that the Operator was in and installed double locks on the door. We rented a copying machine and a clerk from a personnel agency. The Operator supplied one of their employees to be in the office at all times.

We requested every invoice, journal entry, etc (a normal audit is done reviewing a small statistical sample). Every request was routed through 'Mom'. On each of the first and second days we ran into problems where 'Mom' refused to supply info (payroll for instance). We had to have the lawyers go back to the Judge to get the original order upheld. The Operator was represented by one of the sons who was a lawyer and the in-house counsel. On the second or third confrontation with him, the Judge warned him that one more frivolous refusal and he would be communicating with his friends from behind bars.

As every document had to be copied, we went through several cases of paper very quickly. One of my jobs was to compare what was being supplied this time compared to what Shirley and I had originally obtained. Where discrepancies occurred, we were a lot more specific with our info requests. Whenever we left the office (lunch, etc), everything had to be locked up in briefcases or strong boxes.

At the end of three weeks we had copies of just about everything in the Operator's office. Most of it went back to Denver for KPMG to digest and prepare working papers and schedules for Court. Considerably more evidence of questionable operatorship surfaced from this audit."

In October our lawyers conducted preliminary depositions and Examinations for Discovery to verify and supplement the audit findings. My role was the JV technical representative, so my presence was expected at all proceedings.

My acquaintance with the Little America Hotel was renewed for several weeks. In the meantime Chuck camped out at the Marriott at twice the cost. Here was my first lesson working with lawyers on the job. Do not mess with their egos when they are spending your money. If the best exists, then it must be provided in the interests of the case.

My comfort zone was just plain comfort, therefore lavish luxury did not appeal to me. Throughout my career expense prudence was exercised whenever my employer's resources were limited. Such was the case with the JV parties. In my view, every saving was worthy and justified if it helped the final cause. That is where Chuck and I differed.

He would not accept second best. I could not bring myself to accept the expense burden my JV partners would have to bear by staying at the Marriott also. It did not suit me, although it would have been convenient to be close for consultation. As a result, we arranged to meet every morning in the Marriott lobby for discussions prior to meetings or depositions.

Armed with audit, examination for discovery, and deposition results, our lawyers spent the next few months moulding an offense strategy. While it may have seemed like a delay to some of the participants, the pace was sustained and deliberate.

With Chuck's and the local Salt Lake City law firms employed, cost escalation was a concern. While our strategy timetable was on tract, the Court's docket for scheduling a Trial date was still unpredictable. We were confident a judgement would be rendered in our favour. In the U.S. Justice system, however, numerous levels of appeal are available to the accused (see EPISODE 10).

Therefore, the odds were not great for retrieving control of our program, recovering the legal costs, and dispensing settlement funds in the near future.

The financial squeeze was becoming unbearable for some of the JV partners. Oil and gas revenues from the Utah program were accumulating in suspense accounts administered by the oil and gas Purchasers, pending the Trial verdict.

The JV participants, with pain, were forced to restructure their overhead and operating budgets. The casualty that gave me the most grief was the withdrawal of Warren Explorations' Corporate Officers. All were close friends, including Ken MacGregor.

On August 31, 1984 Warren's major shareholders sold their controlling interest in the company to a group of investors from Toronto. It was headed by Michael Cooke, who had considerable experience in banking and corporate restructuring. Beginning with this first gamble in the oil and gas industry, Michael established himself as a successful oil and gas entrepreneur.

"One of my first unpleasant, but necessary, business decisions was to 'fire' Warren's Salt Lake City lawyer and hire a replacement. This strategy was awkward and required conviction, since both the 'fired' and the 'hired' lawyers were Senior Partners in the same law firm. It was a calculated, deliberate move that was not regretted.

Although I was initially unaware of all of the facts relating to the Utah predicament, I remained determined to utilize Warren as a foundation on which to build a successful oil and gas company. To fund the Utah litigation through to a conclusion, Warren's other U.S. delinquent Accounts Receivable were pursued. I persevered during the remainder of 1984 until nearly $500,000 was collected, mostly in Texas."

As for Tripoli, the activity level diminished sufficiently in the fall to concentrate on other U.S. areas of interest. After the hectic and stressful pace of the past six months, it was not obvious to me where the juice and determination would come from to renew the battle in the New Year.

View of Denver, facing west, as it appeared in the mid - 1980s

EPISODE 6: DALLAS - VERIFY, VERIFY, and VERIFY

I
(Mission Impossible)

By October 1984 the Utah dispute had degenerated irreversibly into litigation, the first of many to come. Our Joint Venture legal team from Denver and Salt Lake City now controlled pace and strategy. It had the makings of a long, costly battle and my mind was already weary of daily operational confrontations.

When it was least expected, but most needed, a unique assignment was offered. It spelled E-S-C-A-P-E.

My recollection was being quite apprehensive about meeting the mandatory year end deadline. Since it encompassed all my engineering training and background, however, it was a most exciting opportunity to contribute meaningfully to Tripoli's future.

Tripoli had raised a considerable portion of their seed money from European investors, primarily German Drilling Funds. Through this connection, Tripoli had learned that the U.S. assets of seven large German Drilling Funds were for sale. Five Funds were operated and partially owned by Hunt Energy Company and two Funds by Southland Royalty Corporation, both of Dallas. The asking price of $10,000,000. U.S. was considered a bargain, based on the financial reports supplied for 1981 to 1983.

There was a price to pay for this bargain. An acceptable offer had to be formalized by December 31, 1984. This mechanism would qualify the Funds' European investors for substantial tax rebates according to German tax law.

The spectacle of the Ohio fiasco was still fresh in Tripoli's mind. More recently, the ongoing investigation into abuse of funds in the Utah program had stiffened resistance to any further U.S. participation.

The overwhelming temptation to 'do Dallas' stemmed from the fact that the asking price represented only two and one half years of Cash Flow. In addition, there was also some security in knowing that some of the German Fund holders had indirect investments in Tripoli.

Preliminary reports indicated that the first group of five Funds comprised 113 wells, but only 60 appeared to be producing. Most were multi-zone completions averaging 10,000 feet in depth. Seven States were involved: Oklahoma, Texas, North Dakota, Montana, Louisiana, Mississippi, and New Mexico.

The second group of two Funds comprised eleven wells, fortunately all in the state of New Mexico. Most were relatively shallow, single zone producers.

It was our understanding that a sale to a major purchaser had fallen through at the last minute. The Fund owners, having already elected to liquidate their assets, scrambled to salvage a deal despite the eleventh hour timing. Hence the attractive price tag.

Only financial summaries to 1983 were included in the offering. To avoid repeating the mistakes of Ohio and Utah, it was imperative my homework be thorough and accurate. Committing funds of this magnitude without assurances of future recovery would be disastrous to Tripoli's survival. My major concern was the potential for substantial plug and abandonment liabilities.

On the other hand, it had all the makings of a tremendous opportunity. If oil and gas prices recovered in the near future, this acquisition would look like a stroke of genius. The anticipated cash flow would greatly accelerate Tripoli's debt repayment and thus facilitate more aggressive Canadian expansion.

There was just one ingredient missing. We had practically no knowledge of performance in 1984. This void not only included production, but also operating costs, net revenue, environmental and litigation liabilities, well payout status, and expiring leases to name the more pressing of our concerns.

The records of seventy producing wells had to be screened, evaluated, and summarized in less than two months. The status of the remaining shut-in or suspended wells likewise had to be determined. Reserve and economic cases for numerous contingencies had to be forecast. It may sound over dramatic, but on my shoulders would rest Tripoli's future.

Steady Cash Flows of $4,000,000. U.S. in 1982 and 1983 were impressive. Management was keen to proceed with this purchase, given a favourable technical and financial means test. If my findings were to the contrary, my argument would have to be convincing.

Ohio and Utah had already taught me to be guarded and suspicious of haste and initial impressions. This evaluation, to be effective, had to be comprehensive. The critical timing would guarantee a photo finish with the clock. This was a challenge that seemed modelled after the television show 'Mission Impossible'.

Tripoli, on presenting this assignment to me for consideration, made one criteria abundantly clear. Acceptance meant it had to be completed in full and on time. No exceptions.

The tight deadline was an added challenge that made my involvement that much more exciting. Unlike operations, my energies would be focused to achieve my goal without the constant fear and distraction of litigation.

II
(The Boot)

Although the Dallas assignment was unexpected, it was opportune for combining my skills exclusive of litigation. My enthusiasm for getting started knew no bounds.

The events surrounding the Utah properties were distressing and stressful. As EPISODE 5 noted, some of my close associates were involved in recent bloodletting. Our investment strategy and posture was no better. Utah was beginning to look like a remake of Ohio 1980.

Dallas represented an opportunity to channel my energy constructively, even if only for an interim period, and was readily welcomed.

There was one loose end to tie up in the few days remaining before my departure.

The North American oil industry was desperately trying to recover from three years of uncertain energy prices but high inflationary costs. At Tripoli, particularly, the mood was further influenced by disappointing exploitation results and U.S. asset write downs.

Tripoli's Manager of Corporate Relations had been toying with an idea for boosting office morale and pride leading into the Christmas season. 'Pat' and I had spent several noon hours testing various themes to facilitate a home movie involving all staff.

Pat's hobbies were videos and sound systems, so he was a natural to wear the Producer's hat. He needed a Lead actor, and for some unknown reason, insisted on me. Barring Hollywood intervention, the plan was to unveil the edited version at the company Christmas Party in early December.

Pat deserved all the credit for the success of 'The Boot'. When he first ran the idea past me, it seemed crazy. I vainly searched for alternatives, but relented when Dallas forced me to expedite my commitment.

Of course, the staff deserved a compliment for their co-operation and dedication. It was gratifying to witness a sincere effort by everyone for this common cause.

Considering we spent only about $50 for rental props, and used only half a day preparation and shooting time, Pat worked wonders providing the finished product.

The script went something like this.

- The Lead, whose face is never seen throughout the movie, gets off the elevator wearing a greasy, soiled white smock and carrying a black leather military boot by the lace.
- Instead of walking normally, he is slouched over and shuffles his feet as if his body is totally sunburned. He addresses himself to the Receptionist as the Building Maintenance Supervisor, anxiously trying to find the owner of a new boot found in the building trash container.
- Asked how things were going at Tripoli, the Receptionist , who is wearing a pair of big pink bunny ears, announces 'things are really hopping'.
- Claiming The Boot is not hers, she calls on the Personnel Manager, who directs the Lead to the President's office and asks him to wait. He makes himself comfortable in the President's chair, feet resting on the desk top. The phone rings and the Lead fields a call to the President offering to pay Tripoli $5,000,000 if they will take Ohio back, but it is rejected as the offer was not in Canadian currency.
- On cue, the President walks in at the termination of the call and is confronted with The Boot. He immediately waives ownership as he puts his foot up on the desk to reveal a running shoe, his standard office footwear for keeping an eye on the staff. He points the Lead to the Accounting Department and wishes him luck in his search.
- The door is closed, but the Controller happens by on cue and admits him. The entire Accounting group are in the process of a Bingo game and a winner is just declared as the door opens.

Naturally the Controller is frightfully embarrassed and leaves the Lead to his foot finding feat. No takers from this half dozen overworked Tripoli faithful.

- The Lead is directed onward to the Engineering Department, secluded behind a closed door. Gathered around a table full of beer and liquor bottles, in a tastefully done balloon and party streamer decorated office of the Vice President, again The Boot fails to find its owner. This hard working crew returns to its strategy session as the Lead is guided to the Exploration Department, again behind closed doors.

- The door opens just as the Vice President is throwing a dart at a wall map and is applauded by the rest of the geological staff for selecting Tripoli's next major drilling venture. The Boot is introduced. A few close fits here, but no cigar. On to the Land Department for boot sizing.

- Opening this door reveals the entire Land staff, true to their spirit of bidding up land prices, engrossed in a game of Monopoly. Unfortunately there is no one here who can fill The Boot.

- So it is off to the Contract auditor's office, where he is discovered practising his dice roll on a Craps table. Informed by the auditor that he may have lost his mind today but definitely not his boot, the Lead moves on to the last possible recipient.

- The Executive Vice President is dressed in a Canadian Armed Forces flight uniform, surrounded by model aeroplanes, and is busy checking the sky with binoculars from his many windowed office. When informed by the Lead of his mission, the Executive Vice President raises one foot up on his desk to display the matching boot. In ecstasy, he explains how his wife had feared he had lost the mate forever and was frantically searching Calgary's stores to replace it before Christmas.

- The Lead wails in relief at finding the owner at last and being able to give someone at Tripoli *The Boot* today.

- The script ends with the Executive Vice President giving the Lead the boot in the backside to move him from the office to the elevators where it all began.

While it may seem silly and ridiculous, everyone was a tremendous sport and performed with a minimum of prompting and rehearsal. We made sure all in attendance that afternoon got a guest appearance. By the end of the day, adrenaline was flowing freely. Soon after I was off to the land of adventure - ' JR's ' hometown.

According to my sources, Pat laboured for weeks dubbing in music like 'These Boots Are Made For Walking' and 'Take It To The Top'. He rented a big screen for the Christmas party and **The Boot** premier was the main entertainment.

Although obviously not able to attend, it was brought to my attention later that **The Boot** was such a hit that Pat had to show it twice. Accordingly, each scene was greeted with applause and laughter that did not end with the evening.

No doubt Tripoli would have flown me back for this weekend if requested. Quite simply, that amount of time could not be spared and it never entered my mind.

Pat made video copies of The Boot available at cost and sold out. Fortunately he saved one for me. We still have it and savour showing it to our friends' young ones who get a real kick out of it.

There is no law that prevents you from having spontaneous fun in life. By this little gesture, I was able to make a lasting contribution. Unlike my oilpatch ventures, it remains unblemished and a source of satisfaction. This was one of the recollections that encouraged me to build this book.

III
(Getting To Work)

Before departing Calgary, Tripoli agreed to my appeal to assign one of their Geologists to Dallas for two or three weeks. It was my opinion that my year end deadline would not be met without this assistance. It turned out to be an accurate assessment.

Tim Atkinson and I had worked together before, and on U.S. projects. These two advantages prompted me to request his participation. Thankfully he was available to join me for three weeks in November.

My last time in Dallas was 1978; for Tim it was his first time. The auto traffic took some getting used to, but sharing the navigator duties was a blessing during Tim's stay. We were greeted with warm, pleasant, shirt sleeve weather. Our first night in town, we had an outdoor game of tennis on the roof of the hotel. Calm before the storm. It was lucky for me; Tim was the much better tennis player.

"Tripoli considered the Drilling Fund urgent enough to free me from my ongoing exploration and development activities. My assignment, as I understood it, was to assess the geological quality of existing producing pools and speculate on recompletion and development potential.

Initially we stayed at a moderately priced, west side motel just off a major artery. I think it was a Ramada Inn. Although I am vague on the name, I remember clearly the outdoor hot tubs which we had all to ourselves. Apparently the locals considered the evening temperatures too cold; for us it was just right.

The coffee shop in the motel was our rendezvous each morning. Since we often skipped lunch, we tried to eat a hearty breakfast. The food and service were good, so we did not bother looking elsewhere. Usually, by the time we finished, the freeway traffic had lessened a bit."

Our first priority in Dallas was to make appointments to visit the offices of Southland Royalty and Hunt Energy Company. At the latter we met Stuart Hunt, a thrill since the Hunt family was, generally speaking, legendary in the oil industry. My lasting impression, as we were escorted into his office, was a large framed picture on the wall behind his desk.

As we exchanged formalities, my attention was divided. It was increasingly difficult to concentrate on our business discussion. Sheepishly he was asked to share the secret of his art, followed by my admission to a sincere and lengthy interest in aeronautics and space.

Mr. Hunt was close friends with one of the Apollo astronauts, perhaps many. Their deep loyalty was represented by an actual photograph of the first golf shot on the moon and personally autographed. The frame was professionally designed to draw out the remarkable contrasts of this historical event.

I hesitate to name this astronaut for fear of being inaccurate after all these years, but in all probability it was Alan Shepard. My treasure was just being in the same room, so it was no surprise that Mr. Hunt spoke very proudly of it.

The object of our meeting was to determine two crucial aspects of our potential transaction, assuming Tripoli agreed to purchase the Funds. First were the arrangements to transfer Operatorship and records. Second were the options for the terms and conditions of Closing.

We did not need a long meeting as we were assured full cooperation at the field and administrative levels. Secondly, there was only one rigid condition for sale - cash only and a non refundable deposit by December 31, 1984.

We relayed these findings regrettably to Calgary, knowing Tripoli's preference was a combination cash and share issue. Regardless, it was full speed ahead on the evaluation.

The management firm responsible for daily accounting of the seven Funds was located in the heart of downtown. In addition to the financial records, all the well files were also maintained here. It was to be home for the duration of the evaluation.

The Office Manager, 'Bret', was a retired Braniff Airlines administrator. He was always very helpful and courteous, as was his Receptionist/Secretary. His role, as we understood it, was to process revenues and billings for the Funds in exchange for a monthly management fee.

Our first task was to isolate the top performing wells in each Fund. While Tim reviewed the geology, my role was to evaluate and summarize the engineering data. Once we had conferred and agreed on the credibility of the producing zone (s) in each well, we concentrated on uphole or bypassed potential. An index was prepared for future reference, covering all data available to, and assessable in, our study.

We created a large spreadsheet, listing primary and secondary histories. Since Tim's time was premium, emphasis was on verifying longevity of production and cash flow. Secondly, by screening the best wells selectively, we attempted to quantify the 1981 to 1983 results that had been supplied in advance. This process involved moving a mountain of paper. We had so much to sort out, Tim and I rarely talked to each other until the end of the day. It took a while before we actually felt we were getting a handle on things.

"My daily routine involved screening well files and creating geological structure and net pay maps. I focused on the important cash flow pools such as the Treetop Madison field in North Dakota. We independently concluded that many of the best wells had been overproduced, risking a shortened life.

Neil and I had to confer frequently as our prime objective was to determine upside drilling and recompletion potential. We were constantly aware of the year end deadline, so it was a no nonsense schedule.

Overall I felt that many of the pools had seen their better days, even though the wells were not that old. As I recall, there must have been more than fifty producing and suspended wells in five different Basins that were comprehensively researched and evaluated."

Near the end of Tim's assignment, as time permitted, our focus was directed to randomly selected shut-in or suspended wells. With more than fifty wells in this category, we would have preferred a more detailed evaluation; however the candidates we looked at presented a clear and decisive trend.

Accomplishing all of this meant certain sacrifices to normal routine. We worked through most lunch hours or grabbed a takeout sandwich. We preferred working to six or seven in the evening to avoid the traffic congestion. Saturdays were considered a workday, however Sundays were a day of rest. Since Tim had the shortest stay, he had first choice in choosing our itinerary. When it came to the seventh day, we were usually too burnt out to do much of anything.

"I remember catching lunch on the fly lots of times, usually at a place close by. I had a favourite deli near the Diamond Shamrock building that we frequented. Neil seemed to like all kinds of food, so selection was never a problem. I enjoyed our lunches with Bret as he had a varied background and his stories were always interesting.

I know I spent several Sundays in Dallas, but I cannot remember doing anything special. If we had gone sight seeing or taken in a Cowboys football game, I am sure I would have remembered. Perhaps we were so bushed by the seventh day of the week, we just relaxed."

Bret was very co-operative to our needs and provided an office key for late hour and weekend entry. It was a large office layout for just two employees. We were thankful, as it allowed room for spreading log cross sections on walls or across conference tables. It occurred to us that we must have been in the way and interfering with routine; however nothing was ever mentioned if we were.

IV
(Pastimes)

One day we accepted Bret's invitation to lunch. He had a favourite cafe within walking distance of the office. His hidden motive was to surprise us with his cellular telephone. It was a big thrill for him to use it while we were eating. It never failed, regardless of when we accompanied him, to attract everyone's attention. Back then, this was a very new, creative, and misunderstood technology.

As Bret explained, Dallas was one of a handful of U.S. cities designated to experiment with remote cellular communication. A transmission tower had been erected somewhere in city centre. Calls at any time and from any location within the tower radius, ten miles by my recollection, were now possible to anywhere in the world.

These first cellular phones were burdensome, nearly the size of an adult shoe box and heavy.

Bret had acquired the, or one of the, distributorships for the Dallas area. He was convinced of the future value for a cellular in everyday life and proud to be associated at an introductory stage. There was no disguising how much more excited he was about this venture compared to his oilpatch interests. Tim often discussed it during our freeway crawling.

One afternoon late in December, Bret invited me outside for a break. Standing in the middle of an adjacent parking lot, we called Tripoli's office in Calgary. Merrily expressing our Christmas greetings, we advised each recipient of the location from where we were calling. I could tell, by the lack of enthusiasm, that my colleagues figured some holiday spirits had been sampled too early in the day. It was a little ahead of its time for most people to take seriously.

Tim and I kept changing hotels, hoping to discover a more convenient downtown route. By early evening, the city centre was almost deserted and offered limited affordable and casual dining. In addition, room rates for core accommodation were more than we were willing to bear. Therefore, we concentrated on outlying areas. In the end it worked out best to stay in the north, just off the Dallas Northern Tollway. This is also where we discovered the best bars and restaurants. We took turns deciding what to eat each night. Selection was endless.

"The west side rush hour congestion convinced us to experiment with hotel options elsewhere. Neil had rented an economy car and it hardly had any acceleration. Merging in and out of a half dozen lanes of traffic was unnerving as Neil was either cursing the rental car or the other drivers. Eventually our hotel home became a thirty to forty-five minute drive up a toll road to North Dallas. Although it took a long time to cover a short distance, at least the traffic moved.

I remember "bar hopping" at a nearby strip on more than one occasion, since plenty of trendy restaurants and night-clubs were concentrated here.
Bret's secretary was kind enough to show us the town one night, so we made a mental note of favourites for return visits. One that comes to mind was called Studebaker's. It had many antique cars on display and I believe some were used as a booth for eating or drinking."

The last Saturday of Tim's assignment, Bret invited us out to his home in North Dallas for dinner. We knocked off early to give us time to return to the hotel and change.

Checking the map thoroughly to determine the best route to take, we noted that he appeared to live in a very prestigious part of the city. Bret had never given the impression he was wealthy. Until this discovery, we had planned to dress down to jeans and casual shirt. I had second thoughts and put on my best dress pants and dress shirt. Tim stayed with the cowboy look, ensuring that one of us would look out of place.

By Calgary standards, Bret lived in a palatial mansion, entrance way pillars and all. We waited in the car a moment, wondering if valet service would handle parking or a butler would greet us at the door. One thing was for certain, *I was dressed appropriately*.

Actually clothes were not an issue, although Tim apologized for his as soon as we entered. Bret and his wife were the perfect hosts. In minutes we felt so at home that it probably would not have mattered if we had shown up in bathing suits.

We first toured the house, which took a while. Then we convened around a *big* table in a *big* dining room and had a *big* meal - catered, of course. Yes sir, this was Texas hospitality.

Afterwards, over a few drinks, we shared stories of the oilpatch and listened intently to Bret's recollections of his airline experiences. Since both he and his wife had lived in Dallas for quite a while, they had many tall tales of big city life.

It was late when we left, well past midnight. We were sorry to see the night end.

"As Neil pointed out, Bret's home was very lavish. One of the Hunts lived in the neighbourhood, but we did not get to see which house it was. I do not recall discussing if Bret and his wife had any children. We assumed not, as we did not see or hear of any. We certainly felt like we were treated like family."

The one thing notable about Tim's departure several days later was how cold it was compared to when we arrived.

If you were a fan of the television show 'DALLAS', it is unlikely you ever saw an episode involving snow, ice, and cold temperatures. Well, we can vouch for all three this December of 1984.

Taking Tim to the Dallas/Fort Worth airport, which was twenty-five miles equidistant from each city centre, was as hairy as any field assignment. Frost, the previous night, had deposited a layer of ice. Driving was treacherous, as were the drivers. It was too cool for the clothes we had brought. Tim was not too sorry to be leaving.

"The Dallas weather had turned for the worse. We were even exposed to freezing rain on a couple of occasions. It was not at all what I had expected for Texas, even if it was the end of the year.

Before leaving, I conveyed my general impression of the Drilling Fund assets to Neil. Although there were a few development locations of value, there was not a lot of upside and most of the pools were experiencing high declines. Neil still had a lot of engineering work to do, but his research had uncovered similar conclusions. The Dallas chapter was now over for me and I looked forward to getting home for Christmas."

V
(No Santa This Year)

There was no time to relax after Tim left. We had assembled a mountain of cost and revenue tables, well assessments, production decline plots, Joint Interest Billings, Plug and Abandonment candidates, Lease Schedules, Payout Statements, and prospect maps. There was plenty more data, but it had yet to be prioritized to maintain and schedule.

Instead of allocating time to evaluate all wells, the top third were selectively analysed, in descending value (an average of five or six per Fund). Since our research had determined actual values from 1981 - 1983, future Fund performance was modelled from a combination of data and correlative projections. Graphing future production and revenue against historical totals disclosed inconsistencies in several Funds, requiring expansion of the list of top performers.

Similarly, the suspended/shut-in wells that Tim and I had screened also received detailed interpretation. In all, this list amounted to about one third of this type (an average of two or three per Fund). The significance for this grouping was the potential plug and abandonment liability and it was the source of a few sleepless nights as the clock wound down.

Normally notes and/or summaries were taken home to the hotel each night. My oilpatch experience pondered how these wells (representing 40% of the total) would impact the program if (a) recompletion attempts failed; and (b) oil and gas prices weakened, which in turn would limit cash flow for remedial action such as workover or plugging operations.

Many suspended/shut-in wells were deep tests, 10000 feet or more, in Texas and North Dakota. Since the initial target had proven unsuccessful, it was only a matter of time before funds would be requested for recompletion or abandonment.

One well that caught our attention was a nightmare. A deep test in Mississippi encountered prolonged problems such as hole caving, stuck casing, and fishing for lost tools. Several completion attempts were unsuccessful, despite the optimism of the participants. After plug and abandonment, the Fund sustained cumulative losses of $11,000,000.

It was important to remain objective. Tripoli did not hide their preference to proceed with this acquisition, pending our evaluation. In the beginning we were equally excited. On the surface it looked like a tremendous opportunity. Experience in Ohio and Utah, however, had taught me how shallow this surface could be.

My draft reports for the seven Funds were finalized by December 22, 1984 and collectively forwarded to Calgary. I was cognizant that my recommendation might earn me a scrooge of the year award. Technically Tim supported me. His assessment was equally critical. When an engineer and geologist form a consensus without influence, there is good reason to respect it. Our composite summary was as follows:

		NET OPERATING INCOME (M $)							
	#PROD	1981	1982	1983	1984	1985	1986	1987	1988
FUND	WELLS	act.	act.	act.	est.	est.	est.	est.	est.
	(1984)								
I	12	380	252	268	170	320	79	47	26
II	6	466	284	209	173	128	97	74	54
III	32	4482	2347	1914	1359	958	643	391	193
IV	7	483	185	294	350	240	219	198	179
V	9	464	549	1269	594	399	228	106	14
A	7	174	278	68	1447	737	351	70	0
B	0	29	233	41	(79)	0	0	0	0
TOTALS		6478	4128	4063	4014	2782	1617	886	466

Cumulative Net Operating Income Forecast Total (1985 - 1992): **6610**

Our evaluation included a number of clarifications, such as:
(1)Fund I - 1985;includes Mavis #1 withheld revenue of 47 M$.
(2)Fund V - 1983;includes the sale of two deep wells.
(3)Fund A - 1984;comprises one recompletion and one 300% payout.
(4)Fund B - 1984;last North Dakota well plugged & abandoned.
Our forecast was predicated on conservative assumptions:
*   average oil and gas prices from 1985 - 1988 would remain the same as 1984, or roughly $19.50 per barrel and $1.75 per MCF;
*   included only well abandonments pending in 1984 ;
*   included only recompletions having less than 50% risk factor;
*   assumed no litigation or title disputes.

Revenue was equally distributed between gas and oil. Most of the wells had passed the half way mark in their productive life and were on steep decline. Any appreciable decrease in resource prices would doom my forecast andTripoli's $10,000,000. investment.

Several individual asset sales had occurred during the previous twelve months. As stalwart performers, they had contributed meaningfully to past Cash Flows. As dispositions, the applicable Funds realized major one time only returns.

On its own merit this acquisition would not fly. The potential liabilities were many times the potential recovery. The administration alone represented a major undertaking for Tripoli's size. Cash Flow had peaked in 1981 and only miracles in pricing and recompletion success would avert a disastrous bottom line in future years. It was an Ohio clone, just on a bigger scale.

The Dallas interests wanted to sell and the Calgary interests wanted to buy. My summation put Christmas on hold for both. I had no regrets. Within a year, oil prices dropped to $12.00 per barrel and gas to less than $1.00 per MCF. One of my two axioms for U.S. oil and gas operations, **"Verify, Verify, and Verify"**, proved to be our saviour.

It was impossible to get a flight back to Calgary for Christmas, except on First Class. A Southwest Airlines no frills flight was available to Virginia, so Christmas was spent with friends there. I returned to Dallas before New Year's to pack my research and bid farewell to Bret.

Celebrating the arrival of January 1, 1985 was the last thing on my mind. A much better ending to the old year had been hoped for. With the Utah litigation waiting my return, there were no illusions about the beginning of the new year either.

EPISODE 7: UTAH - EXPECT THE UNEXPECTED

I
(Combined Operations)

Little time was wasted in the New Year mobilizing our forces for the ensuing wars we knew would come. Both sides were entrenched and neither could capitulate without fear of being destroyed. Tripoli continued to bear the bulk of managing and coordinating the JV's interests in ongoing field operations and litigation. It was fortunate that when individuals were called upon to share their energy and talents, all else was put aside. The stakes had become too high.

Litigating in the U.S., whether as a Plaintiff or Defendant, not only demands commitment and purpose, but also a divine belief that your cause is just. It is not good enough, or practical, to engage your opponent in a law suit only for the sake of proving a point.

If Court action does not qualify as sound business judgement, avoid the risks and write it off as experience. This was the toughest aptitude test in my U.S. operations experience.

Before Utah ceased to be an issue, each JV participant submitted to this test of choice. Each would have two options. One was to recognize a compromise and retire from battle with less than desired compensation; both sides wounded but intact. The other was to prolong hostilities, seeking full recovery of Settlement or Court award; punishment for victorious and vanquished alike.

This threshold would be reached many times in my ensuing years of U.S. operations. The advice that served me best was to *'expect the unexpected'*.

Since the New Year objective was to conclude our preparations and establish a Trial Date for the earliest opening, the pace of depositions was accelerated. Depending on the topic of examination, we would call on JV or consultant expertise to educate our legal team and assist in formulating strategy. Furthermore, a representative would be at their disposal during all depositions. While this added to our costs, it was the right decision. We presented a determined, knowledgeable, and united front.

Our legal team rarely failed to score crucial blows at these proceedings. As the months progressed, our case became more solidified and the outcome more predictable. This would prove to be both
encouraging and deceiving.

There is no disputing the competency and capability of our
Counsel leading up to Trial. By no small measure, many individuals
contributed to this success.

Every documented response from the Operator was reviewed
and, if necessary, challenged by Tripoli staff on a priority basis. A
logging system was designed to record and comment on every
telephone call, facsimile, and mailed correspondence.

Concurrently, Mac was addressing the Operator's responses
to the 1984 audits. It was not uncommon for him to revisit an issue
several times before courting an acceptable answer. Despite Mac's
intensity, many queries remained unanswered or ignored. It was a
tedious, frustrating process.

*"Neil is right about auditing, it often takes 2, 3, or 4 tries before a query is
satisfactorily resolved.*

*Luke didn't reply directly to any query. His replies would beat about the
bush, hum and haw, but never directly address the problems. Some minor
housekeeping items were resolved, but only because they would end up being in
the Operator's favour."*

To ensure our assets were not totally neglected, we maintained
a presence in the field through frequent fact finding trips or facility
tours for members of the legal team or JV. The most enthusiastic and
aggressive of the latter was Michael Cooke, the new President of
Warren. His banking background proved of great value for analyzing
personalities.

Michael added new blood and determination to the conflict.
His spirit was infectious and invigorating for the rest of us who had
been bloodied for almost two years. We had ceased to regard the
Operator as the enemy. Instead it was frustration, tedium, internal
friction, and the relentless accumulation of costs.

Michael submerged himself in every detail of our litigation,
studiously researching legal and supporting technical documents.
It was mutually beneficial to confer on a frequent basis.

Despite residing in Toronto, he frequently visited Calgary and
Salt Lake City for briefings. At Warren's expense, he maintained

additional Utah legal expertise and shared his progress. He methodi-
cally investigated the financial dealings of the Operator with significant success. Our team had yet to pursue this aspect in detail.
Amalgamating forces seemed prudent and efficient. Michael offered,
and we accepted, the contributions of his Salt Lake City lawyer to
our legal team.

*"As financial matters were my field of expertise, Warren's attorney and I
subpoenaed all banking documents from the Utah Operator. We discovered
significant transfers of funds from Utah to a Denver bank.*

*The Utah Operator's bank required that the Operator file an annual
certificate verifying that it was not a Defendant in any litigation anywhere in the
U.S. in the past year. When the Operator's in-house Counsel, 'Bill', provided an
executed certificate to the Denver bank, he conveniently and deliberately ignored
the fact that Warren had filed a Statement of Claim in Federal Court several
months earlier. Therefore an untruthful certificate was filed.*

*According to U.S. Banking Law, this false certificate constituted interstate
fraud, which is a Federal offence punishable by incarceration.*

*A Salt Lake City meeting was convened and copies of our Statement of
Claim and the false certificate were provided for pondering. It only took a few
minutes for the Operator and Bill to understand the inevitable consequences."*

As the Utah litigation wore on, mind games developed. I began to visualize the process as an acrimonious triangle of external
influence: 1) us/our Counsel interaction; 2) us/Operator interaction;
and 3) our Counsel's interaction with both sides.

My conscience was always sensitive and cautious of being the
foreigner, the outsider, in this formula. It was helpful to consult and
share strategy with a source in the centre of this triangle. As 'the
new kid on the block', Michael provided the sounding board needed
to relax my guard and examine our position without influence.

*"I shared Neil's sense of alienation in the U.S. theatre. It was fortunate for
me that a business associate, who was a lawyer, was more familiar with U.S.
customs and proved to be a valuable source of guidance.*

*In his words, litigation in the U.S. was a national blood sport and designed
for animals. In Canada, it was strictly a last resort. More than once he cautioned
that a successful outcome against our Utah Operator was a long shot. Despite
this risk, I accepted the challenge of proving a fundamental belief; our Operator
was wrong and should be held accountable for their actions."*

Deposing the Operator's key employees in the spring and summer of 1985 signalled the final phase of our investigations. It was a period of enlightenment for Mac and myself. We could not hide our frustrations at testimony we knew to be inaccurate, despite being under oath. Likewise responses like 'I do not recall' or 'I have no knowledge', were reminders that Trial would be unpredictable.

We vowed not to engage in any business dealings again with these individuals. Several years later my path would cross the path of the Operator's Controller, Luke. This time, armed with past experience, the relationship was severed promptly and unmercifully (EPISODE 11).

These depositions were subjected to the same tactics employed by the Operator during our meetings and audits of 1984. Even the lawyers sometimes lost their temper or concentration. There were times when, as observers, we expected opposing Counsel would initiate legal action against each other.

For example, the Operator's President had to be examined twice, end of June and mid-July. It did not surprise any of us that he was most uncooperative. No matter how bad it got, we knew the Trial phase would screen out these bad habits.

In June, the Operator's Counsel conducted a week long examination in Calgary of our representatives. A lengthy list of the deposed included myself, Mac, Rick Nixon, Michael Cooke, Tim Malo, Richard Bowens, several JV representatives, and numerous unrelated or remotely connected Tripoli and ex-Tripoli staff.

Depositions, conducted in a shotgun and hostile manner, lacked purpose. If anything, these proceedings worsened the Operator's status. We theorized on motive:
1) an expense paid vacation to Calgary with a weekend on each end;
2) stretch the JV's financial resources by extended attendance;
3) intimidate unsuspecting and unprepared ancillary participants;
4) seek weak links to exploit at Trial for confusion; and
5) lack of vision and strategy.

The more answers they got to their questions, the more untenable their case became. The Operator's treatment of our program had become legend and few of the people involved were lost for words relating to it. In the years since, it has often been a topic of conversation with Michael over coffee.

"One anecdote concerning my two hour deposition comes to mind. The Defendant's Counsel came out swinging in an aggressive and cocky mood.

Under vague questioning about banking irregularities alleged in Warren's Statement of Claim, most of my responses were in descriptive financial or legal language. After seven years of banking experience, I was comfortable with this language and examination routine. The Operator's Counsel, however, became quite frustrated with his lack of progress and perhaps from being upstaged. He asked sarcastically, 'Mr. Cooke, are you a lawyer?' I replied, sarcastically, 'No, are you?'

The second anecdote concerns a conversation over dinner that evening. We were discussing the deposition results with our attorneys. One of the lawyers remarked 'The problem with you Canadians is that you're too polite. The Defendant's lawyers see your lack of emotion as a sign of weakness or lack of conviction. You need to get angry and impolite.' I guess he said it all."

Rick Nixon recollected his experience that week of June 1985. He had started the ball rolling with his mini-audit back in mid 1983. As the saying goes, first impressions are important. His observations of the Operator 's conduct made for another interesting deposition.

"My greatest concern was that the rate the principals were taking money out of the company, that no funds would be available to satisfy the position of Tripoli. My recommendation to Tripoli was to first, act quickly and insist on a cash settlement and secondly to divest itself of any further relationship with the Operator."

The only lasting and stressful reservations we had about Trial were financial. A week had been scheduled, but there was no assurance it would not take longer. Being in Salt Lake City meant incurring considerable travel and accommodation expenses.

The JV legal costs had escalated to more than twice our original worst case projection. Knowing that Appeals could delay settlement for years, the pain threshold could still be in the distant future. In the interim the solvency of the Operator, and the JV participants, would be at risk and had to be considered. No doubt these scenarios were subjected to rigorous speculation by the Defendant also.

II
(Escape At Last)

Personally, my future in the industry was concerning, given my prolonged and specialized exposure to litigation. Skills in operations and production engineering demanded constant upgrading and refreshing.

My value would be ranked on expertise in, and knowledge of, horizontal and slant hole drilling, creative fracture stimulation, computer enhanced reservoir modelling, production decline software, advanced logging tools, etc. No need to continue. It was just as obvious to me at the time.

If only to get my hands dirty again on a rig floor, or flow test wells, or supervise a workover - anything but more Naked City drama.

As you may recall, the 1980's began with a stampede of Canadian resource companies to the U.S. to escape the National Energy Policy (NEP). By mid 1985 most of these adventurers had returned, at least those that were survivors. Many had met a fate similar to my exploits.

In October 1984 the Mulroney Conservatives defeated the Liberals, after 16 years of Trudeau rule, and formed a majority government. Support from Western Canada was almost unanimous, based on Brian Mulroney's promise to replace the hated NEP without delay. **Let history show that he delivered on this promise.**

Mulroney created a new hope for the Canadian energy industry. The participants were all too happy and eager to focus attention and investment back to their native land. It was none too soon, for another world oil price collapse would strangle the industry for the last half of the decade. Had the NEP remained, the combination would have been disastrous.

It was extremely rare for any Canadian Independents still to be active south of the border. Likewise, employment opportunities for Canadian professionals specializing in U.S. operations were quite unique. My intentions were to explore my options as soon as Utah was resolved.

On March 16, 1985 an option to my dilemma appeared and it was seized. The opportunity was most unexpected and so was my spontaneous reaction.

'Cage Resources' Ltd. of Calgary (Cage) was recruiting an operations/production engineer for their U.S. properties, mostly in Texas and Utah. The Calgary Herald advertisement that Saturday was too good to pass up.

"Engineering - United States Operations

This senior engineer will assume responsibility for all facets of the Company's operations in the United States. The major properties are non-operated and require constant monitoring to ensure the Company's interests are being maximized.
Responsibilities include reviewing the various properties, identifying and evaluating development opportunities, preparing economic evaluations, reviewing AFE's, and supervision of the preparation of yearly budget and reserve reports.
Individuals who enjoy a small company environment and are prepared to demonstrate their initiative will find this position challenging. Good production operations experience is very desirable.
The company offers competitive salaries, a challenging environment, an incentive plan and a comprehensive benefits package."

My first interview was with Wayne Boddy, the Vice President of Production. When invited to a second interview, I met the President, Bill Harrison. My background seemed to be a natural fit. Wayne thought so too, and recommended my appointment.

Confirmation of my appointment was received May 17, 1985 and my official start with Cage was the first week of June.

While eagerly looking forward to a new page in my career, I was equally cognizant of my responsibilities and obligations to the Utah litigation. To maintain continuity, a compromise was brokered that seemed to suit both Cage and Tripoli.

Cage had significant exposure in Utah, near Tripoli's wells in the Altamont Field. My first priority was to inspect and inventory their field facilities and meet the field staff.

The JV legal team had scheduled several key depositions for June and July in Salt Lake City. The Trial docket remained unchanged for the first week of September.

In exchange for the JV picking up Cage's travel expenses, Cage would donate my assistance for depositions and Trial as necessary. My commitments to both parties were assured at minimal cost.

It was a win-win environment for all and the arrangements were most satisfying to me. With a little luck, the Defendants would not detect a change in our team composition. Otherwise, my sudden absence might have signalled damaging speculation about the JV strategy.

Chuck's letter of June 24, 1985 to Wayne Boddy of Cage indicated a similar approval of the compromize both sides had approved.

"Thank you very much for your co-operation in providing Neil Leeson's services to assist us in preparation for our upcoming trial with 'the Operator'. We will need Neil's help for 'the President's' depositions which are currently scheduled for Friday, June 28, 1985 in Salt Lake City. It is quite likely that we will need Neil's services for a second session of 'the President's' deposition probably during the time frame July 15th through August 1, 1985.
Neil's services will additionally be needed for approximately one to two days of trial time during the week of September 3, 1985 in Salt Lake City.
I am enclosing a copy of my letter to the Controller for Tripoli, establishing the process for Tripoli's payment of Neil's expenses for his work in connection with our case."

Similarly, the other side of the equation was balanced with Chuck's letter of June 24, 1985 to Tripoli's Controller, Rod Mitton. The JV momentum did not miss a beat.

"As you know, Neil Leeson has been an integral part of the preparation for the September 3, 1985 trial of our claims against 'the Operator'. It will be necessary for us to use Neil's services in connection with further depositions and preparation for trial, as well as, testimony at trial. I have spoken to Mr. Bill Harrison, President of Cage Resources, and to Wayne Boddy, Vice President of Production, Neil's immediate supervisor, concerning Neil's assistance in the preparation of this trial. The people at Cage have very graciously allowed us to use a limited amount of Neil's time, provided, however, Tripoli, pays for Neil's expenses.
I have cleared the procedure to pay Neil's expenses with Richard during my last visit to Calgary for the Rick Nixon deposition. By copy of this letter I am advising Neil to send a statement for his expenses directly to you."

The purpose of reproducing these two letters was to demonstrate the ease with which the Canadian oilpatch worked together. From years of U.S. experience, this was one discipline we clearly held a competitive edge over our American counterparts.

Now my new challenges at Cage could be pursued. I was pumped. Finally a chance to finish what had been started with my first introduction to the U.S. in October 1980. For Tripoli and the JV, it was now all up to the Courts.

III
(Options)

In late August, following a recent tour of Cage's Texas properties, a call came in from a familiar voice about a familiar topic. It was Michael Cooke calling from his Toronto office to discuss the lawsuit. Very timely, as I had been giving thought to the preparation and commitment expected of me. The JV participants and the legal team were confident and ready leading up to the September 3 Trial date. My schedule had been prioritized to be equally ready.

The frequent strategy sessions with Michael had been missed since leaving Tripoli. This call would make up for it. This call was the biggest one of all.

Just days before commencement of Trial, a settlement offer was presented to each Plaintiff in the form of two options.

One was a lump sum discounted payment immediately. The other was a payment in full, based on a small advance, followed *later* by thirty-six equal monthly instalments to balance of payout. Consideration was limited to a few days.

In Warren's case this first option amounted to about $700,000. U.S., notably less than the damages sought of $2,400,000 U.S. but still a significant, no risk recovery.

Of greater significance, the costs of Trial and the aftermath could be avoided. The estimate of legal services was expected to double the existing cost to date. While the lawyers would have healthy pay-days, little would be left for the victims.

Michael advised he planned to accept the cash settlement and to Quit Claim (convey Warren's ownership in the wells to the Operator) all interests immediately. He asked my opinion. My response was something similar to the following.

"In a heartbeat I would accept it. By now you are well acquainted with the business practises and reliability of the Operator. Almost anything can happen over 36 months. Forget about Court or prolonged recovery. Take the cash and put the whole messy issue behind you."

He did just that, as did the other JV participants. Only one, however, chose Warren's payment option and tactical withdrawal from Utah asset ownership. Michael recalled the event.

"As the Trial clock ticked down, the Operator decided it was time to negotiate with Warren before we made good on our promise to expose the interstate banking issue. At a hastily convened meeting, settlement documents were drawn up.

I shared the details of our settlement with one other JV party who had expressed their unhappiness with Chuck's progress. They then offered to assume a proportionate share of Warren's legal expenses if we would represent their interest.

At a subsequent meeting, Claimant Release forms were executed and Warren's assets were transferred to the Operator (the wells had become liabilities due to neglect and abuse). After securing Warren's settlement cheque, the Operator was advised of a final loose end. 'One last thing to talk about, gentlemen. Another JV party has asked me to represent them in settlement negotiations with you. They will accept a cash settlement proportionate to that accepted by Warren.' When the proceedings terminated, the Operator vowed not to do business with Warren ever again. The feeling was mutual."

Whether or not all the JV parties consulted with each other is not known. The only universal feedback passed on to me was the distressing magnitude of the legal costs and the fatigue of confrontation. For those who retained title in the wells, it would get a lot worse in the future. As with Ohio years earlier, investment losses totalled in the millions and salvage value was negligible.

Chuck's letter to me of October 25, 1985 closed the book on this ugly incident (for me, but unfortunately not for all the JV). It was a very complimentary letter and it gave me juice for my new role at Cage.

"I assume that you have heard via the "grapevine" in the Calgary Oil Patch that the litigation with 'the Operator' has been completely resolved. I want to express to you my sincere appreciation for the assistance you provided us in preparation for the trial of the Operator's' lawsuit. As I expressed to you during the course of our work on 'the Operator's' problem, it is critical that lawyers have technical assistance from people who are knowledgeable, dedicated and willing to teach. You fulfilled those requirements admirably."

To my knowledge, none of the Operator's family members have resurfaced in an oil related business. The sons moved out of Utah. I kept track only to avoid unknowingly crossing paths. Nothing personal, it just was not my concept of doing business.

Warren used the settlement proceeds, after deducting roughly one third for litigation expenses, to pursue successful oil and gas prospects in Saskatchewan.

In December 1990, Warren merged with two other Canadian junior resource companies, also managed by Michael Cooke, to form an aggressive, medium-sized independent exploration and development company, all under his auspices.

FOOTNOTE: Early in 1986, the 'Operator' filed for Chapter 11 Bankruptcy protection. Included in the lengthy list of Unsecured Creditors were several members of the JV. They had chosen to recover all their damages over the thirty-six month period. **Instead, they received payments for only a few months.** Negotiations with the Court appointed Trustee were still in progress several years later. **Expect the unexpected**.

View of Salt Lake City at night, facing east towards the Wasatch Mountains

Typical north eastern Utah scenery; the Uinta Mountains is the only North American mountain range running east and west

Ski runs near Park City, Utah (35 miles east of Salt Lake City), August 1985

EPISODE 8: CAGE - TURNING OVER A NEW PAGE

I

(*Subterfuge*, Again)

June 3, 1985 was my first day on the job at Cage Resources Ltd. (Cage). Like Tripoli, Cage was Canadian owned and controlled but had significant United States investments in addition to its Canadian operations. All U.S. assets had been structured into a wholly owned subsidiary, Cage Resources Inc. (Inc). Despite a frustrating U.S. track record, an ignorance of subterfuge once again interfered with my gut feeling to escape. My goal of making a positive difference this time was all in my imagination.

Prior to my arrival, Inc had been headquartered in Denver. Staff peaked at forty in 1983. A small subsidiary field office had been maintained in Amarillo until 1984.

Although Inc operated very few wells, it had major interests in the Altamont Field of Utah (twenty-six wells), the Whitte (one hundred wells, Compressor Stations, and twenty inch pipeline), Cob (thirteen wells), and Barn (thirteen wells and five MMCFPD Gas Plant) Fields in the Texas Panhandle, and minor positions in Oklahoma, Nebraska, Mississippi, Michigan, and throughout Texas.

Since 1980 Cage had invested in excess of $100 million U.S. into Inc. On paper the assets were impressive, but in reality the cash flows and production performances were not meeting expectations. The uncertainty in world oil prices demanded improved efficiency and lower operating costs to survive. Cage devised a plan to identify specific symptoms. My role was to assist in determining cures and ensuring they were implemented.

Despite owning a majority interest in most of its properties, Inc was in an unenviable position. As a non-operator, it lacked authority for initiating change. However there was a will and we proceeded to find a way.

The focus of our attention was to be Utah first, then Texas. The Utah assets were valuable for future development potential.

Oil was the primary target and product, although gas gathering systems criss-crossed the Altamont Field (Field). Half a dozen gas plants, with various owners and capacities of up to 50 MMCFPD, linked the interlocking system of wells. The solution gas was very rich in Natural Gas Liquids (NGL), adding a valuable component to the cash flow formula. The mostly barren, desert-like, and flat geography was very conducive to pipeline and drilling operations.

In 1981 Inc pioneered a novel arrangement with the Utah State Oil and Gas Board (Board). Until then the Altamont Field consisted of hundreds of deep Wasatch formation wells. Each was assigned, and assumed capable of draining, a lease of one section or 640 acres. The average ultimate recoverable reserves were estimated at a quarter of a million barrels per well. Most had additional unexploited potential in shallower hydrocarbon bearing sands.

The Green River formation possessed multiple pay zones between 7000 and 9000 feet. The Douglas Creek formation similarly indicated considerable potential between 4500 and 6500 feet. Inc's only shallow test yielded initial rates of 100 BOPD in one of five prospective zones.

Inc's research had determined that only a portion of the Wasatch formation reserves were subject to drainage at a density of one well per 640 acres. They proposed an infill drilling experiment on six of their sections containing producing wells. The new wells would be located diagonally opposite the existing wells, which would be suspended during a three year trial period. The objective was to prove the viability of half section (320 acre) drainage without interfering with original well recoveries.

The Board approved, provided pressures were monitored and reported for each original well during suspension. A comprehensive study was promised in 1984, based on Inc's results.

It was a bold gamble by Inc. At $1,500,000 U.S. per well, the risks were substantial. In the ten year history of the Field, Inc was the first promoter of this optimization method. Since hundreds of sections were developed by single well spacing, the industry observed with caution but also great expectation. Twinning existing wells represented rejuvenation of the Field as well as local and State economies.

Inc's six wells were successes. By 1984 cumulative production averaged 100,000 barrels each. As no pressure drawdown had been recorded at the original wells, the production suspensions were lifted.

Decline profiles had been similar for old and new wells, indicating potential virgin reservoir. All data was provided to the Board; the industry waited in suspense.

Finally in March 1985 the Board issued a Field wide Order officially approving infill drilling. The industry immediately switched on afterburners to accommodate the demand. Inc's knowledge and experience were valuable contributions to this rebirth of activity.

During the remainder of 1985, our strategy was to continue monitoring production and pressures on the twin well sections in the event additional well density might prove feasible. A cautious multi-year program to drill second wells in our other sections was also initiated. As in the early 1980s, this was again a time of uncertainty for world oil prices, which were hovering around $20 U.S. per barrel. We knew from our budget models that a price below $17 U.S. would not sustain drilling, let alone production operations. Fortunately Cage had set into motion a series of precautions to counter this threat.

Drilling at 2-9, Aug 1985, facing southwest (mud pits on left)

Drilling 2-9 Wasatch test, Aug 1985, facing west (mudmixing hopper at left)

As an efficiency and economic measure, Cage elected to close Inc's Denver office and consolidate operations in Calgary. Downsizing began in early 1984 and continued unabated until June 1985. My first assignment was to co-ordinate packing and shipping all files and selective furniture and equipment to Calgary prior to office closure and final staff departure.

Upon leaving Calgary June 12 for a familiarization tour, I had only been with Cage for a few days and was still trying to acquaint myself with personnel and procedure. My return was scheduled in ten days, with the first stop in Denver for three of them.

Rig camp at 2-9, Aug 1985, facing north (Blacktail Ridge in background)

Rig drilling offset well in Section 9, Aug 1985, facing southwest

Mud pits at 2-9, facing east, Aug., 1985

Given Cage's long range reorganization plans, it was not surprising that the Denver office morale and attitude had suffered for the past year.

Inc had provided generous severance packages to help mitigate the pain of layoff. Any furniture and equipment not required by Calgary was available to the staff at attractive prices. A half dozen company cars Leases were bought out by Inc and turned over to the applicable staff.

It was easy to sympathize with the victims, having been there myself in 1983. Time and motivation are healing factors no matter what kind of loss is suffered. As Denver was a vibrant oil industry centre, most were able to relocate or establish self employment.

One employee who chose the latter was the Senior Engineer, whom we shall refer to as Rex. His hobby was boating and, during his final year with Inc, had invested in a marina in Wyoming. To facilitate a smooth transition, Cage had negotiated a part time consulting arrangement paying him $8000 U.S. per month to the end of the year. This seemed to be a very generous fee to me, but Cage had begrudgingly agreed as a matter of necessity. Events were building in Texas that I was not aware of nor anticipating.

On the flight from Calgary my itinerary was planned. Denver was the first of **three objectives** for this assignment.

Immediate priority for the **first objective** was to debrief Rex and acquaint myself with his vision of the assets. Second priority was an exit interview with all other staff to reinforce my knowledge of the properties. Third priority was to implement office closing procedures in accordance with Cage's instructions. Fourth priority was to arrange a familiarization tour of the Texas Panhandle properties with Rex. Finally my fifth priority was to introduce myself to the Denver based operator of our Utah properties, 'Cracker Resources' (Cracker).

The first objective was a tall order to fulfil in three days.

No less tiring and demanding would be the **second objective**, requiring five precisely co-ordinated days in Utah to tour Inc's properties and participate in scheduled depositions for the Tripoli JV law suit.

Two days had been allotted for the **third objective**, touring the Panhandle properties in Hutchinson County, Texas with Rex. It was a large Development project involving three Joint Venture leases in an old field. Of all U.S. assets, 22% of net proved oil and 56% of net proved gas reserves were allocated to the Panhandle.

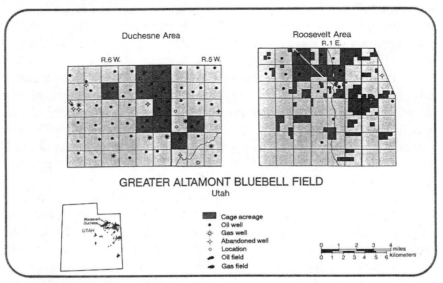

Map of Cage's Utah Properties

My pace would require high energy and patience with precise timetables and agendas. Instead of being nervous and apprehensive, fate could not have been kinder.

II
(Twins, I Presume)

Cage's recruitment ad of March 16, 1985 that solicited my response also included a position for a Development Geologist.

"The successful individual will be involved in a variety of projects in Canada and the United States including supervision of a modest exploration budget, identifying and evaluating development opportunities and assessing farmin/farmout proposals."

This interaction between Canada and the U.S. solicited many more candidates than the engineering position that attracted my attention.

The 'successful candidate' and I began employment with Cage on the same day. His recent experience was also in the U.S., mostly in Kansas. Our benefits included a company car with a maximum value of $15000. Independently we both selected a Chrysler Fifth Avenue, same colour. The difference, known only by the accountants, was his was new from a Dealership and mine was a demonstrator from a Leasing Agency.

We had the same first name. We journeyed together to Denver after sorting out the airline's confusion in assigning us each other's ticket. Our first week at Cage had been so hectic and tailored to our specific positions, we had not even noticed each other. After Denver our paths were to diverge, so we had only a few days to get acquainted.

Any tension that had accumulated prior to my departure quickly dissipated at the expense of my travelling companion. We went directly from the airport to Inc's office (only about a ten minute cab ride from Stapleton Airport; now close to an hour from the new airport) and were at work consulting with the staff by 10 AM. As usual our introduction was good for a laugh and much conjecture.

When we checked into the Denver Park Suites that evening, we were exhausted. In no time the Reservations Clerk nearly brought us to hysteria.

Thinking two rooms had been mistakenly booked for the same person, the hotel had cancelled one. Identical business name, address, and phone number had confused the reservation office. Someone along the network took the liberty of deleting one as a clerical error. Now that we were both in attendance and looking for our rooms, the Clerk had to scramble. On this particular evening there was hardly a vacancy. Neil T. and I had a good laugh.

We both presented CIBC VISA cards for registration and had similar signatures. After all that he had been through, he mixed these up too. It seemed like an hour had passed before we were finally issued keys to our rooms - several floors apart. We didn't argue since we knew only a few were available, although it would have been convenient to be adjacent. Another laugh was shared with Neil T. as we were riding the elevator up.

"Neil was first in line at the Registration Desk. The Clerk could not find his reservation but found mine. He thought mine was in error, cancelled it, and assigned my room to Neil. When I stepped forward after Neil, I had to walk the Clerk through the entire procedure all over again. As a finale, he gave me Neil's credit card imprint to sign.

We both quickly realized that the poor guy behind the counter was becoming increasingly flustered at the endless comedy of errors that was unfolding before him. So we made a noble effort to keep a continuous flow of banter between us. This was not easy, considering we knew absolutely nothing about each other, but was considered essential to avoid getting angry and creating a potentially ugly scene.

It was worth it in the end. The Clerk (and those in the line up behind us) ultimately saw the humour in the situation. One of them commented ' You guys are better than the Blues Brothers. You should take your show on the road.' "

Shortly after laying down on the bed for a few minutes solace, there was a knock at the door. It was Neil T. - with my luggage, and looking for his. Rather than phoning the Front Desk and risking further delay, he undertook Bell Hop duties to ensure a prompt and safe exchange. As he left, I said " well Mr. Thiessen (pronounced Teeson), do you think it matters who offers to pay for dinner tonight? " It was not our first laugh that day.

On the second day we busied ourselves orchestrating the office closure.

Inc's Denver office caught us by surprise. An entire floor of a prestigious office tower dwarfed Cage's Calgary space. Fortunately the lease was expiring the end of June. Vacating saved Inc roughly $40,000 U.S. per month.

The furniture was very impressive, mostly solid oak. Neil T. and I had no trouble filling our quota to accommodate Cage's needs. We speculated on the horse trading that would ensue when it all reached Calgary. The quality was superior and no doubt would go to senior management.

The Denver fleet comprised the elite in custom sports and luxury automobiles. Most had a new price in the range of $20,000 to $25,000 U.S., which was no small benefit. We joked about shipping a couple company cars back and exchanging ours.

"My reaction to the Denver office was similar to Neil's opinion; it was clear that this was not a shoe-string operation. These guys knew how to spend money. I could not wait to get some of the furniture back to my Calgary office.

A rumour surfaced during my discussions with the remaining staff about how the Denver office functioned. A large deal for exploratory lands in New Mexico, a rank wildcat area with very little well control but a large contiguous block in excess of 200,000 acres, was pursued. They were successful and got it.

Less than a month after signing the deal, Denver received a phone call from another company offering all their money back (over $5 million) for a 50% interest in the lands. Considering the risk, and their debt level, they should have jumped at the opportunity. Instead, they refused the offer, electing to proceed on their own. The acreage was never evaluated or drilled, the $5 million to obtain it was lost. "

Neil T. spent most of his time with the Senior Geologist, 'Jordie', who would not be on retainer and therefore not available after the end of the month. That night the three of us had dinner together. We benefited from frank, constructive discussions on the task ahead for us 'twins', as evidenced by Neil T's recollections.

"I was very impressed with Jordie and am to this day. He was honest, constructive, very knowledgeable, and a good communicator. He tried very hard to be helpful in circumstances that were trying at best. Wherever he is today, I wish him well."

Rex had already left for Casper, Wyoming and the weekend at his marina, about a five hour drive. We had agreed to meet in Amarillo in six days.

It was off to Utah the next day, June 14, for a combination field tour and Tripoli law suit depositions. Despite a hectic and tight schedule, objective two went according to plan.

Inc's operations were a model of efficiency and cohesion compared to Tripoli's. The difference was in the operators. Cracker employed a local contract operator, 'Ben', who was a Canadian Professional Engineer. Cage had transferred him to Roosevelt, thirty miles east of Duchesne, in the early 1980s when their infill program kicked off. He ran a tight ship and by the book. In this environment I was to follow rather than lead and it suited me just fine. It was a great relief and I left Utah most impressed with Inc's assets and encouraged for the future.

My return to Denver June 19 facilitated an introductory meeting with Cracker. A well organized, technically staffed office greeted me. After reporting favourable findings from my field orientation, we shared frank discussion.

Our Utah objectives were similar, however all was not well on the technical side. Relations with Rex had been cool for the past year, impeding workover and development drilling progress. Co-operation and mutual respect faded as the end drew nearer for Inc's Denver office, a predictable and natural consequence.

My immediate conclusion was that the restoration of chemistry would be hastened by a more constructive attitude on Inc's part. To that end my support was pledged . It was a relief that all 'seemed quiet on the Western Front'. Next day was south to Texas for Rex's rendezvous, my last objective,.

III
(Panhandle Pandemonium)

Denver to Amarillo was a short one hour flight but a very long day was planned.

As our operations were sixty-five miles northeast of Amarillo, near the small town of Stinnett, so a car was rented at the airport. I drove out to meet Rex and visit with the field staff in my normal mid sized economy car (Taurus or Sable type). His rental car was a Lincoln Continental. An awkward air prevailed. To say our reception was cool would be an understatement. There was feedback from different sources for months. The rest of the story line will be left to imagination, but it took a long time to establish that my own credentials and ethics were based on fairness and equality.

We toured the three fields in separate cars; I refused to be chauffeured in an air conditioned limousine while preaching the need for frugal spending in our operations. My determinion was not to walk in those shoes.

One day was not nearly sufficient to visit 126 wells but we struggled to at least get an overview. As the day wore on, Rex insisted on returning to Amarillo before it was too late for a good restaurant meal. The highway was mostly deserted, isolated, flat, and straight. A speeder's paradise, you might say.

There was one catch. Our route was notoriously patrolled by local Highway Patrol. Speeding tickets were a dependable source of income for the County.

Rex had brought his mobile radar detector from Denver to avoid the cost and delay of being stopped. He volunteered to lead and slow down as a warning of approaching radar.

Sounded good in theory to me. The only problem was that, except for the first few miles, he was out of sight for the duration. My little under powered vehicle laboured to catch up. Without my 'early warning system,' fear of a ticket on my inaugural visit eventually forced me to drive the speed limit. Rex had time to change and shower by the time I found the hotel. This was another story in itself.

Rex always stayed at the Sheraton and had arranged my reservation. It seemed like all the hotel staff knew Rex well as they addressed him by first name. He always stayed in a top floor suite, specially equipped with a large bar, meeting room, television and phone in each room, and complimentary use of Hollywood style white cotton house coats. My standard room, still opulent by my account, was a floor below. Regardless of what the penthouse cost, at $100 U.S. per night for my room, my determination was not to walk in those shoes either.

Rex did not exactly volunteer his knowledge during dinner. Enough sarcasm was pried to justify staying around longer next day on my own. He was on the first flight to Denver next morning, a Friday. Weekends were sacred to him and reserved for his marina. I wondered if smooth sailing was in the cards for me also.

Spending these extra hours observing field operations removed any doubt about what was in store for me. Among my many concerns was a general lack of field activity. Secondly, the equipment reminded me of a page out of the Ohio EPISODE 2. Thirdly, passing references throughout both days featured a threatening political dispute referred to by local oilpatchers as the " White Oil " controversy.

A late flight was caught back to Calgary, via Denver. There was plenty of time to contemplate my ten day assignment. This last objective was most fearful. My conviction was to get intimately acquainted with all the details without delay.

IV
(Scene Of The Crime)

The next several months were spent getting more knowledgeable with Panhandle history and politics. In my opinion it would be painful. My desire was to get it over with.

A quick and unbiased history lesson was needed. It was provided in a 1983 Gas Deliverability and Reserves Study (Study) by an acclaimed Denver based consulting firm.

Oil and gas production was initiated in July 1981 from very low pressure reservoirs. The field reached full development and first gas sales commenced in April 1982.

Based on a pressure build-up analysis for a sample well, the average reservoir pressure was approximated to be **17 PSIG** (very low by industry standards) at the time of the Study. Other reservoir parameters derived from this build-up were average permeability of **1.4 millidarcies** (also very low by industry standards) and Skin of -0.8, indicating a slightly stimulated reservoir. From log evaluation the average net pay thickness was eighty-four feet.

The completion objectives were the Brown and White Dolomites and the Moore County Limestone, all at depths between 2300 and 3400 feet. It was not uncommon for the gross perforated interval to exceed one hundred feet.

Average *initial* production rates per well were twelve BOPD and three hundred MCFPD. Water to oil ratios averaging eight barrels of water per barrel of oil necessitated pumping equipment installation on all wells.

All production was commingled and gas was gathered by a series of trunklines from casing heads at very low pressure. While flow through the gathering line segments were measured, the wells were not independently metered. The gas was extremely rich, yielding an average of one hundred and twelve barrels of NGLs per MMCF.

Because gas was the main revenue generator, the 1983 Study was commissioned to determine what increase in gas production rates and recoverable reserves could be anticipated by installing field compression and improving efficiency of the gathering system.

Within the past year total field output had decreased from thirty MMCFPD to six MMCFPD. Similarly, oil production dropped from 1200 BOPD to 300 BOPD. Alarming, to say the least. Consequently and ultimately, sixteen field compressor installations were recommended by this Study to provide optimum suction to three PSIG reservoir pressure.

A major gas processor operated a fifty MMCFPD plant and compressor station at the apex of the field gathering system. Most of this capacity had been built and assigned to Inc's production. At the outlet, dry gas entered Inc's twenty inch transmission pipeline and was delivered to a major marketing facility eighteen miles north.

Inc's investment in this area totalled $40,000,000 U.S. during 1981 and 1982. In addition to drilling one hundred Whitte wells and building the twenty inch pipeline, twenty-six existing wells and a five MMCFPD Gas Plant were purchased.

The promoter, whom we shall refer to as Rolex, because he never left home without his Rolex watch, was carried for the capital costs and earned a 40% Working Interest in the Whitte Field and facilities. The leases, all freehold, were burdened with royalties of 40 %.

The inequity did not end here. Despite assuming all the investment risk and cost, Inc recovered only $0.36 cents from every $1.00 of gross revenue (typically an investor would expect to net back twice this rate to remain profitable). Then Rolex, who was contractually the operator, depleted much of the remaining cash flow with burdensome overhead and operating expenses.

That ugly word "Turnkey" had surfaced again, to add insult to injury. This time each well had been budgeted out at $250,000 U.S. My observations concluded similar analogies to the Ohio program of 1980:

   *Employing used equipment in lieu of AFE priced and approved new choices;
   *Communal batteries instead of independent facilities;

*Gas gathering and effluent flow lines on the surface instead of being buried;
*Inconsistent or absent painting and corrosion protection;
*Poorly designed and maintained lease roads;
*Pumping unit model and manufacturer inconsistency, and
*Collective sales metering rather than individual wellhead meters.

The scene of this crime had been visited before, only the name of the State had been changed to protect the innocent. It matched obvious and dangerous past trends.

However, as if scripted for a Dallas or Dynasty episode, the most astonishing caper of all involved the twenty inch pipeline. Graphic details from files and third party involvement portrayed how a $5,000,000 U.S. routine pipeline project became a $10,000,000 U.S. Panhandle nightmare.

In researching the promoter/operator, it did not appear that he had a lengthy or distinguished oil industry background. Despite ending up with a significant ownership in the assets, he avoided any risk or investment obligations. It is difficult to be conscientious when one is on a free ride. My concern about Rolex reached a crises when it was learned he not only had a litigating attorney on staff, he was also a partner. I buckled down for the ride.

V
(The Plot Thickens)

From the outset it was amazing that reserves would be projected for hydrocarbon deposits a mere seventeen PSI above atmospheric pressure.

In mid 1983, after the first twelve months of full operations, cumulative production was four BCF and 261,000 barrels of oil and condensate. The 1983 Study predicted additional twenty year recoveries of ten BCF and 550,000 barrels under conditions existing at that time. Furthermore, the Study forecasted increases of twenty-four to forty-six percent after implementation of improvements. In spite of this optimism, during 1983 Inc wrote down the U.S. assets by $15 million, half attributed to the Panhandle properties.

Using inflated estimates of this magnitude for such low quality reservoir reminded me of a magic show. Inc wanted to believe the illusion and there were plenty of magicians who knew how to perform the tricks.

By mid 1984 most of the Study's recommendations had been accommodated at considerable expense. Much weight had been placed on the success of these field improvements. Inc's 1983 Annual Report recognized alarming adjustments to total U.S. Net Proven Reserves, mostly attributable to the Panhandle, as follows:

U.S. NET PROVEN RESERVES	Jan 01/'82	Jan01/'83	% Change
OIL (MBBL)	976	487	-50
GAS (MMCF)	24765	13445	-45

After a year of experimentation and modification, productivity in the summer of 1985 remained far below expectation. The gas decline rate of nearly thirty percent was concerning, but the implications of reduced oil reserves were catastrophic, as we shall discuss in Section VI.

Flushed with enthusiasm from the early years, Inc expanded its Panhandle operations in 1983 and 1984 by purchasing two adjacent thirteen well fields, Barn and Cob. While the production concept was identical, the burdens were less onerous.

Ownership was eighty percent Inc and twenty percent Rolex. Royalties were much less than Whitte, averaging twenty-five percent. The Barn acquisition included a five MMCFPD processing and treating plant which serviced both fields. It had incurred considerable start up and ongoing maintenance expense, mainly due to an inefficient Amine sour gas treating process.

Production was from identical formations and depths, but the fields were located 16 miles north of Whitte and were plagued with 2% - 4% H2S content. Removal of this acid component from the wet gas was required before the dehydration process extracted the NGLs. This dryer gas then entered and blended with the main sweet gas transmission and sales line.

The plant, costing about $1,000,000 U.S., had been prefabricated and moved from the Dallas manufacturer in segments. Like a jigsaw puzzle with a missing piece, it never performed to specification. At the time of my involvement it was shut down, pending improvements to the liquid knockout and Amine facilities. The Texas Railroad Commission (TRRC) had issued an operational restraining order until emission quality was acceptable.

At peak production the throughput rarely exceeded two MMCFPD. Over design was obvious, however it was the inefficiency that earned the plant the nickname of White Elephant. Fuel gas requirements consumed up to 15% of the raw gas production. This situation was intolerable when royalties were applied. Barn Agreements required payment on raw inlet volumes as opposed to the traditional sales outlet volumes.

Rolex had operated for a short time but had lost interest when besieged with technical problems. As a result, production suffered dramatically and was subject to lengthy suspensions.

Curing these problems was paramount to Inc. Gas prices were averaging $2.50 U.S. per MCF as the result of high liquid content. In addition, local royalty owners were complaining about the revenue suspension and were threatening legal action. Rolex, recognizing this show was not worth the price of admission, unexpectedly relinquished operatorship to Inc in the last quarter of 1985.

Each of the three fields had its own unique villain. After identifying the symptom(s), it was our intention to promote the cures promptly and vigorously. Throughout the summer of 1985 we developed a Panhandle strategy.

In mid September another week was spent visiting our operations for a more detailed assessment. Instead of the Denver route, I experimented with Dallas as the stop over. It was a short one hour flight southeast of Amarillo. It was a bad choice. The originating Calgary flight had landing gear problems at Dallas and had to circle for awhile before landing. It was evening but still in time to catch the last commuter to Amarillo. Unfortunately this flight had engine trouble and was cancelled.

Appointments had been arranged in Pampa, fifty-five miles east of Amarillo, for early the next morning. A car was rented for the three hundred and fifty mile drive, arriving there about 2 AM.

The purpose of my meetings was to interview local contract operators. Assuming we were successful in wresting operatorship from Rolex, our strategy was to employ a capable and competent administrator to manage the operations with the following mandates:

BARN/COB
1) Solve the plant design problems and resume operation.
2) Implement routine maintenance/workover programs; meet performance goals.
3) Institute corrosion protection and treatment for prolonging facility life.
4) Contract third party gas for processing through the under utilized plant.
5) Maximize the Barn salt water disposal facility to accommodate Cob.

WHITTE
1) Suspend uneconomic wells (roughly 25%), saving $800/well/month fixed Overhead and operational costs.
2) Establish routine testing to isolate remedial candidates for prompt attention.
3) Design and implement recompletion programs for wells not perforated in all three reservoirs.
4) Streamline operations through staff reductions and efficiency control, such as eliminating many of the twenty field positions and relocating the mobile field office, from ten miles distant, to within the theatre of operations.
5) Maximize the salt water disposal facilities.

Over the next few weeks my interview findings were summarized. One of the Pampa candidates was recommended to Inc in the event of an operator change at one or all three fields. U.S. operations had taught me to be prepared and to **expect the unexpected**.

During this week in the Panhandle a visit was arranged with the Texas Air Quality Control Board in Lubbock. Relations had soured from numerous disputes with Rolex over emission standards for the Barn Plant.

It was only a few hours drive south of Amarillo and I was anxious to put a face to a name. This meeting was valuable in addressing specifically what modifications *had* to take place in order to renew the plant's operating permit. Rolex had encountered a hopeless stalemate, which he then used as a means of justifying inaction.

Quite the opposite reaction was experienced in our constructive and frank review of the operations and the operator. Suggested innovative alternatives to our mechanical dilemmas made the drive well worthwhile. It was not long before their co-operation and assistance would play a key role in resuming plant operations and at minimal expense.

In late September I left the Panhandle, convinced the operations could yet be salvaged from destruction without bloodshed. Not long after returning, Rolex resigned as operator of Barn and Cob. In the midst of euphoria, this new responsibility unfortunately exposed Inc to a new abyss from which there was no apparent escape.

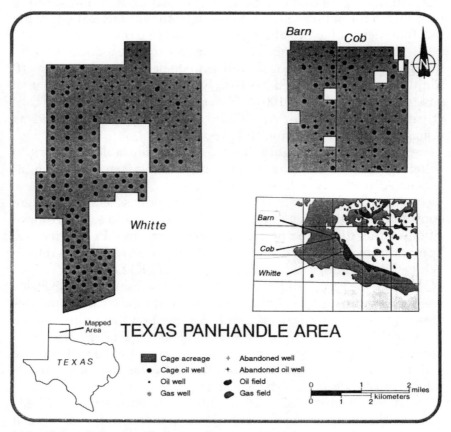

Map of Cage's Panhandle Properties

VI
(White Oil, Black Magic)

It was beginning to look as if all the demons in the oilpatch had concentrated in the Panhandle. The meanest came last.

The Petroleum and Natural Gas (P&NG) Rights to the leases that Inc drilled were sold twice. Historically Hutchinson and neighbouring Counties were rich in natural gas reserves. Decades before Inc's involvement, an extensive gathering and processing network was constructed to market very large gas reserves. As little attention or value had been assigned to oil reserves and production, Lessees were satisfied to acquire only the Natural Gas (NG) Rights from the Lessors.

Inc was promoted into the Panhandle to acquire only the Petroleum (P) Rights that had been overlooked or abandoned in the past search for natural gas. This conundrum was intensified by the fact that identical leases and reservoirs had two ownerships.

Provided Inc produced only black oil and the associated solution gas, harmony existed. To differentiate between solution gas (**P** Rights) and nonassociated gas (**NG** Rights), the Courts ruled that a gas-to-oil ratio (GOR) of 100 MCF per barrel of black oil or less constituted **P** production. Any GOR exceeding 100 qualified as nonassociated gas and thus **NG** production.

Black oil was roughly defined as petroleum liquids dark in colour in their natural state and testing an American Petroleum Institute (API) gravity of less than 50 degrees.

Any petroleum liquids produced with nonassociated gas were considered Natural Gas Liquids and/or Condensates. The composition of this distillate effluent was very high in API gravity and light, or transparent, in colour. Thus the liquids were referred to as White Oil and both products the property of NG Lessees.

Since the P&NG Rights in the Inc's Whitte, Barn, and Cob Fields were shared between local and foreign interests, the local NG owners viewed any gas withdrawals as infringement on their entitlement.

Inc's development of the Whitte Field drew unrelenting suspicions and accusations from the NG owners. Inc considered the White Oil dispute a non-issue since the GOR was well below maximum limits *in the initial development stage*.

When Inc assumed operatorship of the Barn and Cob Fields late in 1985, there was a sudden realization that many wells were at or near the White Oil GOR threshold.

Performance graphs accentuated the substantially higher decline rates of black oil production versus gas production. Most wells experienced high water-to-oil ratios (WOR) which restricted oil productivity more so than gas. Pumping equipment was either too inefficient or inadequately sized to maintain an equilibrium fluid level in the wellbore. While gas was able to percolate up through the water column to the wellhead, oil was restrained.

When the White Oil Ruling was adopted, the TRRC regulated a test program for wells producing black oil from disputed leases. Once a year single well batteries or multiple well batteries had to test and record all produced volumes through the facility over a 24 hour period. Test equipment, format, and personnel had to be approved by the TRRC and results submitted promptly to their Pampa office.

Any well that failed to meet black oil GOR guidelines was immediately suspended. Although not implied in the regulations, legal action by the NG Lessees was a distinct possibility for wells and leases in this category. Recognizing the sensitivity, the TRRC avoided straying from its legislated authority for test results, leaving resolution to Court or Lessee compromise.

Since the Whitte wells were grouped into batteries and tested collectively, the White Oil GOR limit had never been breached by any of the nine batteries. Similarly all thirteen Cob wells were tested collectively at a central battery. The thirteen Barn wells converged at the plant header where they were tested collectively. Neither of these two fields had experienced any "collective" failures either.

Beginning in 1986, based on pressure from the NG owners, the TRRC amended the White Oil test specifications. All wells on disputed leases would have to be tested individually on a semi-annual basis. This new requirement created a monster. Additional costs, administration, field labour, and litigation defence were obvious consequences for Inc.

On the average, an individual well test cost between $400 and $500 U.S. Simple arithmetic equated this mandatory program change to over $100,000 U.S. per year additional expense to test all wells. Failures represented incalculable costs.

When we took over operations of Barn and Cob using my recommended Pampa contractor, each well was independently and unofficially tested. Many were incapable of passing a White Oil GOR test, to our horror. After weeks of experimenting, we designated half our wells as producers, preferring to suspend the remainder rather than risk being recorded as failures.

To solve the Plant deficiencies for the sour gas treating and liquid knockout facilities, we simply by-passed all wet gas directly to the Sales Line.

The sour content was within acceptable limits of the Transporter's guidelines. The Barn output was small in proportion to total line capacity. When blended with the mainstream, most of which was sweet nonassociated gas, it had little effect at the Sales outlet. Thus conflict with the Air Quality Control Board over Plant emission standards was avoided.

The trade-off was the loss of NGL revenue to Inc, which became the gain of the Transporter. Our gas purchaser/transporter received 1450 MBTU (thousand British Thermal Units) quality gas but paid a contracted wet gas price of $2.50 per MCF based on 1200 MBTU quality. Considering the costs and delays that were avoided with this compromise, it was a mystery why the Plant had sat idle for so long .

Rolex had not experienced any difficulty getting these wells passed on a collective basis. We discovered high API gravity condensates were collected in gathering system 'drips' (small storage tanks to facilitate bleeding liquids out of the lines) at the rate of eight to ten barrels per day. Naturally we independently reported and sold these volumes as such.

When in full operation, the Plant liquid knockout facility extracted NGLs from the raw gas, reducing heating value from 1450 MBTU to minimum pipeline sales inlet quality of 1200 MBTU. With average production of 1.5 to 2.0 MMCFPD, 15 to 20 barrels per day of NGL were produced and stored at the Plant. Naturally we assumed these volumes were independently recorded and sold as such.

Legally our thirteen Barn wells had to produce no less than fifteen to twenty barrels per day of black oil to deliver 1.5 to 2.0 MMCFPD raw gas to the Plant inlet. Our test program cut these gas rates in half in line with the maximum black oil production of eight to ten barrels per day.

Despite all our efforts to treat and re-equip selective wells, we could not resume operations at the level of our predecessor. Rolex must have used black magic to achieve past performance!

The New Year, in anticipation that the worst was behind, seemed promising.

EPISODE 9: TEXAS - AMARILLO BY MOURNING

I
(Bond, Max Bond)

New Year 1986 began with optimism. While the Barn/Cob properties were not capable of meeting our budget and performance expectations, at least positive cash flow was being generated for the first time in over a year. Combined rates of 8 - 10 barrels per day oil and 750 - 1000 MCFPD gas seemed paltry for 26 wells, but it paid the bills.

Cage was getting more comfortable with our Pampa contract operator, Kelvin. We were gaining ground with our operational problems and restoring confidence with the royalty owners and vendors. Many of these were still battling with Rolex for 1985 payments. Just the mention of his name was enough to infuriate the authorities, particularly the TRRC.

Kelvin was a well known and respected local. He had an established reputation with the TRRC and seemed to lead a charmed life in getting our disputes resolved efficiently and effectively. Rather than fear the authorities, we exploited our mutual interests.

The majority of the District 10 oil and gas fields were mature and rapidly depleting. Other than ranching, energy was the main employer and tax base. Life without it in this area was unthinkable.

Cage's sizeable investment dictated an urgency to ensure our assets were maximized. Previous studies had projected reserve life to the end of the Century. Now that oil and gas prices were plunging again, realism had shortened this expectation to the end of the Decade. A summary of Inc's well activity had a disturbing trend, even to a novice observer:

YEAR ENDING DEC 31	EXPLORATORY	DEVELOPMENT	PRODUCING	
			Oil	Gas
1981	32	103	N/A	N/A
1982	10	45	215	26
1983	2	0	217	26
1984	1	1	217	27
1985	0	0	216	18

Since we were open and co-operative with the TRRC about our intentions and strategy, my experiences were mostly positive. Granted it took a while to establish trust, as the behaviour of our predecessor would rival JR Ewing.

Kelvin helped tremendously in his capacity as "translator". In a matter of months the feedback from the TRRC was one of welcomed relief for our efforts. In turn, we worked to build an ally in the authorities. The day was coming when, not if, we would challenge Rolex for operatorship of Whitte. Despite the magnitude of reserves and facility infrastructure, productivity had declined at an alarming rate while costs ascended.

There was no doubt from Cage's viewpoint that the only current benefactor from operations was Rolex. His operating overhead was guaranteed at $40,000 to $50,000 U.S. per month. In addition, most ancillary services were provided by his affiliated companies, such as roustabout maintenance, well servicing, and used well equipment.

Having worked closely with Kelvin in the past few months, it was obvious the costs to maintain the Whitte wells was considerably higher than the properties under our control. It did not even require close scrutiny of invoices to uncover a multitude of disputes.

Despite the fixed monthly overhead advance arrangement, Rolex added a processing fee to every invoice. Duplication of billings was a concern. Charges to wells other than Inc's somehow found their way to the billing department. Salaries and benefits for the field staff were generous. It may have been coincidental, but the same office and field staff also managed Rolex's private producing properties.

Some examples were quite worrisome; for instance, several pumpers daily drove the sixty-five to seventy-five miles each way from Amarillo in field trucks, with predictably noticeable gasoline bills.

A routine Barn/Cob workover would employ a service rig for four - eight hours. A similar remedy at Whitte would consume two - three days.

The solution was not in complaining and threatening. We had exerted this pressure for months to no avail. With Rolex as our opponent; we were novice and naive.

The turnaround of our fortunes at Barn/Cob was obvious proof of the need to gain control of operations and costs in the remaining properties. It had already been concluded that additional capital would be required for recompletions and extensive flow line repairs (formation water and gas were acidic, resulting in as many well suspensions as from mechanical ills). Without authority as Operator, it was imprudent for Inc to continue investing "into the wind", in which case the longevity of the wells would be at serious risk.

While I had witnessed what was going on first hand, it was another matter to convince Inc's management of the severity. Ohio and Utah came to mind. This Texas Panhandle experience to this day still has me wondering if some of it was dreamed up. My paranoia about security and trust are lasting consequences of what this EPISODE tells.

After strategy discussions with Bill Harrison and Wayne Boddy, we decided early in the year to tour the operations covertly. We knew the time had come to either change operators or dispose of the assets. The marketplace was not ideal for the latter, but we were prepared and determined to seize whatever option was feasible.

The main objective for this trip was to observe field activity and gather intelligence on Rolex's performance and reputation. To accomplish this without attention, we kept our itinerary confidential. No car or motel reservations were involved. Cage's Calgary office had an alibi for our absence in the event of an inquiry from Texas.

We departed Calgary in mid January on a secretive five day mission. Except for an unannounced visit with Kelvin in Pampa, our intentions and whereabouts would be unknown in the Panhandle. Without these precautions, we risked "set-ups" that were designed to indicate everything was running smoothly. The storage tank painting scheme perpetrated by the Ohio operator for his New York investors (EPISODE 2) prompted these extraordinary measures.

Our arrival in Amarillo was not without incident. As usual an economy car was rented, but at a different agency to avoid recognition. Normally this size of car was quite adequate for me, however with three of us and baggage, this judgement did not make a favourable impression on Bill or Wayne.

It was near dark, so we wanted to travel the fifty-five miles east to Pampa while it was still light enough to see the countryside. Although this drive was mostly featureless, not unlike Saskatchewan in places, there were a few sites of interest worthy of pointing out.

We left the airport excited and enthusiastic about our adventure. For Bill and Wayne this adventure began much sooner than they had anticipated. In fact, we were still within sight of the terminal buildings.

Amarillo International Airport was designed with very long runways capable of accommodating the world's largest airliners. Unfortunately the economy did not expand as predicted (i.e. Montreal's Mirabel or Edmonton's International). Because of this, commercial traffic was light and facilities utilized well below capacity.

Amarillo's flat topography and stable climate were ideal attributes for flight operations, so the United States Military shared the airport for Air Force and National Guard flight training. It was not uncommon to see a dozen or more Northrop T-38 two seat jet trainers lined up on the east tarmac adjacent to the car rental lots. Arrival and departure of fighter jets on their cross country exercises was also a routine sight. With my interest in aviation, sometimes great delight was achieved with only a casual stare.

The Lockheed C-5A Galaxy transport is one of the world's largest aircraft. It would be extremely rare to see one in Canadian airspace, although one was seen on static ground display at the Abbotsford Air Show one year.

On this particular evening a C-5A was on approach from the south, the direction we were heading out of the airport. At first sight of this behemoth, our conversation, the road, and my driving skills were forgotten. Staring right resulted in steering right, on to the shoulder at 40 - 45 mph. Only Bill and Wayne's verbal abuse awakened me from my trance.

After stopping to regain composure, we realized the Galaxy was performing a touch and go (simulated landing). My plan was to witness another circuit, but Bill pulled rank first and ordered me to put my glasses on and get going or change drivers.

Then Wayne followed up, threatening to demote me to passenger status if any further "rubber necking" was engaged in.

The car was silent for a few minutes until they were convinced my concentration was back on the road. To win back their approval, I bragged about the great dinner they would have at my favourite Bar-B-Q restaurant in Pampa. It was called Dyer's. They served Family Style - which meant individually served on large party trays but all-you-can-eat ribs, chicken, sausage, ham, baked beans, potato salad, pickles, rolls, and corn on the cob. There was more, but you get the picture. Most were smothered in home-made sauce. The cost was $8.95 each and it was the best bargain for the best Bar-B-Q food to my knowledge.

They closed the doors at 8:00 PM but remained open until 10:00 PM. With a little speeding, we arrived at 7:55 PM. It was beside the highway at the east city limit and was not impressive from the outside. It was obvious my reputation was at stake by Bill and Wayne's expression. Our only meal had been lunch on the aeroplane, so I was competing with hunger and genuine food critics. Wayne was an avid hunter and a meat lover. Few seasons passed without fresh moose or deer on his table and in his freezer. Still there was no doubt in my mind that Dyer's would pass the taste test.

There was no question we got our money's worth. Wayne enjoyed it so much he picked up the tab. Bill was so impressed that he investigated acquiring a franchise for Calgary.

Little did they know that another treat was planned for them at breakfast.

We checked into a local motel, the Coronado Inn, for a welcomed sleep. At registration, business affiliation was avoided to conceal our identities.

Next day we paid an early morning surprise visit to Kelvin's office. As our Barn/Cob operator, it was important for Bill and Wayne to establish a trust. After a short and productive conversation on project goals and accomplishments, it was suggested we all go to 'Jilene's' Diner for breakfast.

Kelvin had introduced me to the Diner the previous month. It was an ageing trailer on one of Pampa's main streets, a favourite of the locals for two reasons. It had a large dirt parking lot for trucks and the owner, 'Jilene', was a knockout. Perhaps she had left a Hollywood career behind for small town life. She had a very busty physique. My meal was always enjoyable there no matter what it tasted like.

We talked shop with Kelvin as we ate. After the feast the previous night, none of us were really hungry. I admitted my selfish purpose for breakfast was to enable Bill and Wayne to enjoy one of Pampa's 'natural wonders' - wrong thing to say to Kelvin.

As we were leaving, Kelvin repeated my motive to Jilene. She promptly pulled her sweatshirt up to her neck and revealed her two 'natural wonders' for all to see. No hesitation or shyness. Being only inches away, not having my glasses was not an inconvenience.

We were speechless, but it was just another example of how influential Kelvin was locally. It all unfolded as if part of a script. My embarrassment was too complete to return in the future. Bill and Wayne have joked with me about it over the years. It was difficult convincing them that it was a menu speciality that surprised me also.

We explained to Kelvin the necessity for not disclosing our identity or presence, as we planned to survey Whitte operations the next day. He accompanied us to Barn/Cob for a field tour, a pleasant forty-five miles north. Our operations were centred near the small town of Stinnett, the County Seat.

Bill and Wayne were warned of the condition of the equipment and facilities inherited from Rolex. Kelvin had struggled to clean up the leases to the TRRC's satisfaction and I was quite satisfied with his performance.

Barn Gas Plant (left-Amine Unit; centre-Flare Stack; right-Glycol Unit and Compressor)

Barn #12

Bill and Wayne inspecting Barn well (Texas combo - cows and oil)

Barn well adjacent to Plant

Cob Battery

Cob field compressor

Bill and Wayne inspecting Barn salt water disposal facility. (Mysterious water line coming out of the ground was traced to a lease not approved for water disposal)

Our time in the field proved very educational. Wayne, having considerable facility exposure himself, was able to satisfy many of his doubts and misgivings, although his preconceived value of the assets took a beating.

Kelvin left us to our own tuition by mid day, as he wanted to spend some time with the local pumper he hired to tend our wells. We spent the rest of the day scouting the operations of our competitors and the nearby Diamond Shamrock plant where our twenty inch pipeline delivered the Whitte gas.

After a very long day we drove fifteen miles south to the refinery city of Borger. We picked out a motel at random, the Borger Inn. It was about 6:00 PM so we decided to clean up before going to dinner. Wayne and Bill were invited to my room for a cold six pack of beer. That way we could discuss our observations over a cool one in private.

What happened next is engraved in my mind. When Wayne and Bill knocked at my door, a television commercial had just started about a new movie due for release that spring. There were F-14 Tomcat fighters all over the screen to the accompaniment of constant jet noise in the background. The name of the movie was missed, but Tom Cruise's name was mentioned as one of the leading stars, although for the love of me I could not imagine what part he could play. The preview was enough to affirm my intention to see it again. Wayne and Bill were convinced to relax over a beer in hopes of a repeat of the ad. We were all interested .

Not long after, the phone rang. There was no reason for a call, so I suspiciously picked it up. It was the Front Desk, with a long distance call for Bill. We were stunned as no one knew our whereabouts. None of us had even had a chance to call Calgary.

We watched Bill listen in silence for several minutes before agreeing to a meeting in Amarillo on Saturday at 7:00 PM. Bill hung up abruptly, then explained.

The call was from the owner of a drilling and production company in Amarillo. We will refer to him as 'Max'. His company was very active in the Panhandle. He and Bill had many long distance discussions during the past year, but had never met. The topic was always Cage purchasing Max's production, or vice versa. Bill had avoided any serious negotiations until he had a better appreciation of Inc's operations.

Max's call caught all of us off guard. We could not afford not to explore any potential acquisition, divestiture, or merger. Since

Max's company had drilled many of the Whitte wells, he was quite knowledgeable of their history. The strategy behind an evening meeting was to protect the confidentiality of the participants and the motive. That met our favour.

To my knowledge Kelvin did not know Max or our affiliation. In any event, Kelvin did not know our destination that evening, city or town, let alone motel. There was a local Bar-B-Q restaurant in Borger, Sutphen's. Believe it or not , that was our choice for dinner. Our minds, however, were preoccupied in speculating how Max had tracked us down within an hour of checking in. We lost our appetite and my memory is vague concerning how the meal compared with Dyer's.

As expected, the next day's tour of Whitte confirmed our worst suspicions. It was obvious our secrecy was intact, since we never saw a field hand the entire day. This was a weekend day taken to the extreme. The positive side was our ability to roam freely among the batteries and wellsites without being challenged.

As in Ohio, the wells had been drilled and equipped based on new prices. The wellsites that we inventoried and photographed this day comprised mostly used, poorly maintained facilities. Pumpjacks were of every make, model, and size. Numerous flowline leaks were observed. Again, as in Ohio, gathering systems were permitted on the surface. Many wellheads suffered from stuffing box ruptures and multiple barrel oil spills. Several Seven Day Gas Charts were on their eighth or ninth day.

Whitte Section 33 Battery (field compressor on right)

Whitte topography and flow lines

Whitte #33-14 well (model 160 pumping unit)

Lease road washouts prevented us from inspecting several batteries and wellsites. This script was familiar to me, but for Wayne it was a rude shock.

We left the field in time for Bill and Wayne to see the nearby Sanford Dam. It anchored the huge Lake Meredith National recreation Area for the Amarillo district by damming, of all things, the Canadian River. It had been a very large aquatic artery at one time, measuring several hundred feet across in this area. The Dam slowed the flow to a trickle, but huge boulders the size of cars or small houses were visible on the river bed. It supplemented Amarillo's main water requirements, although motor boats and camp grounds were plentiful.

Sanford Dam, 1986

When we arrived in Amarillo we were still a little early for our meeting with Max. The downtown was all but deserted, precluding shopping or touring. So we went to one of my favourite Mexican restaurants, "Paradise Too". Again from the outside it was unassuming, having been converted from an old warehouse, but the food was very reasonably priced and first class.

Sanford Dam and Lake Meredith

The most memorable recollection of our meeting was the entrance to Max's office. On display was a Norden bombsight from World War II. My inquiry about it prior to the meeting revealed it was Max's prized possession.

He had been a Bombadier with the U.S. Air Force in the European Theatre of Operations, flying in North American B-24 Liberators. He had taken part in the infamous 1943 and 1944 raids on the Ploesti Oil Refineries in Rumania.

History will show that the first of these missions, August 01, 1943, resulted in one of the worst loss rates of the War for the Allies. Of the attacking force of 178 aircraft, 54 were lost or 30.3%. There were 22 major raids on Ploesti, mostly by the Fifteenth Air Force. It ranked third on the list of the world's most heavily defended targets, after Berlin and Vienna. These missions produced no less than *seven Medal of Honor recipients.*

These raids were crucial to deny the Nazis use of the largest and most advanced petroleum processing facilities in occupied Europe. At that time Ploesti refineries were producing 170,000 barrels per day of refined products, representing 35% of Germany's needs. Any air crew survivors were due the ultimate in respect for their courage. I had looked forward to meeting Max and was in awe by his presence.

We were ushered into a large conference room where Max had assembled at least a dozen of his senior staff. Following lengthy introductions, Max chaired the meeting. We still did not know the true purpose.

Max had a number of charts and diagrams prepared and clipped to a floor standing easel. They depicted the history and values of his company, including details on the number of wells, production, reserves, active rigs, and staff levels. As each department head completed his presentation, a young assistant turned a new sheet over on cue. On one occasion, his sleeve got caught up on the frame and the whole easel collapsed with a crash.

Max promptly informed the assistant that he was out of a job. He left the room with his head down and we did not see him again. At the first break, my comment to the manager next to me was that it was a clever entertainment skit. He advised me in no uncertain terms that it was no skit, the kid was gone.

It did not take long to realize that the purpose of Max's meeting was to sell Cage on the virtue of buying his producing assets. We had conducted some detective work of our own and determined Max was in financial difficulty. The White Oil Ruling had all but eliminated drilling activity, Max's prime source of cash flow. In addition, some of his producing properties were targets for White Oil litigation and had been drastically curtailed.

We already had our hands full, courtesy of our field tour of Whitte earlier that day. Bill graciously declined, preferring to concentrate our energies on remedies for Inc's ills.

Max's casual reference to tracking us down for this meeting was a bizarre ending to the evening. We did not learn how he managed this feat. Apparently there was an incredibly effective "Panhandle Intelligence Network" in place. To this day it remains a total mystery.

II
(It Takes Two)

Expanding our Panhandle presence to "average down" our initial investment was no longer an option. The constant and distracting threat of litigation over the White Oil Ruling was expensive in energy and money. The last thing we needed was more of the same. Acquisitions, like Max's proposal, were definitely out. In addition, recoverable reserve potential and productivity continued to deteriorate. Product pricing **exclusive to the Panhandle properties** was represented by the following graph:

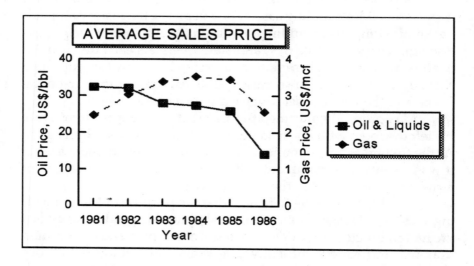

Merging with one or more of the many local producers was considered briefly. The upside to combining operations, however, was too remote to seriously influence our decision. Several candidates' properties were toured and evaluated, but appeared more mismanaged and liable than Inc's assets.

Therefore only one strategy offered potential survival. Inc had to assume control of operations by replacing ROLEX as Operator. We knew he would not resign willingly from this "gravy train". It was time to do our homework.

During the first quarter of 1986 we diligently assembled examples of ROLEX's questionable management and accounting procedures.

Our first order of business was to seek professional guidance and counsel in a local law firm. After considerable scrutiny, we selected a large firm with a distinguished name. It was headquartered on several floors in one of Amarillo's few skyscrapers. 'Roy' was the counsel assigned to our case. Contrary to my general opinion concerning the treatment Canucks received from U.S. lawyers, Roy's services were superb.

His firm had character: very attractive and genuinely congenial receptionists and a businesslike but warm atmosphere. Some Partners had identities other than lawyers, such as John, who was the lead singer in a Rock group of middle-aged impostors called 'The Predators'.

In time Roy impressed me as a family man first. It was a respected quality, a human side of lawyers rarely seen, since most were infatuated with 'the thrill of the hunt". The more identification with Roy's personality, the more comfortable his representation became. Fault was never found with his rates or fee statements, a crucial bond of trust for me. In EPISODE 12 and 14 you will see just how important and revealing this scrutiny is when working with lawyers. If you have seen the movie THE FIRM with Tom Cruise, these later stories will intrigue you.

We had considerable exposure with Roy during our years in the Panhandle. There were times when we addressed two or three litigation issues concurrently, sometimes as Plaintiff, sometimes as Defendant. Despite the stress, strain, and frustration we experienced, Roy always remained conscientious and in control. If he was not, he sure fooled us. He was integral in maintaining our sanity and perspective. It is doubtful we ever really thanked Roy. It is doubtful he would have expected it. He just did his job and did it very well. The Panhandle research that we provided were eye openers, even to him.

One of ROLEX's more annoying practises was in the payment of third party invoices. Inc reimbursed ROLEX for all monthly expenses, usually within thirty to forty-five days of Statement receipt. By now we were accustomed to the local reoccurring field problems and their remedies. Third party vendor invoices, which normally were reasonable and logical, received minimum challenge. We were much more concerned about the authenticity of charges from Rolex's affiliated services.

Reacting to several complaints, subsequent phone calls and interviews revealed many vendors had not been paid for a considerable period. In some cases, the payment delinquency was nearly a year old. Although legal action had not commenced, most had reacted by withholding further services to our Whitte operations. This came as quite a shock to us, as we had no previous knowledge that Inc's funds had been *misdirected*. We determined the accumulated debt of these claims amounted to more than a hundred thousand dollars.

Consequently the health of the wells had suffered and would continue to suffer. Roy's vocabulary had a technical term to describe this novel bookkeeping scheme.

This investigation led to a second discovery. Rolex had his own producing properties in an adjacent County. Work that was performed on some of these wells *mistakenly* got coded to our account. With a little detective work, we prepared a lengthy list of invoice challenges for refund.

Next we documented numerous instances where condensate and NGL volumes disappeared from Gathering System drips and liquid recovery vessels. It was far too dangerous for us to speculate on the destination of these removed fluids. It will suffice to relate that we were constantly under threat of White Oil litigation.

Despite an army of field employees, standard repairs and remedial workovers were sadly lacking. Many days were personally observed where not a soul was seen on our properties after lunch hour. We calculated that each pumper had responsibility for only eight to ten wells, although all were close together. The monthly burdens for salaries, gasoline, and truck maintenance were unconscionable for the services we were receiving or entitled to receive. Rather than a payroll of twelve to fifteen, we could not justify more than five or six personnel. This style of management was bleeding the profits dry.

Finally, the wound that would not heal. Several years earlier Inc's Denver office had generated an AFE to construct eighteen miles of twenty inch pipeline to transport the Whitte gas north to the Diamond Shamrock plant. Although reservoir pressure was very low, the sour component of the gas demanded strict adherence to API pipe specifications. Inc had budgeted for a high grade steel. Somehow and somewhere a "deal" had been discovered for non-specification foreign pipe that could not find a market elsewhere.

On start-up test, the pipe ruptured in a dozen places. The entire line had to be excavated and replaced at Inc's expense. Regardless of origins behind this fiasco, Rolex was responsible for implementing the AFE. We assembled documents, invoices, and witnesses as support.

In spring 1986 Wayne joined Roy and I in Amarillo to present our case for Operator removal before the District Court. The docket was full that day (litigation is an industry in the Panhandle), so our session was scheduled for 7:00 PM.

Our preparation was thorough and we were confident of success. Roy would disclose each grievance and support it with our research . In selective cases we would introduce testimony from disgruntled vendors or ex-employees. It would be a "slam dunk", a phrase Rolex liked to use often.

We were so confident of victory that we scheduled a celebration dinner afterwards, complete with champagne.

Instead we sat solemn faced, starring at each other in bewilderment. Our appetite was gone, but we had a few stiff drinks and discussed alternative strategy. It may have been the only time we witnessed Roy take a drink. My old adage for U.S. operations was reiterated to Wayne - **Expect the Unexpected**.

Rolex walked away from the Courthouse beaming. Our Operating Agreement stated the Operator could only be replaced or dismissed by a majority affirmative vote of the Working Interest Owners (which Inc was) *and* two or more partners. There were only two partners and Rolex was not about to vote himself out of office. Rolex's in-house counsel, Taylor, had added this small condition to an industry standard operating agreement during initial negotiations with Cage years earlier. It was a masterful service for his boss. Cage failed to assimilate the significance at the time.

The Judge had simply refused to hear our submissions on wrong doings and mismanagement without Rolex's consent. The Court ruled on contractual priority, and we never got to first base with our allegations. It was an odd sort of justice and equally odd reaction by Rolex in the days leading up to our Hearing. My mind has remained troubled about that one. It was a very short education, lasting less than fifteen minutes after months of homework.

Canadians are known for their passive, forgiving nature. Let "bygones be bygones" was our reputation - well not these Canucks!

To Roy's credit, we unleashed the one weapon Rolex could not control. All subsequent cash advances were suspended. Actually, in anticipation of relieving Rolex of his duties after our Hearing, payment for the previous several months had been withheld. Using a combination of invoice challenges and excuses, Rolex's lifeline had been cut.

We knew that Inc's financial contributions funded most of Rolex's other exploits. As soon as this source was suspended, he came under heat from all angles. Using a Court injunction based on our allegations, disbursements from the oil and gas purchasers were also suspended. Naturally we sympathized with Rolex's plight and recommended a solution.

By July 1, 1986 the vanquished had become the victor. Rolex sued for peace and a bloodless transition of operatorship to Inc ensued.

It was well into 1987 before all Accounts Receivable were satisfied. We used Overhead fees due Rolex to compensate all the creditors in full. When the account was exhausted, Inc was forced to pay a number of invoices a second time. The sacrifice was considered worthwhile, as it restored trust so our operations would not suffer for lack of attention any longer.

When normal operations resumed, Inc controlled revenue disbursements to Rolex's 40% Working Interest ownership. We neither forgot nor forgave.

Cage's Treasurer, Ned Studer, was assigned the challenge of getting Rolex's financial account in order. His task was both sobering and rewarding.

"My initial involvement with the "Panhandle properties" was to do a joint venture audit on the operator in their Dallas office. I made the requisite arrangements and hired a local auditor, Crowleigh, to assist me. I was well received by the Dallas office, particularly my main contact, Ellen. She and her husband invited me to their home and out to dinner.

The audit straddled the Canadian Thanksgiving weekend and so my wife flew down for three days. On that Sunday Crowleigh made his Cowboy season tickets available to us for a game against the Steelers in Texas Stadium. I found the people of Texas that I dealt with to be very much like folks back home. There were a few bad ones, but the great majority were good people that treated me OK.

I recall that somewhere near the end of the two week audit, Rolex returned from an extended absence. We sat around the board room where I was working and discussed many of the details of our discontent with the US operation. I found him also to be quite accommodating in relating his angle on the events which had transpired over the past few years of our mutual involvement. It was obvious he had taken advantage of circumstances when he had a chance. The main problem seemed to be the operator's fantasy that he had tapped into an endless money supply and he spent our money accordingly. This was indeed extravagant, but until we took steps to replace him after a few years, I suppose he had no reason to think that things should be otherwise.

In the end, as the production declined and his cash flow dwindled, he was hardly able to pay his huge staff, let alone the suppliers. Since we had paid all of our joint interest billings, this was his final undoing and the main condition for removing him as Operator."

III
(Remedies From The Ashes)

The priority order of business as Operator was to establish a small core of dedicated field employees to nurse the Whitte field back to health.

On the first day of transition, Wayne and I drove out to Rolex's field office in my standard economy rental car. Rolex's in-house attorney was there also - in his Mercedes. Not much more had to be said about changes we had in mind for the future.

We interviewed each employee in private. It took most of the day as there were at least fifteen, maybe more. At the end we compared notes. Circumstances dictated prompt and decisive judgement. We advised four to stay behind, dismissing the remainder. There was no expression of surprise or disappointment on any of their faces. They all seemed to have anticipated that the party was over.

The salary issue was addressed first with our four candidates. The compensation they were accustomed to from Rolex was well above industry standard for the area. Our offer was a 10% reduction, but a review within six months, pending improved production performance. Other terms and conditions of our employment offer were presented and explained. Although some of the benefits were identical to Rolex's package, apparently this was the first time they had been explained. Inc's offer seemed to sit all right, so the necessary paperwork was finalized.

It was advantageous that all four lived nearby, either in a rural residence or eighteen miles south in the town of Fritch. The natural leader, David, was young, eager, and talented. We balanced this selection with three of the older employees (50+ years). They had sole responsibility for families or spouses but also met all the "chemistry" we sought.

Our choices were never regretted. It was not a matter of being soft or displaying pity for the older employees. We simply recognized an honest man's offer of an honest day's work. They were challenged but they never let us down. Examples of their dedication will be related here for your appreciation. We consciously avoided faulting the field staff for the miserable state of the Whitte operations; they had been prisoners of a false leadership.

Our immediate goal was to harmonize Whitte, Barn, and Cob operations. This required defining a role that each of us had to play for success to be achieved. We had to become lean and mean and there was no time to waste. We headed out for the second order of business this busy day.

The downside for this strategy meant the termination of our contractual arrangements with Kelvin. It was a very difficult and uncomfortable choice. Kelvin had performed all that was asked of him. We had worked well together and had enjoyed the successes and failures equally. Financial necessity, however, demanded this business relationship be ended.

Wayne offered to break the news, as he recognized my anguish during our forty-five minute drive to Pampa. Since I had hired Kelvin, it was my responsibility to relieve him. A month's notice helped with the transition, but it still did not seem fair. We both recognized our struggle for survival took precedent, and Kelvin accepted his fate with grace. My opinion was that Wayne would have handled it better, but then my mettle would have always been doubted .

Another innovation was to contract out production reporting and invoice processing. Rolex had employed a large staff to provide these services. During the development drilling stage, this was a technical necessity. Field staff turnover, an army of vendors, huge expenditures on a continuous basis, and complex TRRC reporting requirements demanded a proper and adequate support staff.

In our survival mode, most of these services had become redundant. Being open for suggestions, a Canadian engineer who was working out of Amarillo was tracked down. 'Jerry' and I had "served time" concurrently in Ohio many years previous. He was Production Manager for an independent Canadian company active in another County of the Panhandle. As luck would have it, he provided a painless solution.

Jerry had surplus office space and support staff. We agreed on compensation of $1000 U.S. per month in exchange for an office, accounting, and production reporting services for all three fields. It was an ideally efficient and frugal association. Inc acquired an Amarillo mailing address, a central office, document storage for the voluminous files retrieved from Rolex, and receptionist and technical services that more than accommodated our needs.

In 1987, when Jerry's operations were scaled back, we were able to hire his Field Superintendent. 'Luke' was the rigł ¿ person at the right time, steering us through a myriad of operational remedies that only his experience and knowledge could deliver. It also relieved the necessity for my prolonged assignments in the Panhandle.

The next order of business was field transportation. Rolex's vehicles should have been returned to his responsibility from the transition day forward. Almost all were leased, averaging $300 - $400 U.S. per month, and many were quite new and loaded with options. They were much too rich for our blood, even though we had been paying for them all along.

We needed trucks immediately, but Rolex insisted we take the whole fleet or none. Under the guise of negotiating with Calgary on terms and conditions, four of Rolex's trucks were used for a full month without charge . Ohio and Utah had taught me a few tricks.

Inc had no intention of assuming the lease on any of Rolex's vehicles. The month's delay was used to negotiate the purchase of four used General Motors trucks from a local oilfield supply firm in Pampa. They had recently re-equipped with new trucks of different manufacture, therefore trade-ins were not convenient. The deal included three 2-wheel drive and one 4-wheel drive truck for $3800 U.S.

We were committed to accept Rolex's offer by month end or walk away. So his units were parked at the field office lot, with the keys in the ignition. We transferred to our own trucks, then we drove away.

Our short term objective was to minimize costs until the wells had been adequately addressed. We got by with our second hand trucks for six to eight months before negotiating trade-ins on new units.

An arrangement worked out with the Amarillo Nissan deal-ership to introduce their line of compact trucks to the oilpatch. My alternate vehicle in Calgary had been a Nissan and the experience had been positive. So we gambled a bit, since the old soldiers in the patch said they would never stand up.

The Dealer made it worth our while to try. At less than $5000 U.S. each, two of our pumpers were equipped with new 2-wheel drive Nissans. Our trade-ins, despite the worn-out condition, reduced this by another $1000 U.S. each (according to the salesman, they prob-ably would be resold in Mexico as they were too unsafe and unpre-dictable for the local market).

A few months later this strategy was repeated for our last two used trucks. This time we went to Toyota for 4-wheel drive King

Cabs. The extra power and cab space was needed for the more demanding routes. This horse trading was tougher, resulting in final purchase prices of $9000 U.S., but was still a bargain as we averaged $1000 for the trade-ins. We had to tow one of these in from the field.

The major advantage of resorting to these foreign trucks (although they were assembled in the U.S.) was the reduced gas consumption. On the average our monthly gasoline bills dropped by two-thirds. The pumpers complained bitterly at first that they were too uncomfortable for the rough lease roads. I rode with them and agreed; however their main concern was being associated with supporting an "un-American" manufacturer. For a few weeks their reputation took quite a beating. In time the savings in operating and maintenance costs, plus their reliability, silenced all critics.

The next major change came about as the result of listening to the recommendations of our pumpers. The most pressing issue in their eyes was having an accessible field office for Whitte. Barn/Cob was no problem as the plant incorporated these needs. Unfortunately that was fifteen miles north.

Inc owned the forty foot double wide trailer that Rolex had used as a field office. He had parked it, however, on a rented lot ten miles south from the centre of operations.

Our Gas Transporter had an unused serviced location at their Compressor Station, but they despised Rolex and refused all leasing proposals. Since the Whitte gas gathering lines all converged at this site, it was ideal. We had little trouble working out an arrangement. Before the end of the first month of operations, we rented a huge flatbed truck and relocated the mobile office to where it would finally serve a useful purpose.

The spirits and motivation of our staff climbed from that day forward. Until then we had not realized how many deprivations we were suffering. Now there was a place to change clothes, eat lunch, write reports, shelter from the weather (and it really does get cold in this part of Texas in the winter), phone service for routine and emergency communication, and storage for high usage inventory such as valves and pressure gauges. This small adjustment made an incalculable contribution toward optimizing field operations.

From my early days in Ohio, the value of not asking anything of your employees that you were not prepared to do yourself had been learned. This part of my job was particularly enjoyable.

I took turns riding with each pumper as a subordinate, insisting on performing their job. Troubleshooting was the most effective education. Together we identified our weaknesses and instituted many improvements in operating techniques.

First hand experience taught me to dress for and work in 100 degree Fahrenheit mid-year temperatures or minus 20 degree Fahrenheit winter weather. Driving time to all wells in all kinds of weather was experienced. The cruelty of the lease roads on our vehicles and our bodies was realized. In the flash floods or fierce snowstorms of the Panhandle, **I learned** not to expect the impossible.

A dozen pair of jeans were ruined in my first year. The worn out ones were accumulated at the trailer. My problem has always been throwing anything away. The smell even bothered me after a while. When they disappeared one day, no questions were asked. My heart was not in it to do it myself.

An example of our achievements related to weather. During the hot, dry summer violent lightning storms were common on a nightly basis. The aftermath was the necessity to reset the fuses at the power line junction breaker boxes. The Power Company (SWPS) would send crews out next day and we had to wait our turn before operations could be resumed. The breaker boxes were high on the power poles, requiring a telescopic fibreglass rod to reset the fuse(s). The service call was about $100, and we would normally have several knocked out.

David suggested purchasing a tool similar to the fibreglass rod used by SWPS. He researched the market and located a surplus one for $100 in the next County where storms were less frequent. After that we saved thousands of dollars over the summer months. More importantly, our electric pumping units were back operating hours before service would have been restored by SWPS.

Another example of working together occurred unexpectedly in the fall of 1987. Late one afternoon we got a call from the Compressor Station that pressure in our twenty inch transmission line had been lost. The system was immediately shut down and all deliveries curtailed.

Since our gas had a 3% sour component, it was imperative that the rupture be detected without delay. Gas with a sour concentration 100 times less than this could be lethal. Although the line was buried eight to ten feet, in places it ran near isolated residences, under highways, or near cattle operations.

The convenience of our field office enabled us to promptly review a right-of-way map and study topography. It was agreed the rupture most likely occurred in a low spot where liquids accumulated and corroded the pipe wall.

We separated into three teams of two to walk and drive the entire eighteen mile length. It was a calm day and the risk of being overcome by fumes near the leak was a real danger. Because of this, the team concept provided some comfort that the lead walker would be rescued in the most severe case. We had only one Portable Air Supply and mask per vehicle.

We kept in constant communication. Just before dark we isolated the last two mile desolate and likely stretch of corridor not far from the Compressor Station. My partner was one of our older employees, so I walked the lead. As expected, in a low spot, a crater ten to fifteen feet in diameter was located in the desert sand. My body staggered momentarily as the fumes caught me off guard. My partner immediately radioed the discovery and came to my aid. It was a relief that no danger existed for the immediate area.

The repairs were co-ordinated by David. He located a firm in the next County skilled in sour gas line repairs and a local backhoe operator with proper excavation and winch equipment. He also procured two 15 foot sections of replacement pipe.

In 72 hours, after round the clock repairs, we were back in operation shipping 2.5 to 3.0 MMCFPD. Incredibly we had controlled costs to less than $10,000. All our staff pitched in and worked tirelessly. A letter of thanks was forwarded to the vendors and a letter of gratitude to our staff for their contributions, with copies to Bill and Wayne in Calgary.

Another innovation revolved around a strategic purchase early in 1987. It collectively solved several of our operational problems.

As alluded earlier, the TRRC amended the White Oil well test program in 1986. It was now mandatory for each well to annually qualify on an individual basis rather than collectively through batteries or plants. These tests ran one to three days, depending on how close the results were to passing. The labour and equipment required to conduct such a test cost the Producer between $1000 and $2500. The hidden cost was suspension of well operations where success was known to be risky or impossible.

Inc's solution to defraying these burdens was the purchase of a surplus mobile test unit from the TRRC. Their sale was not widely advertised or marketed. We became aware by accident.

With the deadline for sealed offers near, approval was promptly solicited from Calgary for our bid. We were able to discover that very little interest had been expressed and only a few bids were anticipated.

My budget was extremely limited, but $3500 was scraped together by delaying other expenditures. Our offer was considered risky on the low side. It represented half the replacement cost - if a manufacturer could be enticed to tool up to build only one. We held our breath and were delighted when advised our offer had been accepted.

Payout was less than a month. More importantly, we now had the freedom and flexibility to privately test all our wells before being scheduled by the TRRC for monitored official tests.

The TRRC had special ordered a large number of these mobile testers years earlier when the White Oil Ruling was instituted. Before long many wells that had failed the test were shut-in or abandoned. Wells that were suspected of failing were suspended indefinitely. The quantity of active wells decreased dramatically. The last test unit delivered to the TRRC became surplus before it was ever used. It remained in storage at a Government compound for years.

Although the design and construction was simple, as Government inventory we knew the materials and components were of the finest grade and quality.

A propane fuelled horizontal separator accommodated the highest daily gas and fluid rates of our wells. Gas was channelled to a vertical Barton Gas Meter. Once recorded, the gas was routed back to a wellhead sales connection by custom built flex hose. The separator removed oil from the well effluent so it could be accurately measured and stored in a thirty barrel square storage tank. Water had limited storage but could be routed to the wellsite pit, also with flex hose.

It was all compactly assembled on a sturdy four wheeled trailer equipped for towing by 1/2 or 3/4 ton field trucks. The entire unit was protected with a black, corrosion and weather resistant paint. Our purchase included replacement hoses, tires, gas charts, gaskets, and lubricating fluids. We did not have to put another cent into maintenance.

Beginning in 1986 the well test schedule was controlled by the TRRC rather than at the convenience of the Producer. As a result, Panhandle production was drastically curtailed from well suspensions or failures. Of course, the latter meant potential legal action for the owner.

Portable Test Unit at Barn #25

Any oil well suspected or proven to be producing gas volumes in excess of the White Oil limits was promptly the topic of a threatening legal letter. As we learned to our chagrin, independent lawyers willingly represented local clients under a contingency arrangement based on a percentage of the damages sought. Consequently, firms like Cage were in constant defence against these actions at the expense of cash flow and energies otherwise allocated to operations.

The acquisition of the test unit ensured none of our wells were officially tested that risked failure. We determined roughly half the wells in our three fields would be disqualified if subjected to TRRC governed tests. Consequently these wells were indefinitely suspended in the 'Depleted' category and the production lost forever. It was the lesser of two evils.

Within one year of assuming operatorship, we had reduced monthly expenses by $40,000 to $50,000 over our predecessor. Part of the credit is due Cage management for the strategy developed and implemented. The remainder is due the field employees and contracted assistance, without whom the assets would have been worthless. For many years the Panhandle properties had been the major villain in the deterioration of Inc's U.S. asset and net sales values as represented in the following chronology:

ALL ASSETS - CAGE RESOURCES INC

	1986	1985	1984	1983	1982
WRITE DOWNS(million U.S.$)	11.0	13.1	nil	18.5	33.2
NET REVENUES(million U.S.$)	4.40	9.70	10.8	15.3	25.8

Despite substantial changes, combined monthly cash flow rarely exceeded $50,000 U.S. Productivity was consistent with the worst case performance predictions of the reservoir study commissioned in 1983. Installation of field compression had failed to arrest the decline as forecast. The detrimental effects of the White Oil Ruling on well status had simply been ignored. The road ahead promised to be a rocky one.

IV
(Speaking Out)

Because of Inc's increased presence in the Panhandle, the Amarillo Desk & Derrick Club approached me early in 1987 to be a guest speaker at their February meeting. This was an organization throughout North America, dedicated to recognizing the contributions of women to the energy industry. It served both social and technical purposes for its membership.

This request was not considered seriously at first, having no formal speaking experience. It was appealing, however, as an opportunity to share my knowledge of the Canadian oil industry with a willing audience. Constant comparisons between Texas and Alberta and between Canada and the United States were being asked. It also provided a community relations vehicle for Cage.

Once my objectives were affirmed, I was away to the races. My strength was always the determination to accomplish my goals. The consequences have not always been favourable, but once a challenge was accepted, it would be accomplished.

Given only weeks to prepare for the February third Meeting, my research proceeded with a vengeance. My topic was "Differences

Between Canadian and Texas Oil and Gas Operations". The challenge was to avoid controversy and emotion and stick to the facts. Dozens of publications and references were screened from the Energy Resources Conservation Board(ERCB), Alberta Energy and Natural Resources, and past transcripts of speeches to the Calgary chapter of the Desk & Derrick Club.

The hidden reward for my efforts was how much I learned about Alberta and Texas statistics. As the volume and scope of technical data was too overwhelming and dry for oral presentation, numerous view graphs were prepared.

On the evening of my presentation the Desk & Derrick Club treated me to dinner at the Sheraton, a regular meeting location. My apprehension was noticeable, as it was my first time performing before a large group. Speech delivery was allotted 45 minutes, followed by a question period. A timer bell would sound with two minutes remaining.

The first few minutes passed without breathing once. Then the timer went off accidentally and I asked convincingly if my time was up already. It drew a big laugh, broke the ice, and the rest of the evening was pleasant and fulfilling.

Selective statistical comparisons existing a decade ago have been reproduced.

USA vs. CANADA
A COMPARISON OF STATISTICAL DATA

		USA	CANADA
CONVENTIONAL RESERVES	: GAS (TCF)	209	107
	: OIL (billions of bbls)	27.7	7.0
DAILY PRODUCTION	: GAS (BCF/d)	18.2	4.8
	: OIL (millions of bbls/d)	8.49	1.55
INDUSTRY EMPLOYMENT:		1,750,000	650,000
PRODUCING WELLS	:	850,000	109,000
DRILLED WELLS	:	2,500,000	150,000
WELL DENSITY	: (Sq. Miles/well)	5/8	6.25

A COMPARISON OF OIL AND GAS OPERATIONS

		TEXAS	ALBERTA
OIL PROD. - JANUARY 1986 (MBbl)	:	2435	1395
OIL PROD. - JANUARY 1987 (MBbl)	:	2177	1125
WELLS DRILLING - JANUARY 1986	:	592	440
WELLS DRILLING - JANUARY 1987	:	296	209
FINDING COSTS ($/Bbl)	:	8.75	4.66
LOCAL REGULATORY BODY	:	TRRC	ERCB
DRILLING INCENTIVES(Wildcats)	:	none	5 Yr Roy free
% OF COUNTRY'S RESERVES	:	30	90
CONVENTIONAL RESERVES			
-GAS (TCF)	:	53.8	86
-OIL (Billions of Bbls)	:	10.6	5.6
REMAINING RESERVE LIFE AT			
CURRENT RATES (Years) - GAS	:	8.8	23.0
- OIL	:	11.6	11.0

ENERGY RESOURCES CONSERVATION BOARD - HISTORY

STAFF : 110 Inspectors, 670 Professionals, 9 Alberta offices
ANNUAL INSPECTIONS : 30,000

ANNUAL APPLICATIONS : - 9100 to drill wells
                                 - 2300 to install pipelines
                                 - 50 to build gas plants
                                 - 50 to export gas
                                 - 1500 miscellaneous

FACILITY INVENTORY :10,768 oil & gas batteries
                               106,000 miles of pipelines
                               43,000 producing wells
                               517 gas plants (129 sour)
                               6 coal fired plants and 25 petrochemical plants
                               19 surface and underground mines

CORE RESEARCH :720 miles(2,500,000 ft) samples, 4,800,000 cuttings, 59000 logs

At the conclusion of the technical meeting, some public relations plugs were thrown in for the Calgary sponsored 1988 Winter Olympic Games, which were only a year away. Token handout mementoes were provided by the Olympic Committee and City of Calgary in the form of colourful decals depicting the Olympics and Calgary 1988. This unknowingly added an additional difference between our two countries. In Texas it was pronounced *"deee-cals"*.

A lengthy and warm applause was received for my presentation. At that moment I realized it was the first time in my U.S. experience that appreciation was received for discussing our differences. Up to now it had been a thankless job and this feeling was quite unnatural. Finding words to express my gratitude was more difficult than delivering my speech.

As a memento a unique coffee mug was presented. The background was totally black, the foreground was a sea of white derricks spaced close together. Perhaps it depicts the early days of Spindletop. I should have asked. It is still with me today in its original shape and is used frequently. Avoiding a dishwasher has had a lot to do with preservation. The Club's critique the following month was a rare moment of glory for a Canadian in the U.S. oilpatch.

" Our speaker for our February meeting was Mr. Neil Leeson, a Petroleum Engineer with Cage Resources located in Alberta, Canada. Mr. Leeson was well prepared and informative with his speech, "The Differences Between Canadian and Texas Oil & Gas Operations". He related a great many comparisons, but noted that the United states and Canada have the same long range goal - to ensure a safe supply of our natural resources for the long term. He told us that it would be possible to use an alternate but expensive source of oil which has a great deal of recoverable reserves - synthetic or "heavy" oil - if the predicted shortages become a reality. This optimistic idea gives security to those of us relying on the longevity of energy reserves for our livelihoods. His realistic yet upbeat approach to these trying times in our industry was most refreshing. If an abundance of interest exhibited through questions is any indication, this speaker sparked a learning experience for all of us. Our sincere thanks to Mr. Leeson for sharing his views with us. "

V
(TMBA)

In my three years in Amarillo and area, not a single instance of homesickness comes to mind. Despite the frustrating business atmosphere, Amarillo was my home away from home and my memories truly complimentary of its people and hospitality.

A number of attributes were discovered that made the sun shine brighter at daybreak and the air healthier at the end of the day.

For starters, besides the Naked City television series referred to in my PREFACE, I was also a fan of the detective series ROUTE 66 (with Efram Zimbalist Jr. and "Kookie" Barnes). The actual Route 66 runs directly through the north end of Amarillo, much like the Trans Canada Highway is carved through Calgary. The motels and restaurants along this strip are among the oldest in Amarillo. They ooze character. My bet was that they concealed more than their share of scripts for the television show.

Less than six driving hours (360 miles) west of Amarillo is the city of Taos, New Mexico. Thanks to an offer from the President of a local oil producer with properties adjacent to Inc's, a ski weekend was spent there. 'Carl' did the driving; it was my 'rest and relaxation' trip.

Alberta and its ski resorts have always received my support, but Taos absolutely took my breath away. Runs were so numerous that only half of them were skied. The quality and quantity of Beginner, Intermediate, and Expert runs rivalled Alberta's Sunshine and Lake Louise resorts at that time. Snow and weather was incredible. Scenery was superb. Lift tickets and meals were most reasonable. It would not have been believed if not seen with my own eyes.

When possible, the odd game of golf was enjoyed. It was uncommon to get in more than half a dozen games a year, thereby disqualifying me for a handicap. On the rare occasion that my score was under 100, ecstasy prevailed.

The golf courses in and around Amarillo offer all that one could ask. Wayne and I were invited once to play the Amarillo Country Club, where Boone Pickens belonged and lived in an estate home bordering a fairway.

A game was played in Borger one January with 'Teddy' from a local service company. The fairways were spotted with snow drifts but the greens had been cleared and were lush. It was not cold, just sweater weather. It was one of those few times my score was under 100, in spite of the hazards.

The Pampa Course was played at the invitation of an associate producer, 'Dennis'. It was the one and only time my drive that stuck square in the 'Y' of a tree, half way down the fairway. We searched for what seemed like forever, since it was a good hit straight down the middle. In desperation we checked the tree. It could only happen to a Canuck in the Panhandle.

There were no recollections of a bad restaurant meal. Of all the cities in my fifteen year U.S. background, Amarillo is the only one where the names of favourite eateries can still be remembered like it was yesterday.

For Mexican it was Paradise Too or Santa Fe. In either case a meal and a couple of beers rarely exceeded $10.

For steaks and prime rib it was Ruth's (Sunday evening special was large prime rib, salad bar, and glass of wine for $9.95) or Big Texan Steak House (eat a 32 ounce steak with all the trimmings and the meal is free).

For seafood it was Red Lobster (menu, portions, and service superior to Canadian equivalents that have had my patronage) or J Christopher's (fresh oysters at 25 cents each). Canadian restaurants can copy a trend. However, in my opinion, they fail to duplicate the eatery personality that guarantees repeat clientele.

For Bar-B-Q it was Dyer's or Sutphen's (still the bar-b-q kings in my mind).

For pub and deli style it was JJ Muggs or Harrigans.

For chicken fried steak it was The Feed lot.

It would be worth returning to Amarillo just to dine. It was an event, not a routine. Quality food, service, and prices made it that way. Prove me wrong the next time you can arrange a stopover, assuming some or all of these choices still exist.

The indisputable champion of taking my breath away was my accommodation. Although other motels in Fritch, Stinnett, and Borger were used to be close to the field when necessary, the Fifth Season Inn East was always my choice when in Amarillo.

It was a large new three story off Interstate 40. The rooms were spacious, with King size beds. Complimentary morning newspaper and a thermos of coffee (which always went to the field with me) were delivered at your door by 6:00 AM. Breakfast was buffet style, featuring different main courses, and included in the room cost. At night alcoholic drinks were free in the atrium from 5 - 7 PM, with complimentary appetizers from the restaurant.

Often my return from the field was not in time for Happy Hour. Being a regular, several drinks would be set aside for me. No restriction on brand or choice. A few nights, devoid of an appetite and exhausted from 100 degree heat of the day, a few drinks meant near oblivion.

The reception area had a big screen TV. It had large comfortable sofas and easy chairs. When needed, washrooms were adjacent. Besides being convenient for guest watching, it had all the comforts of home.

Ned Studer spent a week in Amarillo during the summer of 1987 addressing Rolex's account. At my suggestion, he also stayed at the Fifth Season.

On the Sunday morning of his stay, he found me in front of this TV, three breaths from a coma. We had discovered Long Island Ice Teas at Happy Hour the night before. Ned knew when to stop but I lost count. He was worried about my greenish colour. The highlight of our activity that day was a leisurely drive to the site of the Hello Texas musical play (a prestigious summer event that is attended by visitors from all over America). It was all we could handle on this day of rest. Ned was getting used to Happy Hour with a sad ending of his own, although not as severe.

"I did get to Amarillo for a few different reasons - setting up administrative structure for operations, property tax appeal, examination of field inventory and equipment installations, meeting with lawyers to strategize successor operatorship, etc. Although the details escape me now, I did tour the field with Neil one time and again later with Neil and Wayne. Generally I found the field installations to be of much poorer quality than the standard which would be considered common in Canada. After we assumed operatorship, Neil was able to make some enhancements within his limited budget.

I was introduced to most of the fine establishments which Neil mentioned. I found them to be pretty much as he described them. The Fifth Season was certainly one of the most hospitable places at which I have had the pleasure of staying. We did indeed spend some long nights there, including perhaps the longest one which Neil described in detail."

The other half of the atrium housed a large swimming pool, Jacuzzi, and sauna. Policy was 10 PM closing, but many nights my return from a well workover was much later. Near midnight one evening, while relaxing in the Jacuzzi, a very big security guard (an armed guard patrolled the premises overnight) challenged me to get out or else, pointing to the "House Rules" sign. Offering him my name and room number, it was suggested he check with the Front desk. He returned soon after to apologize. Because of my patronage, the management did not seem to mind and had waived this rule for me before. Now that's service the Texas way.

The in-house bar was, as you might expect for Amarillo, Country and Western. It was the favourite choice of the local party enthusiasts. Every evening a free buffet was offered from 4 - 7 PM (different theme each night). A live band and a large dance floor ensured plenty of entertainment and Amarillo cowgirl dance partners.

It was in this bar in mid-1988 that Rolex was bumped into by accident. We argued about his reputation, so he was challenged to a drinking contest to settle the dispute. Being opponents next day in depositions, we agreed to limit the intake to one hour.

As a regular, I discovered the bartender had an old bottle of dust covered Chartreuse that no one ever ordered. It had been saved for a special occasion, remembering its conquering power from my Ohio confrontation (EPISODE 2). The trap sprung when Rolex consented to my choice of poison. Rolex was matched glass for glass until he turned green and surrendered. He was anxious to know what had beaten him up. It was a secret my ego was satisfied in keeping.

Next day with the lawyers he was a hurting cowboy, lacking the spark and shrewdness we were accustomed to. Since Bill Harrison had resigned from Cage in October 1987, Wayne was attending these Hearings and depositions in the President's capacity for the first time. Even he noted Rolex's uncommon conciliating nature.

Considering the free breakfast, newspaper, coffee, and Happy Hour drinks - all of which are must habits for me routinely - the savings to Inc approximated $20 - $25 per day. Since the free food in the atrium or bar often sufficed for dinner, my living expenses outside the motel were less than $100 U.S. per week. There were exceptions when entertaining, but not often.

The standard daily rate for rooms on the second and third floors was $39.95 (there were also third floor suites at $69.95). My negotiated rate on a weekly basis was $33.00. The motel/hotel bills for prolonged stays anywhere else would have taken my breath away. Not in Amarillo. It was the best accommodation value in my U.S. travels.

Last, but not least, the movie preview caught in the Borger motel in 1986 was Top Gun. It played in Amarillo for more than a year. The last few months it showed at a dollar theatre. My count was more than half a dozen times. Life could not have been better.

VI
(Final Page For Cage)

Cage's destiny was decided on March 7, 1988 as predetermined by the following PRESS RELEASE of January 29, 1988.

"FOR IMMEDIATE RELEASE
Cage Resources Ltd. announced today that it has received a letter from its bank declaring immediately due the Canadian corporation's entire direct indebtedness to the bank of approximately $80 million. Management expects that the Corporation will not be able to repay such indebtedness by March 7, 1988, the date at which the bank has indicated it will proceed with remedies available to it.

Cage Resources Inc., a wholly owned subsidiary of Cage Resources Ltd., is indebted to the bank for an additional $68 million Canadian dollars which could be at any time, but has not been, demanded by the bank.

Cage Resources Ltd., headquartered in Calgary, Alberta, Canada is engaged in the development and production of oil and gas in Canada and, through its subsidiary Cage Resources Inc., in the United States. The Corporation is listed on the Toronto and Pacific Stock Exchanges."

As expected, the bank petitioned the Courts to appoint a Receiver Manager to oversee Cage's assets. On March 7, 1988 the door locks were changed and the staff formally advised that the company was in default of its loans and therefore in receivership.

By mutual consent with the bank and the Receiver, Inc continued to function as if nothing had changed. Our actions were governed by existing negotiations to sell our Panhandle interests to the Gas Transporter, based near Houston. Although we had begun several months ago a long way apart on purchase price, we were convinced a deal was imminent.

In April Wayne and I joined Roy and several of his associates specializing in corporate divestiture. We began negotiating final price, terms, and conditions on a Wednesday at Roy's offices. Several times in the following days both sides retreated to neutral ground to consider alternate strategy. Near midnight on the Friday we shook hands and left the rest to the lawyers. Cage's financial status did not become an issue and it was not volunteered by our side.

Most of our objectives had been achieved. We were relatively satisfied with the sale price of $3,750,000 U.S. for all Inc's interests in the Panhandle. While there were many technical disputes that threatened to scuttle the discussions, we remained firm that our field employees had to be part of the acquisition. We also received assurance that salary and employment status would not change for at least two years. With this final concession by the Purchaser, Roy and his associates worked overnight to draft final documents for signature in the morning.

We were on a flight back to Calgary by noon. Given the deteriorating state of field operations and Cage Ltd.'s Receivership, Wayne shared his relief that it unfolded as well as it did. It actually was like an L.A. LAW television script but with all the real ingredients.

The bank's Receiver had representatives present throughout the negotiations. The Purchaser, however, apparently did not realize their true purpose or identity. If it had been otherwise, it is doubtful these negotiations would have been successful.

These kind of endings were getting monotonous. We were convinced we got the best possible price for the assets, given their condition. Again, however, we were faced with justifying a recovery of one-tenth our original investment, with minimal profits in the interim. The saving grace was the realization that a liability of 126 wellbores belonged to a new owner.

EPISODE 10 : THE MOTHER OF ALL LAWSUITS

I
(Wolf's Lair)

I was O J-ayed before OJ was cool.

Together with Inc's U.S. lawyer 'Baxter' and his Legal Assistant 'Wendy', we had been engaged in idle conversation for hours. Topics were unimportant, only excuses for taking our minds off waiting. We were getting more testy as this Thursday evening, June 30,1988, dragged on.

Around us were many of the Defendants' eight lawyers and their Legal Assistants. The Court Bailiff and Recorder stood by for duty if called upon. Curious spectators milled about, some of whom had wandered in and out of our Trial during these final days. Despite all the activity, we knew we would soon be saying goodbye to the Courtroom that had been our home for the past three weeks.

A Jury of twelve men and women from Columbus, Texas and surrounding rural areas had been deliberating a verdict since early in the morning. As 8:00 PM passed, we relented to the realization that at least one more day might be required to resolve this eight year dispute. Silently we all prayed this final day of June would conclude this segment of the litigation process. For me tomorrow marked a new month, Canada Day, and an Alberta engagement in Edmonton Alberta.

As if by magic, the Jury Foreman informed the Judge that a verdict had been reached. Counsel for the Defendants and Plaintiffs were assembled and the Jury members returned single file to warm their unenviable bench seats for the last time.

The Judge, after standard oral formalities, read aloud the Findings to the Jury Questions.

Each favourable Answer for Inc, representing a seven party Joint Venture Plaintiff, swelled my emotion and spirits. The efforts and costs all these years had finally paid off.

When the Jury's decision on the closing and most influential Special Issue was revealed, shock permeated both sides of the

Courtroom. The Defendants' Counsel had digested blow after blow from the Answers and dreaded the worst possible outcome. On the other hand, after monopolizing the affirmative Answers, we could hardly believe our ears.

Every Trial has its winners and losers. In our case, however, confusion reigned supreme as neither side was sure who had emerged the victor. The Judge consented to repeat the final Jury Finding. The thought of being captive to methodical, frustrating Appeal Motions for years to come was a dreaded fate. What had gone wrong?

Despite a plethora of convincing fact and testimony, delivered by most capable and aggressive Counsel, our Jury rendered the unexpected. My number one adage for U.S. operations was vindicated again - **Expect the Unexpected**.

Watching occasional clips of the 1994/1995 O.J. Simpson Trial was frighteningly familiar. Evidence stacked against him, motive defined, the absence of any other likely suspect, the Plaintiff (victims) and their Counsel (District Attorney) confident in the outcome. It was all too familiar.

In 1981 Inc, as Operator, drilled the Cage Lair #2, a routine 10900 foot development well in Colorado County, Texas. A November 1979 Joint Venture Agreement committed six other non-operators to a multi-well exploration program.

The primary targets were the Wilcox A-2 , A-3, and A-4 Sands from 8800 feet to 9100 feet. Secondary targets below and above these pay zones were also productive locally. The general area had been active for many years. In-place oil reserves of 400,000 - 500,000 barrels per well per Sand were not uncommon.

Inc's venture involved several forty acre drilling spacing units in the Mustang Creek Field. A Dallas based personnel consulting firm, 'PEC' was contracted to provide an expert Drilling Superintendent, 'Len ' (Defendant #1). General field operations were contracted to a local consulting Production Superintendent, 'Ray'.

The prospective horizons were encountered as anticipated. Core samples were retrieved as verification of pay potential in the A-3 and A-4 Sands. The A-2, traditionally gas prone, was reserved for future exploitation.

Prior to completion of the Cage Lair #2, a Houston based logging firm was contracted to log the hole from 5000 feet to total depth. This procedure was standard evaluation before incurring major expense to run and cement 11000 feet of casing. The logging company, 'DA', was an international giant in the industry (Defendant #2).

While conducting logging operations over the Wilcox Sands, the Rope Socket, part of the logging company's winch apparatus at the wellhead, failed. As a result, the logging recorder tool and 9000 feet of electrical cable fell into the well. Concurrently the power generator, supplying power for all the logging truck's use, shorted out.

Subsequent investigation revealed the integrity of this equipment had been suspect in previous assignments. Recently the rope socket had been inspected and repaired by a Houston based oilfield equipment supplier, 'BTI' (Defendant #3). The generator had experienced mysterious malfunctions, but 'DA' had elected to use this truck anyway due to shortage of equipment.

As Drilling Superintendent, Len immediately solicited assistance. His inquiries resulted in the contracting of a Houston based firm specializing in downhole retrieval of stuck oilfield tools and equipment (Fish). Given the urgency, 'HFT' (Defendant #4) arrived on site with their equipment and crew at midnight to begin recovery operations.

Although the heavy logging sonde was at the bottom of the hole, the top of the electrical cable to which it was attached had been tagged at approximately 5000 feet. A free fall of this distance resulted in a coiled, mangled mess of cable near the bottom but a more flexible Fish at the top.

HFT's Foreman was on his first assignment in a supervisory role.

Against numerous suggestions of his own employees and Inc's contractors, he repeatedly rammed his retrieving tool into the nearest free portion of wire at 5000 feet. Ray forcefully ordered him to refrain from this procedure as it would surely end in the Fishing Tool and the drill pipe becoming stuck. Ray 's instructions were witnessed by several rig hands.

Noticeable by his absence was Len , the Supervisor most responsible for all rig related operations. Witnesses later reported that he was intoxicated at the time, remaining in the Driller's shack nursing a hangover and incapable of supervision.

As predicted, HFT became stuck in the hole and consequently had to sever their Fishing tool and drill pipe to extricate. With this additional steel pipe and Fish, the well was rendered inaccessible.

After several weeks of futile remedial action, Cage Lair #2 had to be plugged and abandoned. The final cost to Inc and its partners was nearly $1,000,000 U.S., including payment of all invoices from HFT, DA, and PEC.

While this disaster occurred well before my employment, Inc's files contained a litany of requests and appeals for compensation and accountability from the potential Defendants. No admissions or settlement offers were forthcoming.

As all verbal and documented efforts were to no avail, Inc's Denver office initiated legal action in December 1982 to recover the costs of Cage Lair #2.

In the interim Inc drilled a replacement well, Cage Lair #3, about 1000 feet north.

Initial production of 125 BOPD had stabilized at 40 BOPD by the time of Trial, matching historic decline trends. Cumulative production for the deepest and only completed Sand, the A-4, was 95,000 barrels. Estimated remaining recoverable oil reserves from the A-4 and A-3 Sands were 35,000 and 145,000 barrels respectively. Total drilling, completion, and equipping costs for this replacement well were $1,492,519. U.S.

Lair #3 half way from Lair #2 lease, June 1988 (left to right : pumping unit, horizontal treater, vertical separator, tanks)

The Cage Lair #2 background was first brought to my attention in late 1986.

Litigation had been in progress for four years before being summoned to Houston that December for deposition. At the time, Panhandle litigation was so preoccupying that familiarization with the Lair #2 details did not occur until reading the well files on the flight from Calgary.

I busied preparing for the following day's questioning, but had no intention of assigning it any more time or energy if it could be avoided. Inc was already embroiled in several law suits filed in Amarillo District Court. Distracting my attention from the 126 Panhandle wells to this isolated well dispute was not my preference.

That attitude all changed abruptly in deposition, which was in the penthouse offices of a very large, prominent law firm occupying one of Houston's tallest downtown skyscrapers.

My face must have had "easy meat and generally disinterested" written all over it. The Defendants' Counsel were aggressively rude and intimidating, young and cocky.

Our Counsel was from Alice, a coastal city 125 miles southwest of Houston.

He was an ageing Partner who, perhaps, resented the spectre of retirement. We were both whipped like mashed potatoes in the ensuing confrontation. Faced with incessant badgering and insults, Counsel for both sides were equally offending. Up to now it had been impersonal, but this adversarial treatment begged confrontation.

At the conclusion everyone was politely thanked for the adventure. My enthusiasm for a return engagement was declared. I consented to being outclassed in the theatrical department, but vowed to stare them down in Court.

There were no misgivings, it was war again.

II
(Public Enemy Number One)

Inc's Lair #2 ownership position was 33 1/3%, 'Robertsland' (Canadian Junior Oil Company in Bankruptcy) was 33 1/3%, 'MAP' of Midland was 16 2/3%, 'JSJ' of Dallas was 8 1/3%, and three obscure "fly-by- nighters" made up the remaining 8 1/3%.

In March 1987 all Working Owners were advised of a pre-trial Hearing scheduled for May 13, 1987 and a Trial date of June 8, 1987. Inc's Denver office had been passive in their pursuit of justice and the case had almost become dormant. Calgary changed that perception.

Although all partners had executed a Litigation Agreement Mail Ballot, our Accounts Receivable records indicated only JSJ was current. Inc had begrudgingly incurred the financial and administrative burdens to this point. With Trial costs on the horizon, it was time for a friendly reminder .

"The enclosed letter of March 2, 1983 from 'MAP' is a representative Agreement to Participate. Inclusion in the eventual outcome can only be assured by payment of the attached invoice arrears from April 1984 to August 1986 without further delay. We appreciate that the lengthy proceedings may have contributed to some confusion of purpose and exposure. Please give this matter your immediate attention. "

As in previously attempted correspondence, no responses were received. Our objective, however, was to establish a paper train for the record. We fully expected a stampede out of the closet once an award or settlement was imminent; for now, though, Inc carried on almost alone.

Despite our objections to the ongoing theatrics of our opposing Counsel, they were successful in delaying a trial docket for an additional year. The curtain closed on their act at a pre-trial Hearing on June 7, 1988 in Columbus, Texas.

The previous day was a Monday and a travel day for myself and Frank Dearlove. Ironically it was also the 44th Anniversary of D-Day, the Allied landing on the Normandy beaches that began the liberation of Europe. As a history enthusiast, the coincidence was reasoned to be a favourable omen to our cause. During the flight, however, Frank *cleaned* me repeatedly in Gin.

Cage Resources Ltd. had been officially in receivership since March 7, 1988. The ongoing actions of Inc, as a subsidiary, were governed and approved by the bank's Receiver Manager. Frank was a lawyer for the Calgary law firm acting as legal counsel for the latter.

Columbus was a quiet city eighty-five freeway miles west of Houston, population about 11,000. As the County Seat for the 25th Judicial District, which included Colorado County, it served as our venue.

The Courthouse was centrally located and a most impressive and distinguished landmark. It was an all white, stone, multi-storeyed building featuring early American architecture. Surrounded by century old trees, strategically placed park benches maximized welcomed shade from the brutal summer sun. Like a sentinel, it was crowned with a domed roof housing a large clock visible from afar. There was no mistaking it, this was the heart of America.

Frank's assignment was to represent the bank's interests at the pre-trial Hearing.

Columbus Courthouse, June 1988

As expected, Counsel for the Defendants entered another Motion for Delay, based on the usual frivolous excuses. Judge 'S', after reviewing the chronology of the action, would have none of it. This must have been quite unexpected, as our opponents had not prepared the Court ordered pre-trial affidavits. Their choice was production within twenty-four hours or be fined for Contempt of Court. The Judge meant business and the parking lot cleared out in minutes.

Columbus "divided highway", June 1988 jogging route

The Judge scheduled the Trial to begin Monday, June13, 1988. He further ordered that voir dire examination and jury selection be completed by the end of this first day, pending resolution by the two sides in the interim.

We were off to a promising start. Frank expected a settlement offer would be forthcoming, now that the courthouse clock was finally ticking.

The next day, Wednesday, was marked by the Defendants' submission of affidavits minutes before the Judge's deadline expired. It also produced the anticipated settlement offer.

It was Frank's call, but I almost choked when "possibly up to $250,000 less the Defendants' costs to date to withdraw our action" was proposed.

We were both anxious for a conclusion, given our knowledge of Cage Resources Ltd's financial status. As in EPISODE 9 and the sale of our Panhandle properties several months earlier, knowledge of our Parent's state of affairs by the Defendants would surely have influenced the course of events.

A quarter million U.S. dollars was an attractive recovery for a few days work, but Frank rightly concluded that Inc would only be entitled to one third. Most of the accumulated legal costs of $72,135

U.S. had been at Inc's expense. Frank did not leave me to suffer and shared his opinion within minutes of his private negotiations.

Relief greeted the rejection of their proposal. My attitude had been mentally prepared to fight this one to the end, no matter how long the Trial lasted. Columbus was my home for the duration.

The remainder of the week was spent preparing for trial. We studied profiles for the list of potential jurors. We inspected and photographed Inc's wells in the Mustang Creek field, less than two hours drive south. Frank and our new counsel from Alice, Baxter, conferred on strategy. Baxter had a busy itinerary, so he commuted to Alice for the two days of his involvement.

In the four days Frank spent in Columbus, he appointed me his Public Enemy Number One. It was fortunate the Trial had not started.

As was my custom, the restaurants and motel accommodation were researched before venturing into hostile U.S. territory for the first time. My travel information on Columbus referred to only two old motels, moderate rates. One was picked at random and rooms reserved.

It was your standard one story, poorly maintained and serviced, bargain room. The cockroaches welcomed us to their home as soon as we opened the door. Drab interior with small, uncomfortable beds were the printable comments from Frank.

It did not impress even my humble standards. The air conditioner was no match for the steamy temperatures this time of year. Only local TV stations were available, and reception was lousy. At $32.95 per night, it was a far cry from the luxury of the Fifth Season Inn. Other than the rates, absolutely nothing else compared even remotely. It was pointless, however, to move as the alternate motel had a similar listing.

Tension between us began to grow as Frank was more adverse to returning to his motel room at night than he was facing his counterparts during the day. He craved exercise, so he resorted to late night, lengthy walks or jogging to escape.

On the third night a miracle occurred; we had a visitor. It distracted Frank from his miserable surroundings and his resentment of me for twenty-four hours.

It was maybe 8:00 PM or so, just after we returned from dinner (we will not get into the restaurant topic as Frank's choice words for accommodation and meals were usually referred to in the same breath). We were each opening our room door when a car screeched up behind us. A black, high performance sports car had parked sideways in the parking lot in front of our rooms. It was either a Corvette or foreign model, like a Jaguar.

An immaculate, expensive suit jumped out and introduced himself. What a relief; I was expecting to be mowed down by gunfire any second (like my Preface alluded, crime shows like Naked City and Route 66 were an obsession after my U.S. operations experience had convinced me that most incidents were real life and not scripts).

'Tug' presented himself as an attorney and the Senior Partner of a Houston investment firm that had acquired all the stock in Robertsland. He was our 33 1/3% partner in Cage Lair #2.

As Agent for Robertsland, he was assisting in the management and operation of its oil and gas properties.

He wanted to ensure his interests were properly represented at Trial the following Monday. He was also aware of the settlement advanced that afternoon. In no uncertain terms, he warned Frank, would acceptance of any resolution be tolerated without his clearance. He reminded us that his interest equalled Inc's.

He was reminded that it was our only common ground, as Inc had paid nearly all the billings and supplied all the administration of the litigation for the past six years.

Smooth talking Tug then informed us that if we expected payment of bills, all we had to do was provide proof of invoicing. Furthermore, he had contracted the services of a partner in our Alice law firm (the attorney referred to previously at my December 1986 Houston deposition). Therefore Inc could not settle or compromise any claim, act on any judgement or other interest, without his consent.

With that said, Tug hopped into his luxury wheels and was off into the sunset. He jumped over the door, rather than opening it, but then all cool dudes do.

The conversation had lasted only a few minutes, and entirely in the parking lot. We were thankful; if we had invited him to our room, the embarrassment would have been overwhelming.

After the encounter with Tug, Frank's curly black hair seemed white and straight.

Frank wondered how Tug had been so well informed and had found us so easily, then realized there were only two motels.

Remembering the Max Bond episode in the Panhandle, my reaction was a simple shrug. In any event, Tug had made a real impression on Frank.

It bought me a twenty-four hour respite from Frank's abuse over our accommodation. The following evening, Frank's last in Columbus, we went for a long walk together while revisiting our memories of Tug. Taking a new route for a change, we were able to cross under the freeway just blocks away from our motel.

On the other side, maybe a ten minute walk from our rooms, was a brand new, two story, brick castle of a motel! It had a walled private courtyard containing a large outdoor pool. Huge trees had partially hidden the entire complex from view.

When we inquired about vacancy, which there were plenty, we also learned that a free host bar was available pool side from 4 - 7 PM and free Continental breakfasts were served every morning. It was painful, but there was more.

Air conditioned rooms included satellite TV, King size beds, and balconies or private courtyards. It was so new it had not yet been advertised in travel brochures. The opening special room rate was $32.95, all amenities included.

One look at Frank and I was done like toast.

It was difficult keeping up to Frank on the way back. He was determined to change motels that night. It was getting quite late and the thought of paying for two rooms on the same night haunted my frugal style. So a compromise was negotiated.

My offer was to drive him to Houston at the conclusion of Friday's activity. We would settle for nothing less than a luxury (sort of) hotel with an exercise room, a Jacuzzi, and a King size bed. Then we would go out for a decent dinner at his choice. He would be driven to the airport for the first Calgary bound flight Saturday morning.

My limited credibility was on the line, so delivery on my promise was assured.

We got to Houston about 7:00 PM and checked into a high-rise hotel on Westheimer, at the western city limits. Our rooms were $95.00 U.S. each, but as far as Frank was concerned it would not have made a difference if they were $950.00.

He spent the first hour in the workout room trying to get me off his mind.

It was after 9:00 PM before we headed out to eat. Surely Frank would get his revenge chalking up a several hundred dollar meal with the finest wine. My fretting was wasted as neither of us were very hungry. We went to a nearby Deli and had a 'decent' meal. Frank kept grumbling while he was eating, but I assumed it was indigestion.

Frank never forgave me.

III
(Never Say Every)

Inc appointed me Trial representative, providing technical and observer support as required. My presence was expected in the Courtroom every day until conclusion.

My key contribution was to testify on the probability that Cage Lair #2 would have been a successful oil well, if completed.

Daily testimony of witnesses were to be analysed and strengths and weaknesses reported to Baxter for future cross examination.

Daily observations of the Judge, the Jury, and the Defendants' Counsel were to be provided also.

Nights would be reserved for conference on the day's activities and preparing for the next day's strategy.

My conscience wondered how I would stand up to the uninterrupted stress and strain for three to four weeks if our litigation proceeded to Trial.

It promised to be a new experience. Although eager to accept the challenge, the intimidating 1986 Houston deposition had forewarned me to be better prepared.

A week before my departure to Columbus, Wayne's approval was requested to enrol in a three day interactive workshop stressing cogent communication. Knowing little about it, selection was mostly by chance and desperation. After reading about it in a local newspaper, the President was contacted for details.

It was designed to identify and promote powerful behaviour techniques that greatly enhance one's interpersonal communication skills.

I was unaware of how or if this program would benefit my Trial responsibilities, but was game to find out. This $200 investment turned out to be a deal of a lifetime. One seemingly insignificant application stoned the Defendants' Counsel cold.

The cogent concept taught me some truly worthwhile tools. We have only to visit a few selective excerpts from my notes to see why.

The success of your communication is determined solely by the quality of the information you are able to gather from your clients, customers, associates, etc. The quality of their information is directly proportional to the quantity of rapport you have established with them.

Establishing physiological rapport provides us with an opportunity to enter another person's space and share their reality.

HANDSHAKE - it should match the other person's in as many ways as possible - strength, firmness of grip, and duration - even when we receive a wet fish grip.

MIRRORING - slowly shift your physiology (body position) until you are providing the other person with a reflection, a mirror image of himself/herself.

TONALITY - modulate your voice tone so as to match the tone, timbre, pace, and tempo (not accent, this is not mimicry) so that you are also providing the other person with a constant playback of their own voice.

LEADING - shift your physiology slightly to another position, such as tilting your head slightly to the right and slightly shift your weight; if performed with correct smoothness, the other person will follow and adjust his/her physiology to maintain the mirror image.

Research has shown that the way in which we position our bodies will determine our internal state. People's behaviour indicates which of the three representational systems (Visual, Auditory, or Kinaesthetic) they are accessing and storing information in during any given conversation. While the majority of people have a preferred modality or "comfort zone", it is useful to realize that everyone has all three systems available. Therefore use the system he/she is in at the time of your communication or negotiation.

ANCHORING - an extension of the stimulus response theory of behaviour; it is a process whereby a given stimulus (conscious or unconscious) causes a response (state of mind, memory feeling, and physiology) and therefore the two become neurological linked so that each time the same stimulus is presented, the same stimulus will occur. Audible Example: Driving your car down the highway, a song you have not heard in a long while comes drifting in over the radio. The song reminds you of a special person or event that took place many years ago. Perhaps it was 'your' song at your high school prom. You immediately drift back to your prom as if it were recurring right now.

WORD TONES - Verbal content accounts for only 7% of all communication. The voice tones that accompany those words account for 35% of our interactions, and by altering our tones we can substantially increase the impact of the words we use.

BACKTRACKING - valuable technique to employ to reduce or eliminate misunderstanding or miscommunication; e.g. bringing a meeting to a halt every now and then in order to confirm everything that has been discussed and agreed to.

PRECISION MODEL - As we convert our pictures, sounds, and feelings into words, we tend to distort, delete, and generalize our output on the assumption that the listener will fully comprehend our statement. e.g.

GENERALIZATIONS:	*ALL - All what?*
	EVERY- Every what, every where?
	NEVER - Never what, never where?
COMPARATIVES:	*EXPENSIVE - Compared to what?*
	TOO MUCH - Compared to what?
	SLOWER - Compared to what?
LIMITERS:	*CAN'T - What would happen if.....?*
	MUST - What stops/prevents you?
	SHOULD - What would it take?
NEGATIVES:	*BUT - negates everything that has preceded it; substituting*
	AND allows for the input of the same information while reducing the possible negative response.

Why were these tools considered valuable and how were they applied at the Trial?

The four Defendants had no less than eight lawyers in Court. When Legal Assistants were participating, the posse on the other side of the courtroom was most intimidating.

When my turn came to take the stand, I had the benefit of observing the proceedings for weeks and was well aware of what to expect. My testimony and cross examination stretched over two days.

Near the end, my faculties were wearing thin. Cogent tools and techniques had been employed where circumstances permitted. Some of the Defendants' lawyers were considered among the best litigation attorneys in Texas. No mercy was expected.

I had been steered into testimony on a technical assessment for which my qualifications were lacking. No doubt my examiner was well aware of this. Admission at this crucial stage would have negated all my previous strengths to the Jury, who were three feet to my left.

PEC's lead Counsel, 'Rusty', had manoeuvred his questioning for more than an hour to trap me and assassinate my integrity.

As his routine had been followed closely over the duration of the Trial, my respect for his ability was most genuine.

He knew the answers to his questions before asking them. Often he would backtrack on controversial issues and repeat the questions. In this manner he had overpowered one of our key witnesses, destroying his confidence and self esteem. Now it was my turn and the heat was on.

Fatigue was a concern, as I was unable to rotate responsibility for answering as my eight opposing attorneys could do with the questioning.

Rusty combined the geological, petrophysical, and reservoir risks of Cage Lair #2 into one final missile. He preceded his long winded, several sentence query with a PRECISION MODEL GENERALIZATION " Mr. Leeson, is it not true that every time .... ".

Agonizing over how answer, but my cogent radar seized on "every time". So the retraction was a question of my own, " *Every time*, ...Mr. Rusty ? "

Rusty was silent for what seemed like minutes before the Judge asked him if he planned to reply, repeat the question, or continue on. " No, your Honour, I'm through with this witness."

I had escaped within seconds of being humiliated and could hardly believe my luck. Looking over at Baxter seated below me and to my right, a genuine smile of approval covered his face. Chalk a big one up to cogent communication.

IV
(Hello Columbus)

My move into the new motel coincided with Frank's departure. Without question, this decision had a lot to do with enjoying a pleasant stay for the duration of the Trial.

Our Alice Counsel and Legal Assistant, the Defendants' Counsel, the Judge, and the Court Reporter all stayed here as well. Believe me it was an odd sensation in the evening when we all convened around the pool to sip on our free drinks and pretend to ignore one another.

On one occasion the Judge came over to ask me about hunting in Alberta (where was Wayne Boddy when needed). Not being a hunter, not much help was offered. Cognizant that all eyes were on us, I was petrified of being accused of seeking Judicial favour. Everyone had been warned to avoid fraternizing.

However, my cogent techniques were actively practised on the Defendants' attorneys, who were fair game.

Author roughing it at motel home, June 8-30, 1988

Defendants' spies, Columbus, June 1988 morning jogging route

At the beginning of the second week Cage's Controller, John Hecht, joined our team. He had been called to testify on the accuracy of the Cage Lair #2 and the replacement Cage Lair #3 well costs. Baxter recognized that John's assistance would be valuable in preparing other financial reports to support cross examination scheduled for early the following week. Fortunately there were no pressing matters in Calgary and John arrived just before Trial began.

"Houston airport was my first introduction to the great state of Texas. I started my rental car to cool it down before getting in - a procedure that was backward to Canadians but a necessity during summer months in Texas.

Driving to Columbus I was struck by a number of things, particularly the maze of concrete freeways. Road construction and law enforcement officers to monitor traffic must have been a major industry! A relatively short trip west to Columbus on a sunny Sunday afternoon was very enjoyable.

Columbus was very old by Canadian standards, and loaded with history and tradition. The courthouse was a grand historic building. The motel was first class and, after a walk around town, I settled down to await the arrival of Neil and the rest of the crew. Neil had made reservations in a 'good' motel, although I had to see it to believe it. Neil was known to have somewhat conservative standards when spending money.

'Orval', formerly an Inc Vice President in the Denver office but then residing in Las Vegas, arrived first in a Budget Lincoln rental car. I had turned one down earlier at the Houston airport, although it was at a reduced rate. Thoughts of what people would think about the car came to mind.

Neil, who had been in Houston that day, arrived next. The motel soon filled with legal counsel and support staff, all amicably residing there despite pending opposition in the courtroom. The parking lot boasted a number of expensive cars from the Houston area. Concern of the Lincoln image dissipated.

After Neil performed introductions and got us all organized, it was time to get to work. The jury was selected during my first day there. A number of residents filed in, no doubt wondering about details of the litigation and who were all the persons in suits! Soon I was excluded from the courtroom until such time came for me to testify. Review of the daily proceedings took place in the evenings.

Baxter was no stranger to the courtroom. After listening to a few hours of particularly animated presentation by the lead defence counsel 'Rusty', Baxter made his views known. At the next opportunity to ask questions, he opened with 'Your Honor, when Mr. Rusty was testifying...'. Of course three or four persons immediately corrected him by stating the witness name as opposed to the defence counsel. But Baxter had made his point. The grandstanding by defence counsel had not gone unnoticed. Even the Judge smiled.

Wednesday morning I was called to testify, primarily with regard to well costs. Having the opportunity to become acclimatized and to testifying on a specific topic, my testimony was straight forward and uneventful. At other times in the trial, the antics of the legal counsel could have been included in Hollywood films!"

As luck would have it, our motel hosted a Miss Columbus Beauty Contest on the Friday evening of John's stay.

Apparently there were dozens of towns and cities in the United States named Columbus. Annually each would choose a Queen as the representative for National Miss Columbus.

John and I were fortunate enough to be spectators at pool side for the entire event. Little time was lost putting a week of Trial behind us that evening. Having heard of Frank's misgivings of Columbus, John anguished through the entire ninety minutes, sipping on a drink in his lounge chair under the warm Texas sun.

On the Saturday morning we headed out early for a game of golf at the local club. We finished play before noon, otherwise the sun was too hot for more than a few minutes exposure. The course was liberally sprinkled with shady trees and sand traps. We quite enjoyed our game.

Author at Columbus Golf Club (early Saturday morning, rushing to complete a round before the sun got too high)

That afternoon we headed south on the freeway a hundred miles to one of my favourite cities, San Antonio. The rest of the day was spent leisurely touring the river walk and sipping Marguerites. We drove to Columbus late that evening after a big Mexican fiesta. John found harmony in blending business and pleasure.

"My involvement lasted about eight days. Fortunately time permitted a tour of some of Inc's field facilities, a visit with our local contract operator, an opportunity to see some of the country, and a Saturday afternoon visit to San Antonio."

Sunday evening we attended a musical play at the local live theatre. We had struck up a casual relationship with two of the female performers, so our presence was introduced as *guests from the farthest destination.* In our honour, the closing song was Ann Murray's 'SNOWBIRD'.

In a small town, community relations were important. John and I speculated that some of the Jurors might have been in attendance. With so much at stake, all exposure that positively enhanced Inc's image had to be considered.

"The town reminded me of rural Alberta in many ways. Good honest people, not initially trusting outsiders, and perhaps being somewhat wary of the number of lawyers and other persons in their town.

The area was so full of history and tradition, and national pride was everywhere. I very much enjoyed the hospitality of the people of Columbus, and hope in turn they thought favourably of Neil and I.

I left with somewhat of a sense of abandoning Neil among the masses of legal counsel, but also knowing it might have been the lawyers at the disadvantage here. Neil was the most tenacious person I knew."

Strategy was also behind my renting an American economy sedan. A conscious effort was made to arrive at the Courthouse early each morning. Parking directly in front, my briefcase would be sorted or rearranged on the hood of my car. As the Defendants' attorneys arrived in their Mercedes, BMW, or Lincoln, they would be greeted with a wave.

My Courtroom presence was positive and educational. Excluding Counsel, I was the only representative in attendance for the entire Trial. Three weeks was a long time for the Jury to be away from home and business. My objective was to show that my life was subject to the same deprivations. The underdog image was prominent every time the Defendants' mob of lawyers ganged up on us.

One of Buster's Jury strategies is worthy of repeat.

The Defendants had hired a professional Expert Technical Witness. To put it more bluntly, he was paid to justify his client's position. Since he testified for a living, he was very knowledgeable, polished, and well compensated. His role was to convince the Jury that Lair #2 would not have been productive even if it had been completed properly (despite the fact that a successful replacement well was only 1000 feet away).

We could not compete with his performance nor could we crack his armour. After several days in attendance, Baxter had him reveal his fee for testimony. At $1000 U.S. per day, his limited three day contribution earned him more than many of the working Jury members made in a month. Expressions of disbelief were observed on some of their faces. Relying on Cogent techniques, I mirrored their look of disgust.

Baxter was a Texas Aggie and a star college football player in his prime. He was still built like a fullback and was a bull in the Courtroom. His representation and dedication could not be faulted.

These precautions were re-examined after the Jury's verdict was delivered on the night of June 30, 1988. Understanding still alluded us.

V
(Beyond Reason - Judgement Day)

It was fortunate for me that July 1 was a *must* travel day. My sister was getting married in Edmonton on Saturday, July 2 and it was my honour to give the Toast To The Bride. When John journeyed from Calgary weeks earlier, he had brought me several transcripts and magazine articles on how best to perform this function. By studying them , a crude speech had been drafted. My concern was disappointing everyone by missing the Wedding. It was close; my arrival at Edmonton International was 10:00 PM Friday. Although exhausted, it was a relief to be able to put the Trial out of my mind for later reconciliation.

It was not long before the events of June 1988 had to be revisited. Inc's Management, the bank, the Receiver, and Frank were all anxious to hear my interpretation. In their opinion it was not a total loss for Inc, but I felt partly responsible for the unexpected and inconclusive ending.

The Jury's reasoning remains unresolved in my mind. It can only be speculated that they viewed us as foreigners, thus influencing their interpretation of justice.

Defendants BTI, responsible for the condition of the Rope Socket, and PEC, responsible for Len's performance, were totally absolved of wrongdoing and released from damages.

Defendants DA and HFT were assessed Principal damages by the Jury, the Courts applied Interest charges, then ordered payment of the following damages:

	PRINCIPAL($)	INTEREST($)	TOTAL($)
DA	83600	63993	147593
HFT	224400	263354	487754
	308000	327347	635347

These recoveries represented 50% of the damages that had been incurred. In accordance with convention, the Courts awarded interest at 10% per annum. Since the original Statement of Claim was filed December 13, 1982, it was compounded annually from that date.

In the Jury's Final Answer on Special Issues, they **deemed Inc to be 50% negligent** and therefore assessed 50% of the damages. The logic was that **Inc had contracted the third party services that eventually led to and caused the loss of Cage Lair #2.**

Neither my expertise nor qualifications were sufficient to challenge the legality of the Jury's Final Answer. It will suffice to offer a personal viewpoint rather than my indignation.

I believed the Jury agonized with the Trust bestowed in them to serve Justice. Punishing the Defendants who had brought harm to Inc simply would have meant turning their backs on neighbours. The Americans versus the Canadians, instead of the guilty versus the innocent, prevailed. Despite the overwhelming evidence to convict, a compromise served as an expedient solution.

The Defendants' Counsel used the confusion created by the final Answer to seek total absolution for their Clients. In his wisdom, the Judge would have none of it; however the legal manoeuvring continued for years.

That is as controversial as *this* book deserves to be. If I were an Officer of the Canadian funeral conglomerate, Loewen Group, perhaps the message would be much clearer. According to a media quote from Raymond Loewen, founder and CEO of the second largest funeral operator in North America, it was *"an aberration of justice"*.

As you may recall, Loewen was accused of defaulting on an $11,000,000 U.S. franchising contract with the O'Keefe family, an independent funeral home owner from Ocean Springs, Mississippi.

The local Jury awarded damages against Loewen of $550,000,000 U.S. Despite the plea that bankruptcy would ensue, the Courts upheld the judgement. The out-of-court settlement reached in January 1996 amounted to $175,000,000 U.S. The Toronto Globe and Mail edition of January 31, 1996 summed it up best. *"An outlandish jury award for what was essentially a breach of a small business contract."*

Only in America!

The virtually unlimited financing of our Defendants funded every conceivable Appeal for the next four years. Likely they spent the equivalent of the Damage Award on legal services.

On November 20, 1988 the 25th Judicial Court upheld the Jury Judgement of $745,347.59 U.S. It further ORDERED post-judgement interest at 10% per annum compounded annually from December 1, 1988, until paid.

A Motion for Mistrial was filed by the Defendants on January 18, 1989.

The District Court of Texas denied the Motion for Mistrial on March 8, 1989.

The Defendants posted a Bond for full Judgement on March 18,1989.

The Defendants finally filed their Appellate Brief Arguments to Dismiss on September 4, 1989 after three extensions.

In November 1989 the Defendants, after learning of Inc's Chapter 11 Bankruptcy and Reorganization Plan, offered a settlement of $250,000 U.S., which was rejected by Inc. and the participants that we were able to contact.

In 1990 the Texas Supreme Court denied the Defendants Motion for Mistrial.

The legal posturing continued until mid 1992 when the Defendants' final Appeal was rejected by the U.S. Supreme Court.

. The award at the time of payout in December 1992 totalled nearly $1,000,000 U.S. The Joint venture partners, some of whom had ignored invoices for a decade, were at the Courthouse with their hands out.

Legal costs which totalled $96,000 U.S. in December 1988 had increased to nearly $150,000 U.S. at the time of settlement. Inc had carried much of this load. Only one partner, JSJ of Dallas, was the only non delinquent account from the very beginning. Most of the earlier disputed billings remained unpaid and were absorbed by Inc.

So after more than a decade, Inc was able to recover its initial investment in Lair #2, less about $50,000 U.S. in costs. Had these funds been invested in an interest bearing account, rather than risking them in Colorado County, Texas, Inc would have tripled its investment.

As in previous EPISODES, the fairness and ethics of U.S. oil and gas operations escaped me. It was a constant reminder of how the oil industries of our two countries differed. It was a difference that no amount of money could change. My view was echoed in John Hecht's opinions which he expressed while summarizing his recollections of this experience.

"The impression I had from the trial, and from dealings with other people south of the border, was mixed. Without their business hats on, I always thoroughly enjoyed my time with the persons I was in contact with in the U.S. oil and gas industry. With the business hat on, it was not always the same story. It seemed basic trust was a bit old fashioned, and you could never be too careful with your dealings.

In Calgary, by comparison, there is more trust and confidence in the scruples of your industry partners or competitors. In the U.S., I sometimes wonder if the oil and gas industry environment is such that it has matured to the extent that companies are now preying more on each other, as opposed to focusing their efforts on exploration, development and production."

Main street, Columbus, Texas

Author at motel after a typical work day - "another day, another lawsuit"

EPISODE 11 : CHAPTER 11 - LIFE IN RECEIVERSHIP

I
(Pre-Petition Trilogy)

My ingredients for surviving a bankruptcy are generous amounts of dedication and sense of humour. There are no regrets about this period of my career. The education and experience were a bonus. To paraphrase the outcome, "it was like having my cake and eating it too".

Although Cage Ltd. was formerly placed in Receivership March 7, 1988, Cage Inc did not seek U.S. bankruptcy protection until the Chapter 11 Petition was filed with the Texas Courts on June 30, 1989. In the interim, operations carried on as close to normal as circumstances warranted. In U.S. Operations, however, circumstances were rarely normal by Canadian standards.

Rumours persisted internally and around the industry that this would be a very dull, painful period. Personally it was found to be quite the contrary.

There were so many loose ends to address that my days were perpetually busy. There was no time to complain or feel sorry for my predicament. These contributions were the most meaningful and rewarding since joining Cage. While every day that passed was one day closer to the End, each day was fulfilled with a sense of purpose to reach that End.

Like my associates, the future encouraged apprehension. A life beyond Cage was welcomed but my obligation to see Inc through to its final demise was also recognized. There was no attempt to kid myself about the End. There would be no White Knight, no resurrection from the ashes. My dedication was anchored by the opinion that neither the bank nor Cage owed me anything. It was just business and I was determined to do my best until my best was no longer required.

The first of this two year period is referred to as the Pre-Petition era. Under the Receiver Manager, we struggled to clear up **three areas of potential conflict** for Inc's Plan of Reorganization and Disclosure Statement. They were, without priority: (1) outstanding

Accounts Receivable; (2) Inc-operated asset dispositions (acquisitions were not an option); and (3) resolution of litigation (a major challenge considering there were normally several lawsuits in progress at any one time).

Any one of these categories harboured a million stories (well OK, less than a million, but more than one). Two have been selectively chosen from each to demonstrate how unforgiving the ownership of U.S. oil and gas assets could be.

II
(Accounts Receivable - Win One, Lose One)

Inc's major gas reserves were attributed to two deep wells, 'Aitken' 2-20 and 1-259, in Hemphill County, Texas. At 25% Working Interest, average rates of 1.5 to 2.0 MMCFPD translated into significant revenue. Since initial completion in 1982, operations had been trouble free. Production was allocated to a Take-Or-Pay (TOP) Contract with a major Gas Purchaser and Transporter which will be referred to as 'Passport'.

Beginning in 1986, Passport reduced their contracted volumes to benefit from much cheaper Spot Market gas supplies not under contract. Inc maintained a dialogue with Passport in an effort to document and recognize volumes "Not Taken". The long term plan was to make up the shortfall with increased future contracted volumes or negotiate a cash settlement. The pending Chapter 11 Petition lent an urgency to the latter solution.

Effective April 1988, with the Courts facing a barrage of TOP litigation from Producers, FERC (Federal Energy Regulatory Commission) abolished future TOP requirements by implementing Order 500-C. This rule introduced cross crediting, under which Producers had to reduce pipelines' TOP liability in exchange for open access transportation. Data filed with the U.S. Securities and Exchange Commission indicated TOP liability totalled $7.2 billion U.S., mostly Outer Continental Shelf gas. Eventually most TOP obligations were resolved through private negotiations and only four pipelines accounted for 50% of total liability.

Inc's calculation of TOP compensation exceeded 100 MMCF . We submitted a claim to Passport at $2.50 per MCF, the average of the contract prices when the delinquencies were accumulated. The excess deliverability had been sold to the Spot Market at prices ranging from $1.00 to $1.25 per MCF. Provided TOP dedications were waived in a settlement, as we expected they would be, our actual damages would be much less.

As 1988 drew to a close, we held out little hope of any recovery. Cage Ltd's bankruptcy was widely known by now and it was no secret that Inc was a subsidiary. Common sense favoured no reaction from Passport until the inevitable Chapter 11 Reorganization. In past restructuring scenarios my experience had been that debts were forgotten, forgiven, or more frequently downgraded to a few cents on the dollar (i.e. Tripoli versus the Utah Operator).

We traded phone calls and letters in the fall of 1988. Inc agreed to amend the volume and value of the TOP claim, but it was assumed these negotiations were simply political posturing or convenient stalling.

Late in the afternoon of Friday, December 23, 1988, a courier delivered Passport's TOP settlement cheque of $120,000 U.S. The volume represented was equivalent to our Spot Market sales. We had recovered full value for our gas on the Eve of Chapter 11. Christmas Eve was a secondary celebration.

It was such a thrill I called the bank's Manager of Special Loans, 'Parry', at his home to advise him of our windfall. He was still in transit from work, so a message was left with his wife that "Santa had delivered big time", knowing he would understand. What a Christmas present! It took days to come down to earth .

At a time when Inc's revenue was drastically reduced due to property sales in advance of Chapter 11, this TOP payment had an influential year end impact. Whether Passport was aware that we were a bankruptcy candidate, before Inc released notice in the New Year, remains a mystery. It was never addressed in our conversations or correspondence, nor did we volunteer it. Not that the settlement was not owing, the timing was just so uncanny. A few weeks delay and we would have been fortunate to collect a fraction of the entitlement. It was no secret that when the Courts became involved, increased administration pretty well negated recoveries due from Pre-Petition accounts.

- - - - - - - - - - - - - -

As if to balance our optimism, we encountered a very strange operational and accounting fiasco late in 1988.

Inc had a 20% Working Interest in an additional Hemphill County, Texas gas wells 'Bones' Estate 1-11. From the productivity viewpoint, it was not a significant contributor. Inc's net of $3000 - $4000 U.S. monthly, however, could not be ignored. But that is exactly what the Operator was guilty of.

The Operator was a large U.S. energy company based in Houston. We will collide with them again in EPISODE 14, where they really stole the show. A promise had been made to myself, from this Bones Estate experience, not to engage in any future business relationship at any cost. That cost was annihilation in 1994. We shall refer to these warriors as 'ACE Petroleum'.

It was my custom to periodically verify revenues and billings on all Inc properties. When Receivable exceeded three months overdue, accounting was requested to follow up for details. An innocent inquiry was usually sufficient to correct the situation.

Lack of revenue from the Bones Estate well for four straight months raised my suspicions. It had been a consistent performer for years. Furthermore, payment of ACE's operating invoices had been approved and processed for these months. There was no indication of down time or well suspension from the billing statements.

Daisy Kwan was Cage's Accounting Manager for Ltd. and Inc. At my request, she undertook to contact ACE on several occasions for a period of weeks. ACE did not respond. She documented and telecopied our queries and concerns for attention. Again no response.

Persistence eventually led to the discovery that the Vice President of Finance at ACE used to hold a similar position at Inc's Denver office years previous. Conversation on a first name basis with 'Dan' resulted in a list of designated contacts in ACE's organization with the authority to rectify the problem. Again we were frustrated with a lack of co-operation. Daisy supported my suspicion of mischief.

After a series of phone calls and supporting letters to the Land Manager, Manager of Gas Contracts, and the Production Manager, it was obvious ACE did not recognize that there was a problem. In their words, "everything appeared normal". As verification, they sent us copies of the State Production reports. This resolved nothing, as we were already in possession of them and they reported normal production volumes.

At our request, ACE checked their internal accounting and realized that none of the parties in the well had received revenue distributions in over six months. Again, at our request, they discovered that no sales had been attributed to our Contract for this period either. Our relationship deteriorated, since ACE was openly confused and without direction. It was difficult to reason with their lack of urgency to identify the culprit.

Investigating from our end, we learned that most of the production was dedicated to a Contract, however a small portion was also allocated to the Spot Market. The wellhead had the capability to deliver to two Purchasers simultaneously.

In 1988 there was a divestiture involving a minority owner's 0.5% Working Interest. The new owner arranged Spot Market sales for *his share of production*, presumably. ACE permitted 100% of production to be delivered to Natural Gas Clearing House, a Spot Market transporter. Apparently ACE did not have an account with this transporter. Consequently the 0.5% owner received *all* revenues for *all* production during this period of confusion. If Inc had not pursued clarification, it would have continued indefinitely.

ACE's attempted recovery of funds was futile; the minority owner disappeared. The transporter refused pleas for compensation, claiming rightly or wrongly that it was the Operator's responsibility to control delivery.

As expected, Inc was left holding the bag. We estimated one hundred years at current production rates would be necessary to make up the shortfall from the minority owner's interest, assuming reserves were adequate.

ACE refused to accept responsibility and we did not receive any compensation prior to filing Chapter 11. Afterward, as Debtor In Possession, we submitted a Class B Unsecured Claim in the neighbourhood of $30,000 U.S. To my knowledge, we did not recover any of it. One up, one down.

III
(Asset Divestitures - Close Encounters)

The strategy of the bank and Receiver was to divest Inc of *all* operated properties prior to filing for Chapter 11. The liability as operator was more binding and complex. This was not only true for contracts with Vendors and Working Interest Owners, but also with employees, contract labour, and State and Federal authorities.

We received full support from the Receiver for our efforts to sell the Whitte, Barn, and Cob assets in April 1988. In Inc's shop, R-E-L-I-E-F was spelled "Panhandle Property Sale Closing".

There remained only two other Inc-operated assets to sell. Each had a memorable ending.

Just west of the Oklahoma City limits Inc owned 100% Working Interest in a pumping oil well, Luger 36-1. Of all places, the location was in Canadian County. It generated a little cash flow, averaging 15 BOPD, but had been on decline for several years. The surface and downhole equipment was in constant need of maintenance, such that we rarely netted more than $1000 to $1500 U.S. monthly.

In Colorado County, Texas, near the Lair wells, Inc owned a 40% Working Interest in a gas well, Johnson #2. Assisted by a small rental compressor costing $1200 per month, it averaged 250 - 300 MCFPD. Under the tending of our contract pumper, 'Dean', it had been maintenance free. Inc's cash flow was similar to Luger, averaging $1000 to $1500 U.S. per month.

Johnson #2, June 1988 (left to right: gas meter, author and pumper, separator, rental compressor, and wellhead)

Johnson #2, June 1988 (Sales meter delivery station)

Obviously neither was a barn burner and both would be diffi-cult to sell.

The search for a Buyer was tedious and unproductive. In the fall of 1988 a weekend was spent vacationing in Las Vegas. Coinci-dentally I ran into a retired Inc Vice President of Production from the Denver era, 'Orval'. He had left Inc in 1982 after cashing in his Stock Options for a considerable profit. At the time, Cage was trad-ing in the $25 U.S. range.

Orval invested his profits in oil and gas prospects and had been quite successful assembling operated assets in a small, inde-pendent company.

Over a few drinks we discussed Inc's financial status and the necessity to dispose of the last remaining operated wells. Since Orval had been instrumental in acquiring them for Inc initially, he was familiar with their background. He indicated a genuine interest in their acquisition.

Early in the New Year we began negotiating offers. Orval in-spected each property personally. At the Receiver's insistence, de-posits were submitted. We finally settled on purchase prices roughly equivalent to three years cash flow. Again, as with the Panhandle, the bank and Receiver were delighted.

By early spring we Closed on the Luger well after a cheque for the balance owing was deposited in the bank's U.S. account and had cleared. A cautious and prudent policy by the Receiver, as events would soon prove.

The very next day Orval called to ask if Inc had carried Operator's insurance. He was advised that we had, but that it was cancelled upon Sale Closing. Then he asked if it was too late to cancel the deal. Again he was advised it was too late. Naturally my curiosity begged to know why.

Over night Luger 36-1 had been struck by lightning during a violent thunder storm. The previous month's production had not yet been shipped. The resulting fire at the battery had destroyed most of the facilities. Orval had not yet arranged insurance. He was out of luck this time and considerably out of pocket. As a courtesy, the circumstances were reviewed with our Insurer but they declined compensation as expected.

- - - - - - - - - - - - -

The bank and Receiver were relieved again when the Johnson #2 sale Closed a few weeks later.

Simultaneously, productivity declined abruptly to 25 - 50 MCFPD with, for the first time, small amounts of water. The latter was most concerning for Orval, as it played havoc with the compressor.

After a few months at these uneconomic rates, Orval designed and conducted a recompletion of an uphole gas sand. He commingled both sands and initial rates were encouraging.

Within a month, however, water encroachment had rendered the well uneconomic. Most of the other Working Interest Owners elected not to participate in this workover, therefore Orval was out of luck and out of pocket once again.

It was a sad ending for this well which I had been particularly fond of.

Our pumper, Gene, had been loyal to Inc and always accommodating to our instructions. During the Lair #2 Trial in 1988, I had driven down to spend half a day touring our operation. He and his wife had treated me to a fabulous All You Can Eat fresh seafood buffet at an isolated rural restaurant south of El Campo.

In addition, one of the Working Interest Owners in Johnson #2 was John Winnant, Jr. Reading a history book revealed that he was the son of a U.S. Ambassador and the first American B-17 bomber pilot shot down over Europe in 1942. He had spent nearly four years in a German prison camp before liberation at the end of the War. It was an honour to have a long telephone discussion with him one day about his adventures. As an ideal and reliable Joint Venture partner, there had been no other reason to visit.

The eleventh hour sale of these two wells was like a Close Encounter. Witnessing an American being stripped naked by his own investment was a new experience. It certainly was possible for lightning to strike the same person twice in the U.S. oilpatch.

IV
(Litigation -Trust Is King)

If you get a charge or a high from courtroom confrontation, then U.S. Operations is for you. There was rarely a time since the early Ohio days when I was not preoccupied with litigation. At this point in my career the sudden emergence of a new law suit was taken in stride. The fact that we were mostly on the defensive as Plaintiff was a subtle reminder of how we misread the intentions of our hosts and partners. Looking back, there was nothing personal, it was simply the way oil and gas operations were conducted.

In order to survive, it was essential to honour the motto - Give No Quarter, Ask No Quarter. We will explore an example of each.

In 1981 Inc had Farmed Out some of its fringe Altamont Field acreage to a major U.S. oil company, which we will refer to as 'Knox'. AFE's for two deep Green River wells, Unit A-1 and Common B-1, were generated by the Operator, Knox, early in 1982. The budget for each completed well was around $1,500,000 U.S.

As Farmor, Inc elected an Overriding Royalty position in the former. In the latter, Inc participated for 25% Working Interest but retained the contractual right to withdraw at Casing Point (decision point or depth after which the well is deepened or cased for completion).

Inc's Open Hole evaluation (formation samples, log interpretation, Drill Stem Tests, drilling characteristics, hydrocarbon shows, etc.)

favoured abandonment. Based on considerable drilling and completion experience in the Uinta Basin, Inc's technical consensus considered both wells to have penetrated high risk, low quality reservoirs. The stakes had become too high for the added expense of continuing.

Despite the requirement for documented election beyond Casing Point in the B-1, Knox completed both wells without approval from Inc. After numerous recompletion attempts, the final costs were in the range of $2,000,000 - $2,500,000 each. Within two years both wells were uneconomic and suspended. Cumulative production for each well was less than 25000 barrels and both investments were failures.

Inc had contributed to Dry Hole Costs to Casing Point in B-1, but refused to incur any additional expenses.

In 1985 Knox threatened Inc with litigation for non payment of their 25% Working Interest share of B-1, approximately $700,000. U.S. Inc's position was that Knox had failed to comply with the terms and conditions of their own Joint Venture Agreement. Since Inc's obligation for costs to Casing Point had been met, no further conciliation would be considered. The dispute went away but our trust was tested.

In 1988 Knox served Inc with a Statement of Claim seeking to recover in excess of $850,000 U.S., interest included, for B-1 operations and abandonment. Our consultations and confrontations dragged on into 1989 and eventually until our Chapter 11 Filing.

For expediency, we agreed to include Knox as an unsecured, hostile Claim. Basically it was ignored after that and our energy was applied to more legitimate claims. Besides being dormant for years, none of the Denver participating staff were available for consultation. This was a case where the Courts were protective.

Knox's recovery was a few cents on the dollar, based on a weighted percentage of funds set aside for disputed claims. Given the circumstances, even this treatment was generous.

- - - - - - - - - - - - - -

Within a few months of Cage Petroleum Ltd. being placed in Receivership, Inc's Utah revenues mysteriously ceased. Our crude oil Purchaser informed us that our account had been moved to a competitor. As no such instructions had been issued, this immediately raised my suspicions.

With assistance again from Daisy's Department, we determined our Utah Operator, Cracker, had orchestrated this manoeuvre after learning of Cage Ltd.'s. The motive was sinister and without precedent.

In 1982 Inc had sold Cracker an undivided 55% Working Interest in all producing Utah properties for $15.2 million U.S. and relinquished Operatorship. Inc remained a signatory on the oil and gas Division Orders (binding contracts between Working Interest Owner and Purchaser whereby the latter recognizes the Owner's Net Revenue Interest and agrees to pay monthly production proceeds directly). It was illegal for an Operator or Purchaser to amend a Division Order (DO) without expressed permission from the Owner.

Cracker's purpose for changing oil purchasers was to execute new DO's recognizing Cracker as the 100% Owner. The new Purchaser willingly accepted this change and all revenues flowed directly to Cracker.

When we challenged Cracker on this, they claimed protection was needed for future Joint Interest Billing (JIB) payments now that Inc was in Receivership.

We quickly corrected their *misunderstanding* and demanded reinstatement of the original Oil Purchaser. Cracker urged our cooperation in remaining with the new purchaser since they had promised a fifty cent per barrel premium as a new account incentive.

The fact that the new purchaser had so readily accepted unilateral DO's from Cracker was most disturbing.

Furthermore our research verified that the fifty cent premium applied only to the first month of sales. Credits for subsequent months were equal to, or even less than, our original Oil Purchaser prices.

In following up on apparent illegalities, it was discovered that the new purchaser's Controller, 'Luke', was an old adversary. He had been the Controller with Tripoli's Utah Operator during their litigation from 1983 to 1985. Luke was particularly resented after Mac and I had attended his depositions in 1985 and witnessed several instances where Luke failed to impress us with his testimony. Based on this experience, Inc's declared intention was not to have any further involvement with the new purchaser. If necessary, we would take our share of production In Kind (assume ownership at the wellhead and manage marketing and royalty reimbursements separately).

As a courtesy, a call was placed to Luke to share our opinion of his integrity and thus our conviction to avoid any business with his employer. Luke did not return my call.

Cracker's Vice President of Finance in Covington, Louisiana was responsible for authoring the new DOs and signing up the new purchaser. He was advised that Inc would not tolerate these arrangements. He agreed to return oil marketing to the status quo once a confidential letter was provided, acknowledging why Inc refused to conduct business with the new purchaser.

This was considered to be a reasonable request, particularly since it would remain confidential. There was no holding back our explicit opinion of Luke and we reiterated that without trust, any business relationship was doomed to failure.

This Vice President forwarded my letter by courier to Luke, who promptly phoned me in Calgary. In between vulgar language were numerous threats to my safety and health.

His anger did not bother me, since my reaction would have been similar if the shoes had been reversed. My revulsion was with Cracker's Vice President. When he was confronted, he claimed my letter was mistakenly sent in a mail pouch with other correspondence to the new purchaser.

As a member of the Senior Management team, with ethical and fiduciary responsibilities, his conduct was intolerable and inexcusable. He displayed little concern and offered a weak apology. It was a low point in my appreciation of professionalism in U.S. oil and gas operations.

Cracker had confiscated several months of Inc's revenue illegally and without provocation. Our JIB account had been current. For a change, Inc assumed an aggressive, offensive role and instigated litigation against Cracker.

With the receipt of the first threatening legal notice, Cracker terminated their contract with the new purchaser and reactivated our old DOs. Funds due Inc were promptly provided.

It was uncommon for Inc to be carrying a big stick. No matter how we detested litigation, there was a time and place for it. This caper was the beginning of a deteriorating relationship with Cracker. As an organization, they never earned back my trust.

V
(Then There Were None)

Fate had been kind to Inc in 1988. Our goals and objectives were met and surpassed with hard work, dedication, and a little luck.

As 1989 began, we had no illusions for the crucial struggle ahead. Limits of patience and determination would be taxed if Inc was to prevail.

The immediate challenge was how to maintain momentum after expending so much energy in the Pre-Petition era. Motivation deserved a breather after nine uninterrupted months. Before the final battle began, Inc unleashed a hidden weapon. It was the second ingredient to bankruptcy survival.

'Stan' was an accountant with the Receiver. He had been assigned to Cage's offices in March 1988.

Stan was a veteran of many receiverships and appreciated the sensitivity of the climate between *us* and his employer. In our presence, he conducted himself firmly but fairly. We gradually became accustomed to each other and accepted our different roles. He was particularly skilled at being available most of the time for consultation but remaining aloof and unobtrusive. While a man of few words, he left me with the impression of a deep thinker. He was the perfect candidate for what I had in mind.

Every Tuesday morning Cage held a joint management meeting to discuss Inc's and Cage's performance. Stan attended as an observer and contributed the Receiver's instructions or opinions as required.

Coincidentally with our regular weekly meeting February 9, it happened to be Stan's birthday.

When Stan arrived at Cage's offices, he was greeted only by our Receptionist, Dana. Bewildered by the absence of all fifteen staff, he learned from Dana that we had had enough of Receivership and had organized a group ski outing for the day.

As we were told later, Stan took this in stride at first.

Then 'Josh', the Receiver's Senior Vice President in the Calgary office, called Stan to assemble everyone for an urgent management meeting. Stan choked but did not break. He had no inkling that Josh was an accomplice.

On cue and at Josh's request, the Receiver's Toronto office called Stan to advise of a purchase offer for all of Inc's properties. Having been submitted through the highest channels, it was a dream offer too good to be true; however acceptance was required by noon.

Now Stan had to react. Frantic phone calls did no good; Josh made himself unavailable. Stress, previously a stranger to Stan's character, crept into his voice. He searched every office repeatedly looking for bodies.

We assumed that by mid morning all the damage that could be done, was done. We had assembled at a next door coffee shop for breakfast. En masse, we all discharged from the elevators. Stan had been pacing in the hallway and was momentarily lost for words.

He grabbed all the managers and ushered us directly into the conference room. Flustered and red faced, he insisted on knowing where we had been and what we thought we were up to. He proceeded to list the urgencies, but we interrupted by claiming not to be ready for the management meeting yet.

He walked over and slammed the door shut, then he read the riot act and his predicament. We calmly announced that it was just the kind of panic one should expect on his birthday. In unison we declared "Happy Birthday Stan", then all walked out laughing.

Stan did not laugh and did not move. Minutes later he was still standing where we had left him in the conference room. We had Josh call to snap him out of his nightmare. Then Toronto called to rub in some salt. Eventually all clues pointed to me as instigator. It crossed my mind that revenge may have been going through Stan's.

At Stan's expense, this prank had given me the juice needed to carry on. My attitude was refreshed and again ready for battle.

VI
(Post Petition Pink Slip)

By spring 1989 all Panhandle business had been finalized and was behind us. Negotiations were nearing conclusion to sell the remaining operated wells. With these major obstacles removed, preparations for seeking Chapter 11 protection began in earnest.

At our suggestion, Roy's firm was employed to co-ordinate the Plan of Reorganization and appropriate bankruptcy filings.

The bank wanted to restructure as soon as possible in order to market Inc's non-operated U.S. assets and capitalize on millions of dollars in tax concessions.

We were preoccupied for months compiling lists of creditors and debtors, then classifying them into secured or unsecured, contested or uncontested. All assets had to be declared, ranked, and valued. Budgets had to be prepared for restrained operations during Chapter 11 and resumption of normal operations afterwards. Likewise our Plan of Reorganization, Disclosure Statement, and List of Executory Contracts were drafted and redrafted.

Finally on June 30, 1989, our Chapter 11 Petition was filed with the Federal Courts.

Tradition called for nine to twelve months to complete the legal processes for an entity the size of Inc. Roy succeeded in the record time of four, much to the bank's satisfaction. Roy's efforts were assisted by the bank's willingness to recognize and compensate in full all Secured, Uncontested Claims. Although rarely the case, it assured minimum challenge and saved a lot of legal fees.

In late October the bank's Manager of Special Loans, Parry, accompanied me to Amarillo. Meeting up with Roy, we drove to Lubbock for the Court's final blessing of our Reorganization.

Parry was treated to the Fifth Season Inn before flying back to Calgary next day. I splurged for the first time and reserved both of us a third floor suite at $69.95. He seemed extremely impressed with the value. Pains were taken not to risk my, or the motel's, credibility by disclosing how much cheaper it was for the next floor down. The next day Inc would celebrate its freedom and a new phase in its history could begin.

My role at Cage was now considered at an End. The bank had decided to transfer responsibility of Inc to a local oil and gas management firm, beginning December 01. This strategy was intended to facilitate the marketing of Inc's assets without interfering with Cage's destiny.

Consistently my desire had been to depart, to get the *"pink slip"*, as soon as my job at Inc was finished. Cage honoured my request in style.

The End for me was Thursday, 30 November. That afternoon my presence was requested in the conference room to exchange good-byes and friendly pontifications. Then a gift was presented to me that was well deserved. The staff *challenged* me to try it on. It was so creative, I went into an adjoining empty office, changed, and wore it into the conference room to everyone's surprise. Once again, humour was the right ingredient at the right time.

The thought of Stan's birthday prank haunted me at first. A hidden movie camera or an unannounced visit by the bank's or Receiver's Senior Management was nervously expected. Anyway there I was, dressed only in my underwear and a mini pink slip. Live by the sword; die by the sword.

My going away party and Cage's office were exited for the last time, but an optimistic future beckoned me. An invitation had been accepted to consult to the management firm chosen by the bank to oversee Inc's Post-Petition restructuring. Energy prices were strengthening and confidence prevailed that the bank would yet manage a decent recovery from the remaining properties and tax pools. That was not to be, as EPISODE 12 will disclose.

EPISODE 12: INTERIM MANAGEMENT-
NO PATTERN, NO PURPOSE

I
(Trooper Knows Best)

Beginning December 1, 1989, my first month as a consultant to a Calgary oil and gas management firm, 'Firm', was exciting but mundane. Now that sounds hypocritical. In truth I looked forward to the freedom of self employment but dreaded the administrative toils of relocating Inc's records and modus operandi.

Hundreds of boxes of Accounting, Land, Geological, and Engineering files had to be sorted and identified according to the Firm's unique labelling criteria. It was a time consuming, laborious chore, requiring sacrifice from most of the staff for weeks. Floor to ceiling, tracked filing cabinets were purchased and installed to accommodate these voluminous records. The confined storage space overflowed.

This new home was intended to be a temporary home. The bank had been clear in emphasizing the immediate need for divestiture at optimum price. Conversely my attitude was challenged into accepting the Firm's extensive preparations to consummate Inc's operations. It was assumed this marriage of convenience would be a short one. The 1989 Cash Flow was less than $1,000,000. U.S. and projected to decline at 15 - 20% annually. Clearly this account could not sustain lengthy administrative burdens and still return a semblance of recovery to the bank.

Armed with this knowledge and appreciation of my objective, confidence in achieving my purpose and goals was secure.

While my body was captive to physical office alterations, my mind raced ahead to ponder creative approaches for developing and marketing the U.S. assets. Every exploitation opportunity had to be judged on its merit for enhancing value in the near term. Several attractive investment options had surfaced during the dormant Petition months and now demanded selective participation.

Our major New Year undertaking would involve grouping the widely scattered properties into congruous geographical areas. Three distinct Post-Petition, self sufficient, entities would be created. The bank's advisors dictated these independent companies would be referred to as CRI (TEXAS) INC, CRI (UTAH) INC, and CRI (MICHIGAN) INC. The acronym 'CRI' stood for Cage Resources Inc. The bank wanted to distance itself from Inc's negative past, but the naming logic was not clearly understood. Value had to be synchronized with the allocation of tax credits, an issue handled by the bank's New York office. While not privy to the details, I prepared myself anyway for maximum effort and pace to meet the bank's deadlines.

Prior to committing my energies to this task, the travel industry motto "I Need A Vacation" victimized me. As a firm believer that the most productive leisure experiences are the unplanned ones; when your subconscious tells you to get away, do not fight it, just do it.

My wife was from Wise, a small town in south-western Virginia. To me it had no significance other than it was her birthplace. Given the need to get away, we decided to spend Christmas with her folks and escape the Calgary winter for two weeks.

It was not long before we had second thoughts. We were greeted with record breaking freezing temperatures. Frequent snow storms provided a very uncommon white Christmas and snow drifts several feet deep. Cars and drivers were unprepared and unaccustomed for this treacherous side of Mother Nature. As a result, we were practically housebound for the first ten days.

When conditions finally improved, my wife convinced me to accompany her to Lexington, 235 miles northeast on Interstate 81, to visit an old college classmate. They had been in touch by phone over Christmas and both were anxious for a reunion.

Had it not been for the prolonged confinement due to weather, this proposal might not have been entertained. There was one other incentive, however, for visiting Lexington and it satisfied my hunger for history.

In the opening EPISODE, my positive experiences travelling and meeting people throughout Texas and Louisiana were related. During my New Orleans weekend I met 'Jed', a close friend of one of my classmates. He was also a Shell engineer, based there and working on offshore projects. In our discussions he disclosed he was a graduate of Virginia Military Institute (VMI) in Lexington, Virginia.

Naturally the 'military' reference caught my ear, so he was pressed for more information.

Founded in 1839, VMI was noted for the excellence of its military and academic programs. Enrolment was prestigious and limited to 1300 candidates who had a choice of twelve disciplines for a baccalaureate degree. In addition to a demanding academic schedule, four years of ROTC (Reserve Officers' Training Corps) courses were mandatory. Graduates could choose careers in the Army, Navy, Air Force, or Marine Corps. Its' alumni body was renowned for Rhodes Scholars, Medal of Honour recipients, and Nobel Prize winners. Graduates had taken a prominent part in every military confrontation since the Mexican war of 1846.

In one of the outstanding heroic acts of the American Civil War, VMI cadets fought as a corps at the Battle of New Market on May 15, 1864. Averaging only 18 years of age, they held the front line for half an hour against seasoned troops. Their valour helped to defeat a numerically superior Union Army under Sigel.

Jed must have made a favourable and intriguing impression. Now more than ten years later, there was an excitement to matching this obscure incident with reality.

During the four hour drive, my wife teased me with local historical facts.

Wise was the home of George C. Scott, the Hollywood actor. In 1970 he played VMI graduate and U.S. World War II General George Patton, naming only one of his distinguished roles. General Frank McCarthy, a VMI graduate, received an Academy Award for producing the movie "Patton".

The adjoining town of Pound was the home of Francis Gary Powers, the American pilot shot down in his Lockheed U-2 high-altitude reconnaissance jet in May 1960. At the height of Cold War tension with the Soviet Union, his capture and interrogated confessions created international headlines for months.

Then she informed me that Lexington was the home of the George C. Marshall Museum. Besides being a VMI graduate and a Nobel Prize recipient in 1953, he had also been Army Chief of Staff for U.S. Armed Forces during World War II. Lexington's roots also include three other renowned American generals - George Washington, Robert E. Lee, and Thomas J. 'Stonewall' Jackson. The latter two, Confederate heroes, had homes there and are buried in the historic town. For military enthusiasts like myself, this was a "must see".

What was meant to be, never happened.

Despite numerous calls throughout the day, we never established contact with my wife's friend (we learned months later that one of her children required emergency hospital treatment).

To salvage our trip, we assigned the last hours of the day touring VMI and the Marshall Museum, which was within the VMI compound. Almost by accident, we were attracted to the adjacent Washington and Lee University. Founded in 1749 (incidentally, by comparison, the founding of my hometown Halifax), the architecture was unique and boasted "the sixth oldest institution of higher learning in America". The famous Civil War Confederate General Robert E. Lee was President during the last five years of his life.

Not knowing what possessed me or why, it was decided to stay overnight in a motel rather than returning to Wise. My curiosity was driven to determine why the first President of the United States was immortalized with a Southern hero of the divisive 1861-1865 U S. Civil War.

Next day as much time as we could spare was spent touring the University and its historic buildings. Civil War displays and artefacts captivated my attention. As if it had been yesterday, a flashback of the Maryland speeding incident eight years previous (EPISODE 2) emerged.

The State Trooper's face was vivid, as was his 'yarn' about an obscure Civil War battle called Antietam. Despite bragging that his Civil War enthusiasm and adventures were as fulfilling as his law enforcement career, the boast was not seriously considered or believed. Why would it?

This day in late December 1989 was momentous for grooming my aspirations in life. The more knowledge of the U.S. Civil War, the more desire to discover. It monopolized the discussions on our drive back to Wise. If we did not have airline tickets for two days hence, our stay would have been extended.

My last day should have spent socializing with my wife's family and friends. Instead I barricaded myself in the Wise Library and poured through the Civil War section.

My enthusiasm for this era has not diminished to this day. It has been a source of escape, of excitement, of satisfaction, of purpose, and of accomplishment. Whether the road on my career path has been rocky or smooth, this retreat has been medicinal. No movie, book, or article has escaped my attention. The details of this conflict absolutely fascinated me. Why, might you ask, should this appeal to a Canadian?

A few facts may surprise you.

Between opening shots at Fort Sumter on April 12, 1861 and Lee's surrender at Appomattox Courthouse on Palm Sunday, April 09, 1865, unprecedented confrontation cost 630,000 American lives, equal to combined United States military losses in all wars before or since.

Many of the 22 Northern and 11 Southern States were ravaged during 76 full-scale battles, 310 engagements, and 6337 skirmishes. This incredulous struggle occurred less than three generations ago in our own backyard, not in Europe or Asia. The last Civil War veteran, Walter Williams, died in December 1959 at the age of 117. The adversaries belonged to the same country. Population of the USA in 1861 was 31,503,000, roughly equivalent to Canada's in 1996.

This conflict has been a favourite of military historians as it ushered in a new era in warfare. The FIRST....practical machine gun, repeating rifle, mobile siege artillery, land and naval mines, ironclad ships, submarines, portable telegraph, and manned balloon reconnaissance were some of the inventions 50 years and a World War ahead of their time.

The preceding was not an attempt to show off my research. If you are stimulated or suspicious of any of these 'facts', as in my case in December 1989, then let the natural thirst for *new* knowledge influence your destiny.

At a time in my life when meaningful challenge and purpose was considered hard to come by, this hobby was an inspiration. Combining this passion with leisure has resulted in countless "miracles of happiness".

Many of my vacations have since emanated from the desire for more Civil War knowledge and assimilation. The hallowed battlefields of Gettysburg, Antietam, New Market, Cedar Creek, Perryton, Richmond, Petersburg, Cumberland Gap, Lookout Mountain, Missionary Ridge, and Chicamauga were personally visited, to name a few. Having studied each in detail first, the sensation of closing my eyes and imagining the events of 130 years ago was gainfully experienced. This imagery has never failed to amaze and satisfy me.

My passion to learn more resulted in the discovery of the Chinook Civil War Round Table Club, a Calgary history group which held meetings periodically to discuss the war. The President, Kathy

Brown, was actively involved in determining the final resting places of Civil War veterans in Western Canada. Here is an example of the interest this military conflict still generated with the public. Kathy's research revealed an insight into one soldier's military career, how lucky he was to survive the war, and why he was buried so far from home in rural Alberta.

"Private William Barnett was the last known Confederate survivor of the infamous Pickett's Charge. He was born in Virginia in 1843, enlisted at eighteen with F Company of the 11th Virginia Infantry and was taken prisoner near Richmond in 1862. Private Barnett was put in hospital twice, with pneumonia and fever. After being exchanged for a Union prisoner, he fought at Gettysburg and survived Pickett's Charge on July 03, 1863. He was called upon to serve as a colour bearer during this battle - a target that the Union army soldiers trained their muskets on first because he was carrying the symbolic Rebel flag into battle.

In this infamous battle, General George Pickett led 12,000 Rebels across a mile of open field to attack entrenched Union troops on Cemetery Ridge. In the face of heavy fire, Pickett's Division charged the hill and broke through part of the Union Army line. Hand to hand fighting ensued and Pickett's men fell back after suffering great losses. Less than one-fourth of his command returned unhurt to Confederate lines on Seminary Ridge. This one hour charge became known in the history books as the "High Tide of the Confederacy" because it marked the deepest major military intrusion into the Northern States. From this point on, the South was on the defensive until the war ended April 09, 1865.

After the war Barnett became a farmer in Virginia, raising five children. Two sons moved to Bottrel, a hamlet thirty-five miles northwest of Calgary. On July 17, 1933, three weeks into visiting with his sons at Bottrel, he died of a heart attack at the age of eighty-nine.

His grave was unmarked until the Chinook Club informed the U.S. government, which sent a granite headstone for the site. On Sunday, March 21, 1993, we organized a military ceremony re-enactment, complete with authentic Civil War uniforms and weapons, honouring this Confederate soldier. With minimum publicity, several hundred people attended, despite the cold and wind. The amount of cars and media overwhelmed the local cemetery facilities. His only known descendants are grandchildren in the U.S. ..... but suddenly he had a lot of people who cared for him in Alberta."

Other than Gettysburg, which was awesome, it was difficult to rank one battlefield/museum ahead of another. Each was distinct and rewarding. However, of the destinations that impressed me most, Chattanooga, Tennessee was always my favourite for genuine hospitality and two minor examples relate why.

In 1991, together with my wife and her sister, we drove to Chattanooga from Wise to tour the many local historical sites. It was near dark when we entered the suburbs and promptly exited on an isolated side street to get our bearings. We were looking for a prominent geographical feature, Lookout Mountain.

Momentarily a car pulled up beside us and blocked our path. Thinking we were done for, in my stereotypical paranoia, a gun was expected any second. Would we speed off or passively submit to robbery? The doors were locked and my window lowered a few inches. A large black man got out and walked over to our Blazer.

The gentleman noted from our license plate that we were from out of town and looked lost. We declared our destination and desire to get there before closing. He motioned for us to follow him. Still reluctant, we drove behind at a safe distance "to allow for a getaway if it turned out to be a trap". Before long he stopped and pointed to a road leading south to a large hill (Chattanooga is inundated with hills). He yelled out instructions, waved, and was on his way. Some bandit!

A short distance away we found the museum in time to get details on tours. My enthusiasm was barely contained for all there was to see next day. Because of our tight schedule, this incident was valuable in planning the rest of our itinerary.

Two days later we were trying to squeeze in one last stop before leaving the city. We were "confused" about the directions to another battlefield on the eastern outskirts, Missionary Ridge.

We parked out of the way on a gas station lot to study maps. After walking over to a nearby street corner to check the sign, we were still lost. An elderly attendant at the gas station witnessed our dilemma, walked away from pumping gas, and asked us how he could help. He pointed out a shortcut that we would have missed.

Again, with time of the essence, genuine hospitality saved the day. Besides being an historian's paradise, no other comparably sized city, American or Canadian, has impressed me so. Chattanooga means "rock coming to a point," in reference to 2,126 foot-high Lookout Mountain.

During the Civil War, Union forces occupied the city and participated in three major engagements. The battlefields of Lookout Mountain, Missionary Ridge and Chickamauga have been preserved in National Military Parks. It was from Chattanooga that William

Tecumseh Sherman began his march in May 1864 through Georgia to the sea, burning Atlanta on the way.

Tennessee River sightseeing cruises are a must. Amusements such as the Chattanooga Choo Choo Museum, Rock City Gardens, Tennessee Aquarium, and National Medal of Honour Museum offer something for everyone.

In 1981 it pained me to be stopped by that State Trooper. The hour travelling time we lost and the speeding ticket it cost were agonized over and over.

If you also believe in mysterious coincidences, you may also have had similar experiences where only the down side was realized initially. Like me, you dwelled on the negative aspects, then put it all behind you. Perhaps you were fortunate, as I, to have had a second chance to cash in on one of life's free gifts. If not: pity!

II
(In No One We Trust)

The dissection of Inc into three entities proceeded rapidly and constructively during the first few months of 1990. By spring the workload had subsided. If there was a plan where to go from here, it was not apparent. Taking advantage of the delay and confusion, other projects were pursued to broaden my scope.

Compliments of the Firm, my services were engaged by 'PMT', the Receiver Manager for a bankrupt Canadian oil and gas junior, Propetro Corp. The Receiver was anxious to sell the minor U.S. assets belonging to a subsidiary, Xanadu Resources Inc (Xanadu).

My extensive Utah background and experience supported my candidacy for evaluating and marketing these properties. After agreeing on a commission rate, a 30 June 1990 Closing Date, and a $30,000 U.S. minimum Sale Price, files were assembled and my research began enthusiastically.

If the assignment could be termed simple, then the results should be termed shocking.

At stake were four deep Wasatch/Green River oil wells in Duchesne County, Utah. Working Interests were non-operated and ranged from 9.375% to 25.0%. Since each well held 640 acres, development drilling to 320 acres was an attractive option. Only

5% of the lands were Tribal, therefore royalty burdens were at the lower end.

Summarizing 1989 operations, **Net** daily production averaged 16 barrels of oil and 13 MCF of gas, translating into $4300 U.S. monthly Cash Flow.

The Operator, Miramar of Denver, offered the Receiver $5000 U.S. to assume Xanadu's interests. It was rejected. Even to a Receiver desperate to divest, this hardly seemed appropriate. Miramar supported their offer with numerous hypothetical gremlins that threatened to discount future value. That is why and when my involvement was solicited.

A February 1987 Miramar Letter Agreement was recovered from Xanadu's files. It referred to litigation against Shell (proof that the American oilpatch sues itself when it runs out of Canadians) for shortages of casinghead gas and Natural Gas Liquid (NGL) payments. The production period covered March 1982 to June 1984. The gross value of the recovery was estimated at $700,000 U.S. Xanadu executed and returned this document February 6, 1987, confirming it was a participant.

There were no further references to this legal claim in the files. When Miramar was approached, they were vague and uncooperative. No worry; a decade of U.S. operational experience governed my actions.

This issue was suspicious, so my extensive Utah network was relied on to provide the answers and verify the outcome. As expected, there had been a full settlement between Shell and Miramar early in 1989. Mysteriously no one had notified Xanadu.

Following the sharing of my research with Miramar, a letter of explanation was eventually forwarded to the Receiver on May 07, 1990. It included a cheque for $17,327 U.S., representing Xanadu's entitlement from the total distribution of $356,562 U.S. Working on contingency, *Miramar's attorneys received $183,315 U.S., or 33 1/3% of the $550,000 gross settlement.*

The magnitude of dollars from only two years of gas and NGL underpayments, secondary revenue streams, was an eye opener. It encouraged me to check out another contentious source of revenue, the Balance to Payout for each well.

Miramar had earned a Carried Interest (as in Panhandle - EPISODE 8) as a fee for promoting Xanadu into these wells. The burden on Xanadu's interest was halved when a well reached payout of the initial investment plus cumulative operating costs. My preliminary review indicated payout was achievable in two additional wells (one well had paid out several years earlier). Confirmation would lead to a higher Present Worth assessment than the Receiver had booked.

In April, after discussions with Miramar's Accounting Department, telecopied Balance to Payout Statements were received for two wells queried. As expected, one of the wells was shown to have reached and exceeded payout. The cumulative balance, and thus credit, was at ($270,665) U.S. If verified, Xanadu would be due considerable recovery. This message was conveyed to Miramar and the Receiver.

Several days later Miramar provided a "Revised Payout Status Report" with a different table of calculations. This time the cumulative balance was $738,686 U.S. still to be recovered from operations before Payout was achievable.

Needless to say, this dispute was not resolved. Only an audit from initial production in 1982 to present was capable of providing an accurate Balance to Payout. There were no illusions that attempting to schedule one in the near future would be next to impossible. In any event, the Sale Deadline intervened and terminated the discussions.

It reminded me of the fish story where the big one slipped away.

With the Firm's assistance, a comprehensive Divestiture Package was prepared. After distribution to a dozen prospective clients, four offers were received by the 7 May 1990 deadline. Miramar had increased its offer substantially, but was still shy of the Receiver's imposed minimum. Of the three acceptable bids, the successful Purchaser was 'District' Gas and Oil of Kelowna, a private Canadian company.

Ned Studer, my old Inc associate, had relocated to Kelowna late in 1987. As a consulting oil and gas accountant, he brokered this acquisition for a group of local investors.

It was a relief to be working with a Canadian acquaintance to negotiate the transaction. We expected it to be trouble free and it was. A month after the Closing of 29 June 1990, Ned and his partners became very satisfied customers, thanks to 'Uncle Sadam'. Timing was everything, as Ned explains.

"I had stayed in touch with Neil after the Cage days mainly on a social basis. Since I still had some minor involvement in Utah through a client company, District Gas & Oil Inc., it wasn't uncommon for Neil to relate his latest tale of woe when we got together for a drink. I don't remember exactly how we first explored the idea of my bid for the Xanadu assets but I suspect it was over a beer.

My partners and I decided to use District as the vehicle for this bid. It was a Montana incorporation which had little left in it after an earlier foray into the minefields of US oil and gas participation. We put our bid together and by the deadline we were scrambling to put the Closing financing together. This was also about the time of the failed (thank God) Meech Lake Agreement Accord so the Canadian dollar was on one of its many roller coaster rides. Since we would be borrowing Canadian currency to Close a US dollar deal, I tried to outguess the roller coaster. Despite the dire predictions, this turned out to be another financial non-event in Quebec-Canada relations and I was sucked in like everyone else.

As Neil mentioned, we received an unexpected birthday gift (at the expense of the Iraqi people) when Iraq invaded Kuwait in August, 1990. Oil prices rocketed like US Patriot missiles for about six months. This was long enough to generate sufficient cash flow to pay out the debt we had incurred to do the deal. Oil prices reacted somewhat like Iraqi Scud missiles when the incursion was over and we were back to the real world. These marginal producers (given the cost of operating 10,000 foot wells and low net revenue vis-à-vis the working interest) resumed generating marginal cash flow.

I had contacted the operator a few times during our period of ownership but their response was always that these wells were following normal decline rates and we couldn't expect much more. The real problem was the heavy promotional fees due the operator, which we had inherited, making our economics much more burdened than the operator's.

After a couple of years of alternating positive and negative monthly revenues, I bought out most of the partners for the equivalent of all their initial investment plus interest. My original District partner and I then proceeded to see if there was any market for these assets. We eventually disposed of them over a period of two more years and walked away with a small profit for our efforts.

I would describe my personal experience with owning these assets as OK, but it certainly had the potential for disaster many times. We seemed to be blessed with good fortune at exactly the right time in every case. The real miracle was that we came out of a US oil & gas deal unscathed and slightly ahead. We could have got skinned had something unpredictable happened to one of these deep wells during our period of ownership."

In the end everyone was happy; the Receiver, the Purchaser, and RESULTS USA - my consulting trade name. My old adage, **Verify - Verify - Verify**, had again enhanced my performance.

III
(Red Flags And The Blues)

An ominous black smoke infiltrated Inc's space in the second half of 1990. As the saying goes, where there's smoke, there's fire.

We were enveloped in an agonizing quiet spell while the bank and their legal advisors debated when and how to sell off the assets. With the previous years' divestment of all operated properties, the remaining value realization was painful. As in my Ohio and Utah experiences, recoveries of twenty cents on the dollar were the norm. Procrastination had an ugly way of making it worse. My frustration with the delays was no secret.

My role had been considered a one year assignment, after which new ownership would be obliged to deal with the seemingly endless reversals of fortune.

Maintaining a prolonged inactive, non-operated, profile had two disadvantages:

1) the cash flows and property values steadily declined; and

2) U.S. Operations had a mystical attraction for unique disputes (Red Flags) when standard confrontations were no longer practical.

Recognizable by their power to totally usurp control, these Red Flags never failed to shock and infuriate me. What saved my sanity this time was the right person, in the right place, at the right time.

The Firm's Vice President of Finance, Ryan, was experienced in International operations. Although gifted with key negotiating skills of patience and determination, he too would suffer at the mercy of these stamina taxing Red Flags. It is dreadful to speculate how much worse this period would have been without his involvement.

Our first 'joint operation' pitted us against the Internal Revenue Service (IRS) in late summer 1990. Without warning, we received an intimidating notice requiring payment of approximately $55,000 U.S. in Interest and Penalties on Inc's overdue Corporate Tax account. With no knowledge on my part, we referred the vague invoice to Cage's Accounting Department. Again, with little to go on, bewilderment reined supreme.

After numerous enquiries, Ryan determined that foreign accounts were administered from the Philadelphia office. Putting his negotiating skills to the test, he painstakingly threaded his way through the bureaucracy to discover a closely guarded secret.

In 1989, in the midst of Cage's Receivership turmoil, Inc had been credited with an $18,000 U.S. refund on the previous year's assessment. As one would expect, Cage booked the windfall and deposited the cheque in Inc's account. Now two years later, the IRS declared a clerical error erroneously issued the refund instead of invoicing an $18,000 billing.

Accordingly, Inc now had to repay the refund, plus the revised assessment, and $20,000 U.S. in Interest and Penalties. Non payment in full within a specified period would result in additional heavy penalties.

It took a while to verify the 'erroneous' refund. No explanation was attached to the cheque copy that was eventually located in Inc's files. Given the major transactions that occurred in 1988, no one doubted that the refund was plausible and legitimate. Regardless of how deep we delved into Inc's financial past, we could not justify the IRS's assessment claim of $18,000 U.S. owed.

Ryan prepared a comprehensive defence for convincing the IRS to waive the Principal, Interest, and Penalty. In the interest of settlement, we agreed to return the initial $18,000 U.S. Unfortunately, by the time we conveyed our position, the IRS had relocated their foreign account office to San Juan, Puerto Rico.

After witnessing days of negotiations and dialogue lapse into weeks, Ryan deserved pity. He would no sooner get his IRS counterpart on side, then personnel would be rotated.

After several months of unproductive energy by Cage and Inc, our deadline neared where matters were bound to deteriorate further. Progress in convincing the IRS of our position was painfully slow. To close out this Red Flag, Ryan negotiated the best compromise he could under the circumstances.

My focus would have dissipated long before. Even though we were being stripped naked on this financial issue, my hat was off to him for minimizing the pain.

- - - - - - - - - - - -

Continued decline in world oil prices at the end of the decade spawned a unique made-in- America solution to deteriorating cash flows.

Inc's Utah wells were predominately oil with inordinately high operating costs. Production was mostly attributed to Tribal Reserve lands, where royalties were much higher than Freehold burdens. Until 1989, production revenues were subject to a State of Utah 8% Severance Tax and a 4% Withholding tax.

As Utah oil prices hovered between $13.00 - $18.00 U.S. per barrel, the Producers, the State, and the Tribe all witnessed drastic reductions in revenues. For most investors, these deep, labour intensive Wasatch wells had a break-even oil price of $18.00 U.S. or less.

As a consequence, drilling ceased, workovers diminished, and marginal wells were suspended or abandoned. The most common practise for two-well 640 acre leases was to shut-in the least productive well. On one-well sections, the lease would be jeopardized unless production occurred for at least one 24 hour period during the calendar month. Since most wells were equipped with steam powered Triplex pumping units, such well operations, while necessary, were extremely expensive.

To compensate for the loss of royalties, a unilateral production tax of 8% was instituted. The application was parallel to the State Severance Tax. Despite organized protests from the Producers, the Tribal Severance Tax became reality. The failure of the authorities to be responsive and creative was a foreboding Red Flag. On a Provincial comparison, an election might have ensued.

Needless to say, royalties ranging from 25 to 40% and taxes from 16 to 20% left very little of the pie to the one and only oilpatch patriot - the investor.

As expected, lean and mean operations became the battle cry for survival. The challenge was not how much profit could be generated, but if it could be achieved at all. The results were disastrous for Inc's Utah investments. A massive write down in asset value was required.

The delay in marketing Inc's properties proved to be very costly.

- - - - - - - - - - - - - - -

One mitigating approach by Inc to arrest the cash flow drain was to identify and design inexpensive recompletions that would prolong economic life until pricing improved. The detrimental effects of dual taxation was immediate and torturous. The industry began aggressively lobbying for incentives like royalty free holidays for new wells and tax credits for workover investment. Rumours persisted that the State and the Tribe were listening, they just had different hearing sensitivities.

Abandoning a Wasatch well could and did cost up to $100,000 U.S.; therefore any remedial measure to 'buy time' was worthy of consideration. However, in repeated discussions with our major Operator, Cracker Resources, little or no progress was achieved. The main deterrent to compromise was attributed to the wholesale staff turnover in Cracker's Denver office. In addition, the working relationship and respect of previous years had vanished with the abuse of trust by Cracker's Covington office as related in EPISODE 11. Our relationship had become stressful and complicated.

During 1990 one of Cracker's silent partners sold all their interests in the Cracker operated Utah properties. The private purchaser was a new player in the energy field from Salt Lake City. We had many meaningful discussions during the year over prudence of operatorship. Eventually we formed a chemistry, a bond.

The owner, 'Jack', paid a visit to Calgary to negotiate the acquisition of Tripoli's Utah interests. These were the debris left over from the litigation and subsequent bankruptcy of their Operator in 1986.

We spent a great deal of time discussing our mutual interest in improving the value of the Utah properties. One respect where we differed was my strategy for short term gain to facilitate asset marketing. Jack's was for the long term, which in my mind was considered a healthy sign. He indicated his desire and willingness to operate our joint venture properties. He also pointed out that our combined Joint Operating Agreement vote was sufficient to effect an operator change.

It was food for thought, but offering my full support was resisted, pending more verification. I was intrigued with the concept, but cautious of his personality which was foreign to me. It was necessary to get closer to form an opinion. Jack was invited to be our house guest for the week he was in town.

If he was genuine, he represented a solution to Inc's Utah crises. I was also eager to sever my ties with Cracker, maybe too eager.

Against the expressed judgement of close associates and the Firm, my efforts promoted Jack as a successor operator for Utah.

Red Flags, such as inexperience and aloofness, were waving but perhaps my focus occurred only when the winds were calm.

An Operator's meeting was arranged for Cracker's Denver office in November 1990. In Jack's presence, Cracker's performance was comprehensively and critically reviewed. The late arrival of their Vice President of Finance from Covington in mid afternoon only aggravated the tension. Cracker's unco-ordinated, unprepared submissions for future operations sealed their fate in my assessment.

After the all day session, we agreed to disagree. Cracker, as expected, ignored criticism of their operatorship. It followed that they would not consider resigning. We departed amicably, but the writing was on the wall. My decision was to mark time for a couple of months while the implications of our strained working relationship sunk in.

Fate intervened and accelerated the process. Cracker's contract field operator, who had attended the Denver meeting, submitted his resignation several days later.

To maintain the pressure, Bulldog Bender was recalled to audit Cracker's financial records in Covington. His three week assignment resulted in numerous controversial issues. Mac translated his queries into six figure claims for compensation.

"I had never met Jack and accepted the audit assignment based on Neil's assurances that he was good for payment of my services. My arrangement with Jack was that he would advance what we estimated would be the expense portion of the audit. Because timing was so short, Jack agreed to meet me at Salt Lake airport with a cheque.

I bought an airline ticket to New Orleans and arranged for a hotel and car. Covington was across 24 mile wide Lake Pontchartrain from New Orleans (via the only bridge in the world where you are out of sight of land for 8 miles).

Jack never showed up at the airport on the Sunday I was travelling. On the Monday I went to Cracker's office and phoned Jack. I told him the cash advance was needed immediately or I would take my lumps and return home without delay. He apologized, saying his car broke down on the way to the airport, and promised to courier a cheque.

I started on the audit but had a contingency travel plan ready if Jack failed a second time. The cheque arrived the next day made out to my company. Normally it would be impossible to cash this Utah cheque, made out to a foreign company, in Louisiana. I wondered if Jack had considered this. With the help of my Cracker audit contact, I was able to cash the cheque at Cracker's bank. I didn't relish the thought of carrying around $4000 cash, but I was not going to stay without at least this amount.

Lake Pontchartrain Causeway connecting New Orleans with the highlands to the north (8 of its 24 mile length are out of sight of land)

In Cracker's office I was set up in a nice big workroom overlooking 5 acres of 'bush land'; a very nice setting. I didn't have any specific problems conducting the audit. Cracker was the typical U.S. Oil and Gas 'Fund' company. They tried to make as much money from their operations as they did from selling oil and gas. They were very gracious to me as an auditor, despite knowing I would catch a lot of their 'tactics'. I presumed they were prepared to reverse the 'errors' (after a good fight) and carry on till the next audit.

Are you ready for another snake story?

The complex Cracker occupied consisted of 3 office towers 5 or 6 stories high on 160 acres of bush/streams/ponds in the middle of nowhere - at least 3 or 4 miles from any town.

One day I noticed a lot of activity around one of the ponds right outside the building I was in. This went on for quite a while. I asked my audit contact if he knew what was going on, which he didn't. He phoned building security and found out they were the guys who were running around outside.

Apparently a 6 or 7 foot water moccasin had got into the pond and was eating the baby ducks. As a lot of the employees ate their lunches on the grass surrounding these ponds, security were afraid someone was going to get killed with this big deadly snake in the area so they were trying to catch it with snare sticks.

I learned later that the whole area, woods, ponds, etc., were 'full' of water moccasins that were native to the area.

I spent a couple of days in Salt Lake, on my return, trying to educate Jack's accountant. Since I was unable to get a cheque from Jack for my services, I kept the queries and backup for finalization when I got back to Calgary. Although the *queries were finished before I left Salt Lake I had no intention of turning them over to Jack before his cheque cleared my bank account.*

After a couple of weeks without a cheque, I phoned Jack and told him 'no cheque - no queries'. He wasn't very happy with this turn of events but he recognized the potential recoveries were substantial and without the queries he wasn't going to get anything. Eventually he sent a bank draft by courier. When the payment cleared my bank, I sent the queries by courier to Salt Lake. I never heard anything more about the audit after that."

By February 1991 Jack had succeeded Cracker as Operator. For better or for worse, our brief courtship had progressed into marriage. Now what are the odds against marriages of convenience working to the advantage of both parties? We shall see in EPISODE 14. Had I not been so blinded by my emotions, the Red Flag the Firm was waving would have given me this answer a lot sooner.

- - - - - - - - - - - - -

My November trip to Denver served two purposes.

The bank had assumed ownership of additional U.S. oil and gas assets, mostly in California, as the result of another Canadian energy firm bankruptcy. Parry was still the Manager of Special Loans and was on a one week U.S. tour to deal with diverse banking issues. Part of his assignment was to satisfy the requirement for additional legal counsel to represent the bank in a potential environmental dispute in the recently acquired California properties.

Our itineraries would intersect in Denver overnight. Parry was updated on the Tripoli litigation experience in Utah with Chuck years before. My offer was to co-ordinate an unofficial information session for the three of us. Current events in Utah indicated Inc might need counsel as well.

Chuck was informally advised that his services might be of value to the bank, to Inc, or to both. Since it would require his 'infomercial' for us to assess the chemistry of our needs, an after work dinner was suggested for November 16 when Parry was passing through Denver. Inc would pick up the meal tab provided there were no fees from Chuck's law firm and no committal obligations on our part (it was window dressing generosity on my part since the bank ultimately paid Inc's expenses anyway). All parties agreed to the arrangements.

Chuck picked out a trendy, pricey French restaurant, Tante's. The discussions were cordial and constructive. My thirst and appetite dissipated when the second bottle of $40 wine was ordered. My principle of governing my business expenses, as if it were my own money, was unshakeable. Parry and Chuck both recognized my discomfort and encouraged me to relax and savour the moment. Well all 150 of those moments cost $222.46, more than my normal expenses for an entire week on the road. Realizing it was for a valuable and strategic cause, however, I did my best to disguise the pain.

This *was not* the Red Flag. My affiliation with spending habits of bankers and lawyers had been dismissed long ago.

Upon my return to Calgary, Parry informed me that the bank would not be pursuing a business relationship with Chuck's firm. His response was diplomatic and avoided implicit justification.

During the next several months Chuck performed minor legal services for Inc, including the Utah operator change. In his first billing statement was an entry of three hours on November 16, 1990 for approximately $500. Red Flag with a bull charging through!

Chuck was challenged immediately.

His explanation was that he logged chargeable hours in one diary and non-chargeable in another so the firm knew all his itineraries. His Secretary must have inadvertently combined both. He agreed the November 16 charge was non-chargeable and inappropriate. It was deducted from the invoice balance, with a note of clarification for the record.

There was far more to this slip-up, as you will learn in EPISODE 14. Failing to recognize the importance of this Red Flag would result in my ultimate assassination.

The Firm also expressed grave concerns about Chuck's billings. Countless $50 range entries added $400 to $500 to each month's invoice. On examination we verified these charges as phone calls. Many were one minute duration or less but charged at a minimum quarter hour litigation rate. In some cases no contact had been established; in others they represented mutual public relations.

Begrudgingly we had a conversation about this sensitive issue. Several logical solutions were offered, but the only effective adjustment was a drastic reduction in phone calls. In my mind, it was the least desirable and accommodating.

In U.S. operations, **Verify-Verify-Verify**, there are no exceptions.

- - - - - - - - - - - - -

Early in 1991 the bank commissioned updated Reserve Reports for Inc's three CRI entities. With an effective date of January 1, they would represent the first independent asset evaluation since 1988. The complexity of tax credit allocation, combined with the uncertainty of economic proven and probable reserves, prompted this action on an urgency basis.

Although we had internal assessments, asset marketing required a Security and Exchange Commission (SEC) engineering evaluation format.

I had worked with several firms in the past, mostly out of Denver. My contacts had been informed of the tendering terms and conditions. It was clear that cost was a governing factor. The industry was hungry and the two bids we received were very competitive and within my price guideline.

Another lesson in judgement was learned here that was unnecessary. Although both firms were knowledgeable with Inc's properties and had prepared previous evaluations, the contract was awarded based on the lowest bid. The competitor was only $4000 U.S. higher, but was more sophisticated in production data base, decline graphics, and economic evaluation software.

In the small to mid-sized energy production and service companies, Canadian equivalents were far more computer skilled and equipped. From my experience, our Regulatory authorities like the ERCB and NEB were superior in data control to their U.S. counterparts. Because of these shortcomings, considerable time and energy was required on our part to supplement the accuracy of the evaluations.

It was not that the final product was not acceptable. Quite the contrary; however, in the end the financial savings did not justify the means.

The three Reserve Reports were completed by 31 March 1991, on time and on budget. Each one represented an alarming Red Flag.

The estimated proven and probable Present Worth Values, discounted at 15%, were well below the bank's expectations. Optimistic pricing scenarios were influenced by near record high oil prices; yet the bottom line results were frightening and discouraging.

CRI (Michigan) Inc was valued at $60,000 U.S., hardly worth its share of the evaluation cost. CRI (Texas) Inc at roughly $6,000,000 U.S. and CRI (Utah) Inc at roughly $2,000,000 U.S. were less than half the values needed to substantiate ten of millions of dollars in tax credits.

To verify the accuracy of these evaluations, detailed 1991/1992 Cash Flow Forecasts were prepared. CRI (Michigan) Inc's contribution was insignificant, at $6000 U.S. CRI (Texas) Inc ranged from $340,000 - $462,000 U.S. and CRI (Utah) Inc from $28,000 - $62,000 U.S. The wide range of revenues were dependent on workover implementation and success.

Without considerable investment, which was not a preferable option, annual production decline would continue to average 15%. On the other hand, the Gulf War had resulted in the highest crude oil prices in a decade. The aftermath created temporary political and military uncertainty, both valuable ingredients for oilpatch optimism. The timing for aggressive marketing of Inc's assets was unique. A Red Flag flapped incessantly. To do nothing would oversee the demise of the bank's investment.

My immediate reaction was to promote the sale of these properties without delay. Too much valuable time had already been lost. A divestiture plan among the bank, the Firm, and RESULTS USA was long overdue. The longer the powers in control hesitated on a commitment, the more it seemed my assignment would lead to failure. Energy was vainly expended; in the end it was beyond my control to influence.

- - - - - - - - - - - - -

In the spring of 1991 Ryan and I teamed up against another first time opponent.

The Utah Minerals Management Service (MMS) was a Federal Government agency assigned to protect resource exploitation on Tribal lands. It administered drilling licenses, collected taxes and royalties, provided legal and financial auditing services to the Tribe, and regulated environmental legislation.

We had no argument with the concept. In Canada, activity on Crown lands was subject to similar scrutiny. The major difference, and advantage, separating Alberta from Utah was our independent vehicle of appeal to settle disputes or render judgements.

Ryan and I found out, from exhaustive frustration, that a decision levied by the MMS is a fait accompli. The more logic we introduced into our argument, the more convoluting and damaging the consequences.

The MMS invoiced CRI (Utah) Inc for roughly $65,000 U.S. in royalties due from production during the period 1981 to 1983. A *unilateral new* accounting procedure was introduced to determine Tribal royalties on natural gas. Payment was demanded from all Operators on Raw Gas volumes produced at the wellhead. This burden was in addition to royalties paid on Sales Gas volumes by the Producers and NGL volumes by the Plant Owners.

The industry referred to this "royalty re-assessment" as the Dual Accounting System.

To everyone except the MMS, it was obvious that proper royalties had already been submitted on all sales products. To apply these royalties to raw gas prior to transportation and processing was simply unjustified, a double penalty.

CRI (Utah) Inc was singled out for these specific three years because Cage Resources Inc was Operator of Record during part of this period. Failure to comply with the MMS payment schedule would bring harsh penalties to the Operator. At least, that is the message that was implied. In defence, the industry maintained it had honoured, and would honour, royalties on any product that *achieved revenue*. Again, to all but the MMS, raw gas in itself did not represent a revenue generator.

Ryan, exhausted himself researching old Inc financial records and preparing a submission. Not only did he verify that royalties had been paid on all sales, he also determined that Inc had been overcharged by roughly $45,000 U.S. during the period. It was further disclosed that Inc relinquished operatorship to Cracker in the middle of the period in question.

Ryan used tact and diplomacy in dealing with this issue day after day, but with little apparent headway. Eventually the MMS relented. They accepted that Inc had, in fact, been overcharged from 1981 to 1983 and was not liable for the entire period.

It was then reasoned that the gas volumes applied to the Dual Accounting calculations were overstated. Factoring in these amendments, the MMS claim against Inc was reduced to $25,000 U.S.

To our disappointment, the MMS insisted Inc provide a cheque for the $25,000 surcharge. In exchange, they would then consider refunding Inc's $40,000 U.S. overcharge. The Interest due on the $25,000 would be forgiven.

Right, and the Tooth Fairy would deliver our refund in person.

I fought with Ryan not to comply. Tantrums were thrown to emphasize my point that recovery of our refund would be more complicated if we paid the MMS *first*. Logic dictated the only payment due was $15,000 U.S. from the MMS to Inc.

Inc paid the MMS $25,000. Our pleas to reciprocate with our $40,000 were unsuccessful. Yet the negotiations were considered a success! Why?

The outcome was not a Red Flag, since it was expected. The lesson learned from Ryan was to focus on the bigger picture.

Each month we duelled with the MMS cost Inc thousands of dollars in legal fees to Chuck's law firm. Every correspondence had to be subjected to legal scrutiny. It was the only authority the MMS would recognize, since they had their own legal department and were prepared for prolonged disagreements. Meanwhile the Operators bled white.

These costs could have continued indefinitely if Ryan had not negotiated an acceptable compromise. Our obligation would have remained $65,000 or more. We would have burnt ourselves out in frustration, despair, and costs. Any attempts to sell the Utah properties would have met with interference and resistance.

In this coin toss, Tails we lose, Heads the MMS wins. We could not win, only limit our losses.

This was the Red Flag that was synonymous with my U.S. operational experience. Ryan helped me open my eyes to reason, even when it hurt.

IV
(Purpose Denied)

With each passing day of 1991 we dug deeper to get to the root of our Red Flags, only to discover we were farther from the surface without a ladder.

Cognizant of the new Reserve Reports and Red Flag alienation, Inc's assets were actively marketed. Not that I had specific instructions or support to do so; given the circumstances, doing anything otherwise would be considered counter-productive at the very least. The temporary surge in energy prices during Desert Storm was a window of opportunity.

Relying on an extensive network, purchase offers were solicited from a lengthy list of candidates. CRI (Texas) Inc drew serious interest from seven U.S. industry players. CRI (Utah) Inc drew four enquiries. CRI (Michigan) Inc was a three State, nine well liability of small Working and Overriding Royalty Interests - a door prize for the successful bidder of Texas or Utah.

By setting an early summer deadline for offers, the hope was to cash in while merger and acquisition optimism was still king. I worked diligently and tirelessly to bring in written offers that would be acceptable; $2,000,000 U.S. for CRI (Texas) and $450,000 U.S. for CRI (Utah).

My prayers were that the oil market would hold up long enough to consummate the sales. With offers representing six to eight times Cash Flow, it never occurred to me that my logic and ambition to sell was without support. It was a cruel irony. Rather than praise for taking the initiative, indifference and alienation greeted me. Asset values had deteriorated so dramatically and quickly that neither the Firm nor the bank were prepared for the shock of these offer levels.

To my knowledge, both offers expired without serious dialogue. This failure was taken personally. It was difficult to imagine how future offers could be more creative or generous.

The months that followed were difficult in my career development. While Inc required a great deal of accounting and lease administration, the needs for my engineering services were limited. As a distraction, numerous Placement Agency and Classified employment ads were entertained.

To walk away would have been the easy way out. After making peace with my conscience, it was decided to see my assignment through to a conclusion. The stronger my commitment, the more determined was my goal setting.

In early November 1991, I flew to Austin, Texas to attend a TRRC Hearing. 'Newbirth' was the operator for one of our deep Hemphill County gas wells. They had petitioned the TRRC to approve pooling together their group of recently drilled gas discoveries.

CRI (Texas) Inc had a 20% Working Interest in the newest well, Aprilson #1. In the other wells, Newbirth not only operated but also owned most of the interests. These wells were very prolific and were allocated most of the gathering system capacity. Several had exceeded 1 BCF of production and were experiencing steep decline. Now the reserves assigned to Aprilson #1 were about to be shared under a pooling arrangement that would legalize the drainage and minimize our value.

I had struggled for half a year to convince Newbirth to acidize and fracture (stimulate) our completion in order to compete with the productivity of their offsetting wells. Countless letters and phone calls had failed to get Newbirth's attention.

The TRRC Hearing was brought to my attention accidentally through one of my sources in Amarillo. Newbirth was advised that Inc would intervene if a stimulation workover AFE for Aprilson #1 was not forthcoming. My engineering counterparts were cordial, but they *never* delivered. Our relationship degenerated as my calls went unanswered. It was time for a stronger voice of reason.

Through the bank's network Inc hired 'Bates', an Austin law firm. By design, my early afternoon arrival preceded the Hearing. There was just enough time to tour Austin, another one of my favourite American cities on a par, scenery-wise, with San Antonio. A meeting had also been scheduled with Bates 's attorney assigned to represent Inc next day, if necessary.

'Sharon' had studied the Aprilson #1 background thoroughly and was well prepared to protect our interests. We respected each other's preference to avoid litigation. On the other hand, it was reassuring that Sharon would be a most competent counsel if called upon.

Next morning we introduced ourselves and our mission to the shocked and disbelieving Newbirth counsel. He claimed to have no knowledge of our 'stimulation' dispute, but he was most distressed at the spectre of Inc challenging his Pooling presentation to the TRRC.

Unlike my past failed efforts, Sharon ensured our well performance concerns were taken seriously. A frantic series of phone calls ensued with Newbirth's Head Office. Minutes before the Hearing began we received written confirmation that a workover would be designed and submitted for approval within fifteen days. This commitment was fulfilled.

Sharon's representation was most impressive. We observed Newbirth's presentation, which was an eye opener, but we did not challenge. Our objective was obtained at minimal cost and effort. What a difference a dedicated lawyer makes! It symbolised a generic secret to U.S. operations; no lawyer, no respect.

One goal down, two to go.

Most of the bank's technical decisions for their U.S. oil and gas assets originated with their Houston office. I drove from Austin to Houston to specifically spend a few days with the bank's Senior Petroleum Engineer, 'Huey'.

Parry had been sympathetic with my views for selling Inc's assets as soon as possible. Since the Houston office had an influential say in the matter, he recommended my convincing begin with them.

In advance of scheduled meetings with Huey, copies of Inc's 1991 budgets and 1992 forecasts were forwarded. Technical property assessments and Red Flag summaries supported my views. Huey's active involvement during preparation of the Reserve Reports precluded lengthy duplication of their input accuracy.

Our discussions were very constructive and frank. We addressed the major Texas and Utah properties in detail. We concluded the recent Reserve Reports were far too generous in allocating probable value to recompletions and undeveloped acreage. In the end, Huey agreed with the pessimistic future of my predictions.

With the Gulf War long over, the strength and stability of oil prices had disintegrated. We independently concluded that 1992 would be a Cash Flow disaster. Any hope of selling Inc's assets for a positive recovery rested with immediate leadership.

By the time of my return to Calgary, the bank had conferred with Houston. In addition, Inc had become the last "Special Loan" account. Eliminating these assets and closing the books was now an urgency. Hasty sale of the properties was encouraged.

Two goals down, one to go.

Wasting no time, a second round of purchase offers were solicited. Being creative with the Effective Sale Date forced the successful bid for CRI (Texas) **up to** exactly half the rejected summer offer. Closing occurred on 31 December 1991 to accommodate beneficial tax implications. The successful conclusion was a relief, but agony over the amount of money left on the table in just six months was painful.

Much of January 1992 was spent packing and labelling over a hundred boxes of files and records for shipment to Tulsa. Not only were there no bites on CRI (Michigan), we could not even give it away with CRI (Texas).

In the meantime sale negotiations continued slowly for CRI (Utah). There were more gremlins in the Utah closets, many without immediate solution. At the end of January I flew to Salt Lake City for presentations. The double severance taxation heat had finally forced the State to announce a tax credit program for the first $50,000 capital investment per well. While confidence was still a long way off, at least it was a step in the right direction.

A sale was concluded after bargaining for the inclusion of CRI (Michigan), which had now become a liability. Closing for CRI (Utah) occurred at the end of March. Again the successful bid was half the rejected summer 1991 offer. The Firm supervised post sale adjustments and shipment of files, as they had handled CRI (Texas).

In early April it was pointed out that my role had become redundant at the Firm. My departure did not bother me, knowing that a few more months delay in selling the assets might have reduced the values half as much again. The recoveries, while exceeding my interpretation of worth, were a fraction of December 1989 expectations.

My third goal of achieving total disposition had been achieved. In my opinion, however, there were no winners. In assessing the purpose of the bank's assignment two and one half years before, it was a purpose denied. My agony was the responsibility for letting the bank down.

An April 03, 1992 letter from the bank lessened the pain and frustration considerably.

"I would like to thank you for the excellent work you performed in managing and selling the oil and gas assets of Cage Resources Inc.

While I realize that there were difficult times during this process for you, your perseverance and determination ensured that the job was done in a professional manner.

Should you ever require any references for future employment do not hesitate to use my name for this purpose.

Thanks again.

Parry"

An uncertain future in the world of consulting, at a vulnerable time in the industry, was my reward. No severance packages in this line of work!

Expecting to office out of my home, I inquired whether the bank would sell me the furniture that had been used at the Firm. It had a long history. The sturdy, solid oak construction had caught my eye during the Denver office closure of 1985. Although it was relocated to the Calgary office, there was no opportunity to use it until Inc's relocation to the Firm in December 1989. My attachment was the thought that it represented the end of an era - the last vestige of U.S. Operations and misery.

EPISODE 13: PARTNERSHIP-DARE TO BE DIFFERENT

I
(Deck Sense)

If only it had been raining that warm mid-May afternoon. I was sunning on my deck, marvelling the unimpeded mountain view and nursing a cold beer. A cordless phone was beside me to avoid disturbing my tranquillity by running for any calls. Not that any were expected, but my resume had been passively circulated during the past month.

It had been four or five weeks since the final Closing of the CRI assets and my departure from the Firm. A change of career opportunities should have been chased more diligently, but relaxing in the fresh air, admiring Nature, was too peaceful an alternative.

The ringing phone startled me but even more so was the sound of 'Donald's' voice. He was the President of a small private Salt Lake City oil and gas investment firm. He specialized in farming in on exploitation prospects and promoting the drilling costs to investors for a fee or Carried Interest. Donald's focus area was Nevada.

" Any progress with Lake Valley? "

During the past year we conversed several times, but this was our first connection since my becoming unemployed. Donald was always cordial and our topic predictable. Less than a year had transpired since the gambling bug had bitten me.

In June 1991, I was approached by 'Rob', the President of a Geophysical firm in Calgary. We had worked together at Shell in the late 1970s. Over the years we confided on our career paths. Rob was well aware of my U.S. background and experience.

A Geologist friend of Rob's from Okotoks, Alberta had exchanged his technical services for a small overriding royalty in an eastern Nevada exploration play promoted by Donald's firm. Solicitation of Joint Venture participants to drill a discovery well by 1992 was actively pursued on both sides of the border. Rob was helping his friend out and provided me with a technical brochure which included extensive data on a large acreage package called Lake Valley.

It was a strange coincidence.

Inc had recognized the potential of eastern Nevada in the mid-1980s. After subleasing 100,000 contiguous acres in Lincoln County, comprehensive geological and engineering studies were prepared for a multi-well drilling program.

Coincidental with the closure of Inc's Denver office and Corporate restructuring, Inc's exploration budget was all but eliminated by the bank; therefore Inc was unable to take on the costly seismic and drilling commitments. Subsequently several prospects, called Page Creek and Pioche Creek, were Farmed Out to an American suitor. Unfortunately the Farmee was a merger victim a year later, and all Lincoln County acreage expired without any progress.

It was astonishing that Inc's old prospect had been resurrected and renamed after six years in obscurity. Based on my familiarization in 1986, my opinion was optimistic for the potential. Two deep wells had been drilled by Amoco between 1981 and 1983 within a five mile radius of Donald's projected new drilling location. A consortium headed by a Canadian junior, Brent Energy, drilled a later offset two and one half miles directly west in 1984.

The attractiveness of this prospect stemmed from the fact that each well had encountered hydrocarbons in numerous horizons. Lost Circulation problems (loss of quantities of whole mud to a formation, evidenced by the complete or partial failure of the mud to return to the surface as it is being circulated in the hole) during drilling resulted in each well being grossly over budget and under valued. There were, however, plenty of technical signs that successful adventurists seek.

In our discussions, Rob was informed that the bank intended to divest itself of all U.S. oil and gas properties. In fact, purchase offers for the CRI assets were being actively solicited. I undertook to present it as a participation opportunity anyway, given its plagiaristic roots. As expected, the bank was not interested in this high risk, capital intensive venture.

After reviewing the latest prospect information Rob provided, I advised him of my willingness to seek investors on a consulting arrangement. He put me in touch with Donald and we worked out verbal compensation terms. RESULTS USA would earn one and one half to two percent (1 1/2% - 2 %) Gross Overriding Royalty for Working Interests solicited by my efforts.

The failure of my initial attempts to sell Inc's assets afforded an opportunity in late summer 1991 to test the market for Lake Valley. My contacts throughout the U.S. were networked, particularly 'Mikael' in Amarillo, 'Kimberly' in Houston, and 'Duggan' in Denver. No serious enquiries materialized from these solicitations. When the bank's urgency to dispose of Inc transpired in November 1991, Lake Valley was put behind me.

Now in May 1992, Donald's call wetted my thirst like a cold beer. He caught me at my most vulnerable time; pondering my future. Donald updated me on his plans.

Seismic and gravity studies had identified an attractive structure for drilling. A noted local Geologist specializing in Nevada had prepared cross sections. Several hydrocarbon formations were targeted for the initial well, which was 40% committed. A Drilling Permit was in progress for a late summer spud date.

In what would prove to be a most tragic response, Donald was assured some investors were being considered and priority would be assigned to soliciting their interest. Talk was cheap. Although several local participation candidates came to mind, convincing them of the prospect's attributes was another matter. After all, it was a *U.S. operation* and no one need have heeded the warnings more than me.

Although unemployed for only a short time, my conscience was already getting restless and critical of my lack of purpose. Sunning on the front deck and admiring the Rocky Mountains had grown stale. Even so, lacking the infrastructure and industry contacts associated with an office environment, it was unclear where and how to start marketing Lake Valley.

May 1992 was one of the warmest in years. Probably more beers were consumed relaxing on my deck in one month than in all previous months since we acquired our home in 1987. For several days after Donald's call, my routine involved more of the same....and pondered.

II
(CRI To The Rescue?)

The CRI (Utah) Inc and CRI (Michigan) Inc assets had been purchased by an international consulting 'firm' with headquarters in Calgary. The ownership had an extensive background evaluating

Utah operations dating back to the Altamont Field discovery in 1972. The subsequent success of many Wasatch wells was owed to the firm's innovative completion techniques.

In the decades since, significant technical research and improved computer simulation had perfected the firm's services. They gradually concluded it would be opportune to apply their expertise and contributions as an investor.

The firm's acquisition of Inc's Utah, Michigan, and Mississippi assets was their first foray into owning and managing producing properties. Apparently it turned out to be more challenging than anticipated.

On May 20 a phone call was received from the President of the firm. It was followed up by a letter.

> *"I was quite surprised when I telephoned you this morning at the Firm and I was informed that you are not with that company any longer. The girl who answered the phone very kindly gave me your number at home, and that is how after some thought, I decided to give you a call.*
>
> *Neil, as I indicated by telephone, I have been thinking about hiring an engineer to assist me with the Utah properties and in some other consulting projects that we anticipate will come mainly from China and Vietnam. I think that with your experience you would be an asset to our organization.*
>
> *If you think that you might be interested in this opportunity, please send me a copy of your Resume. Once I have an opportunity to review it, I will give you a call to set up an appointment so that we can discuss these possibilities in some detail.*
>
> *I will look forward, with interest, to your reply."*

The connection between my search for a Lake Valley candidate and this opportunity could not be ignored. It was too premature to assume the firm would be interested in Nevada. At the very least, however, the option for immediate employment and a base of operations for my consulting services was in my control.

Once again, against my better judgement and conscience, it was back to U.S. operations. An escape door was wide open, but I kicked it shut. The pain remains in my toes to this day.

My last chance to reason my way out disappeared with the execution of a June 1, 1992 Letter Agreement from the firm.

> *"As you are aware, the firm has acquired the petroleum and natural gas assets of CRI (Utah) Inc.*

Respectfully, the firm requests the benefit of your engineering and management services and is prepared to compensate you as per the fee schedule attached to your letter of May 25, 1992. Subject to your approval, it is requested that you continue to represent the firm in the capacity of U.S. Operations Manager.

To properly effect the management of these properties, we would expect your services for approximately 40 hours per month.

Should the forgoing opportunity be acceptable to you, please so indicate by signing and dating below returning one copy to the undersigned."

My first day "back to the future" was June 08, 1992 , as heralded by the following inter-office memorandum of that date.

"Mr. Neil Leeson, P. Eng. has joined the firm as U.S. Operations Manager. Mr. Leeson will be looking after all oil and gas properties in the USA and will provide consulting services as required.

I would appreciate the assistance you can provide Mr. Leeson to fulfil his tasks in an efficient manner."

III
(CRI (Michigan): Door Prize To Booby Prize)

Having extensive knowledge of the Utah and Michigan properties was a major liability. It was a drawback that had not been considered.

My daily routine was not challenging enough to satisfy my new-found ambitions. Two months of freedom had ignited uncharacteristic expectations for *new* adventures. The sooner the current operations were mastered, the sooner the firm's participation in Lake Valley could be solicited.

From this point on, all my strategy was geared towards creating a favourable financial balance sheet to facilitate expansion into Nevada while the opportunity lasted.

CRI (Michigan) lived up to its' administrative inconvenience reputation. Considering the annual accounting, management, and Government reporting requirements, breaking even represented a major accomplishment.

Two solutions were presented to the firm and both were accepted after consideration.

Firstly; the CRI (Michigan) Inc account included an extensive inventory of proprietary Michigan seismic tapes and records. Acquired at great expense by Inc during the early 1980s, it was used to purchase significant acreage and drill several exploratory wells on the 'Clark Hoser' prospect. Several millions of dollars were invested and lost in dry holes. In the mid-1980s the unexpired leases were turned over to 'Klinger and Associates' of Tulsa, the original promoter, in exchange for waiver of outstanding drilling and management fees.

Since then this seismic inventory had remained stored at 'Many Data', a climate controlled facility in Denver. The annual fee of $600 U.S. included marketing and leasing services. Unfortunately, to my knowledge, no revenue was ever generated from sales or rentals. Likewise, Inc had been unsuccessful in this endeavor.

The firm had neither the finances nor inclination to reprocess seismic tapes representing nearly 200 miles of data. Furthermore, we were unprepared to utilize any results to drill high risk, deep tests in Michigan. A previous experience had alerted me that valuable oil industry data was in demand by universities for technical training purposes. Donations to accredited U.S. schools qualified for Federal Income Tax Credits to the value assigned by the beneficiary.

Beginning in September 1992, Petroleum Engineering Departments of northeast universities were sent a letter describing our seismic assets. For good measure, selective distinguished western U.S. schools in Colorado and Nebraska were included. We proposed donating the entire inventory in exchange for Federal Tax Credits. Since all seismic lines were shot in Michigan and Pennsylvania, the acquisition would appeal mostly to schools in those two States.

By the beginning of 1993 we had addressed half a dozen serious enquiries. In March we received a Letter of Intent from a university in Ohio. With the assistance of Many Data, samplings of the tapes were checked for quality and documents for completeness. Satisfied, the Ohio university offered Federal Tax Credits in the amount of $330,000 U.S., provided we pay for shipping from Denver.

Our transaction was finalized in May 1993. We rid ourselves of an unwanted liability in exchange for packing and trucking costs of $540. U.S. Again Many Data's assistance was invaluable. Given the annual storage fee, payout of this cost was less than a year.

The Federal Tax Credit Policy stipulated application of the value immediately, phased in equally over five years. There was no provision for carryover on expiry. If the firm's Revenues could be increased to a level where these Tax Credits kicked in, substantial savings in U.S. Income taxes would be realized.

The Ohio university, on the other hand, had in-house facilities and expertise for reprocessing and evaluating the seismic tapes. In addition to the training value, private investment and Federal Grants were available for oil and gas exploration in the event their efforts exploited overlooked potential.

It was a deal that served all parties well. There were no regrets.

- - - - - - - - - - - - - -

Secondly; during divestiture negotiations for CRI (Texas) in late 1991, Parry returned from a U.S. banking tour and passed on an investment prospectus. One of the bank's clients in Denver had approached him for participation in a Pennsylvania development drilling project. Parry immediately discounted the bank's involvement, but offered it for my personal review. He left it up to my discretion to ignore or investigate.

It was a very comprehensive and professionally prepared report. As a courtesy, the company President, 'Barry', was phoned in Denver. Although no participation candidates had come to mind, he was advised of my general interest. We agreed to revisit when appropriate.

In November 1992 Barry's business card caught my attention. I decided to give him a call and introduce the firm, my new association, and inquire about Pennsylvania.

As luck would have it, the second phase of his drilling program from the previous year had been finalized recently. It had been aggressively marketed, resulting in 70 percent subscription. The prospectus was delivered by courier within a few days for my evaluation.

Although a long way from home, Barry's company was well positioned in Indiana County, Pennsylvania. He operated over one hundred wells, many of which Barry's company had a Working Interest. From my experience, it was a reassuring sign when an operator put his money where his mouth was.

The drilling targets were multiple but thin gas sands from 3000 to 3500 feet. Standard Drilling and Completion AFE costs ranged from $140,000 to $150,000 U.S.

Supply and demand in the gas starved U.S. northeast States supported a healthy gas market. Prices of $3.00 U.S. per MCF in winter months were common. Otherwise, $2.00 U.S. per MCF for the remainder of the year was more than sufficient to sustain positive cash flows.

Although average well deliverability was only 50 to 75 MCF per day, Pennsylvania taxes were among the lowest in the United States. Operating costs, under Barry's management, historically averaged an impressively low $500 U.S. per well per month or less.

Despite the obvious similarities with my Ohio nightmares of the past, technical evaluations of Barry's completions revealed substantially unrecognized opportunity. The firm's expertise in completion techniques could improve performance and recoverable reserves.

As well, our log research revealed a thick, porous, shallow hydrocarbon sand. No well had attempted completion at this depth. No reference to its' presence was detected in our review of well files or in our conversations with Barry. Our reservoir calculations, *assuming* gas, indicated recoverable reserves of 1.75 to 2.00 BCF per 640 acres. Barry's wells were drilled on 80 acre spacing units.

To wet our appetite even more, numerous local wells containing this attractive reservoir were uneconomic as a result of depletion of the deeper sands. Many more were suspended, pending plugging and abandonment. Keeping this discovery close to our vests for the time being, we queried Barry on the feasibility of acquiring shut-in wells for salvage value. Barry responded that he was negotiating to add approximately forty such wells to his operations at the completion of the current three-well drilling program.

Our caution with participation abated. We insisted, however, that our investment be on a per well basis rather than committing to the entire program.

In return for subscribing to the entire remaining 30% participation in the next well, Barry agreed to grant us latitude on the completion design. Furthermore, if our technical theory held true, we would be rewarded. The 10% promotional fee on our Working Interest would be removed at payout, which the firm anticipated in less than a year.

Using advanced computer modelling of offset well logs, we identified two distinct deep sands of high quality. Our proposed design guaranteed that each would be completed and tested separately.

The standard approach used by local operators was to independently perforate and fracture stimulate half a dozen sands and then co-mingle their production. Initial rates of 75 to 100 MCF per day invariably declined to 50 to 75 MCF per day by the end of the first or second month. Within six months of steady production, these rates traditionally stabilized in the 25 to 50 MCF per day range. Average life in excess of ten years was not uncommon.

We were eager to test our research. Our first Joint Venture well, VH #3, was spudded in December 1992.

The deepest of the two sands identified in our study was independently perforated. Instead of high strength HCL acid and large volumes of sand used in local completion designs, our strategy called for only 3% KCL water. Interpretation of technical data convinced us of the presence of natural fracturing in this sand, precluding elaborate and costly stimulation requirements.

Rates in the first month averaged 125 to 150 MCF per day.

In the second month the completed sand was isolated with a retrievable bridge plug (RBP) (a downhole tool composed primarily of slips, a plug mandrel, and a rubber sealing element, that is run and set in casing to isolate a lower zone from an upper zone). The upper sand was then perforated and sand fractured as it had less permeability. After a month of independent testing, this sand also had averaged 125 MCF per day.

Since the winter was winding down, we wanted to capitalize on seasonal $3.00 per MCF gas prices.

We proposed a workover program to Barry for removing the RBP and installing tubing with a packer to isolate the two sets of perfs. The lower naturally fractured sand would produce up tubing. The upper stimulated, tighter, but lower pressured sand would produce up the annulus between tubing and casing. The two sands were approximately seventy-five feet apart.

As agreed, Barry prepared the AFE as we proposed and telecopied it for our approval.

Remember my adage for U.S. Operations from other EPI-SODES; **Verify - Verify - Verify.**

In the design and manufacture of downhole packers, the BAKER trademark is synonymous with quality and performance.

The workover presented no complications. It was a routine operation and was accomplished in one day.

After less than a week of combined deliverability of 225 to 250 MCF per day, the packer mysteriously released, permitting pressure communication between the two zones. Water and frac sand infiltration from the upper sand was the immediate result of pressure equalization between two unequally developed reservoirs.

Everything possible to retrieve the malfunctioning packer was attempted in the first few days. By the end of the first week, the downhole situation deteriorated rapidly.

With less than one hundred feet of Rat Hole, stimulation and/or formation water from the upper sand permeated past the packer and restricted gas production from the lower set of perfs.

As the top sand discharged frac sand in minor amounts, it accumulated on top of the packer and eventually interfered with production from the upper perfs.

The combined gas rate quickly declined to 100 MCF per day.

A second week of remedial efforts did not accomplish anything other than additional cost. The tubing string was solidly seized in the hole, aided by water and sand flushing out of the upper completion. The combination of these two effluents made it impossible to dislodge the packer.

We considered the option of cutting off the tubing above the packer with mechanical or chemical cutters, but this operation was risky, expensive, and still would not extricate the packer. That would require an additional step of drilling out the hardened steel and rubber tool, also an expensive and risky venture.

Based on my conversations with Barry and reports from the field, it appeared the quality of local expertise and equipment was not unlike my Ohio adventures. It was devastating.

In the end, after a month of soul searching and experimenting, we resigned ourselves to our fate. Well performance was less than half our expectations and remedial packer recovery attempts had added $25,000 U.S. to the well costs.

It was disheartening, since our innovative and simplified completion design had reduced the drilling and completion costs from the AFE budget of $145,000 to actual expenses of $125,000. Initial performance translated into an unprecedented one year payout or less. How, why, what, and where did our plans go astray?

We and Barry eventually learned that the 'BAKER' packer was not a BAKER packer. Budgeted at a new BAKER price in the AFE, it was actually a hybrid of salvaged used packers and mediocre spare parts. After assembly in a backyard garage in Parkersburg, West Virginia (yep, you guessed it, my old haunting grounds from EPISODE 2 and you could not imagine my distress on learning these details), "Mr. Baker" sold them privately. Barry had no way of knowing and was equally despondent.

Subsequently we discovered that many of Mr. Baker's packers had similar failures and he was at a loss for the reason or corrective solution. Naturally there was no warranty and therefore no recourse for compensation.

Barry and I had more than one aggressive discussion about equipment quality, downhole or otherwise. In the future, we both agreed my old operations adage would apply.

Verify - Verify - Verify!

We did go on to drill a second well in November of 1993. This time, we designed an open hole completion in the naturally fractured lower sand for VH #4. The average rate of 85 to 100 MCF per day was less than expected but still remarkable for the area. In addition, we further reduced drilling and completion costs to $100,000 U.S.

When Barry forwarded an AFE for a third well in March 1994, we were vehemently opposed. Our research indicated it was too close (centred in an adjacent twenty acre lease) to our most recent producer and would drain reserves already adequately exposed.

Bolstered by our first two successes (even the troubled first well remained legend), Barry had little trouble getting investors to assume our 30% share.

As we predicted, this latest well encroached on our VH #4 , reducing our deliverability to less than 50 MCF per day. VH #5, lacking our involvement and completion expertise, watered out after a few months and had to be suspended. Meanwhile our VH #4 never recovered to full health. As a result, the payout forecast was extended to five years from one and one half.

In all this time we continued to query Barry on the availability of purchasing or farming in on suspended wellbores. We wisely concluded the drilling game would strip us naked. For a quarter of the price and much less risk, we could recomplete the shallow sand and add substantial reserves to the books of CRI (Michigan). Talk was cheap. Barry was never able to consummate any of his intended deals; at least that was our understanding.

In April 1994 we addressed a letter to all the local Operators and Working Interest owners. Our offer included options to sell outright or farm out their interests to us in wells scheduled for plug and abandonment. There were no takers.

This ended our ambitions to build CRI (Michigan) into a viable, self sufficient entity. Despite being granted control of these Pennsylvania operations, we ultimately realized it was a hollow authority. CRI (Michigan) assets had been included in the sale of the Utah assets as a Door Prize. By mid-1993 they had become a Booby Prize.

It was naive of me to have expected otherwise.

IV
(UTAH: Round Three - Down And Out In Wasatch Hills)

Utah operations by far were the most time consuming and critical component of the firm's acquisition from Inc. Most of the 22 wells were operated by Jack and on Tribal leases. This combination had the potential to be unpredictable and dangerous.

As with the CRI (Michigan) assets, my approach to the Utah assets was to minimize the workload and operational costs. My aspirations remained focused on the potential of Lake Valley. An optimization strategy was presented to the firm which was readily adopted.

Instead of a plan for long range success, it turned out to be the first step in a nightmare of failure. These were my recommendations, however, and the buck stopped with me.

Given the firm's expertise in reservoir simulation and completion design, contemplating a future Working Interest position in Nevada was natural. Initial well costs were estimated at $750,000 U.S. Existing acreage participation another $50,000 U.S. Unless drastic measures were implemented, the firm's Cash Flow would be unable to facilitate the 10% - 20% ownership envisioned for Lake Valley.

My first proposal was to sell a portion of the Utah assets to Jack, whom I knew was eager to acquire additional holdings in the Uinta Basin.

Nevada did not totally influence my judgement, nor did desperation. Since my initial exposure to U.S. Operations in Ohio, operators with little or no personal commitment in the properties they managed represented Red Flags.

From my research and forecasts at the Firm, it was known that significant workover investment would be required to maintain

Suspended 'Kay' well, facing southeast (note lease size)

Suspended 'Kay' lease, facing north (Blacktail Ridge behind)

East side 'Forrester' well (triplex pump house and treater on left, separator on right)

production levels. In addition, at least one well was scheduled for Plug and Abandonment each of the next three years. The first one, OH-1, was subject to an existing State Plugging Order. My theory was that the more Working Interest Jack owned, the more diligent and responsible would be the operations. The firm was in agreement.

Jack's ownership in our Joint Venture properties averaged 17%. He had also recently acquired majority interests in twenty other area wells from major U.S. oil companies that were vacating the Basin.

On the last day of June 1992 we flew to Salt Lake City to meet with Jack. We offered to assign 33% of the firm's Utah assets for one third of the original purchase price. After some discussion with Jack's attorney, it was a done deal. While it still remained a personally guarded secret, the first step to financial integrity for Lake Valley participation had been achieved.

My second proposal involved putting *my* money where *my* mouth was!

Since 1980 a percentage of my salary had been exchanged each year into U.S. dollars as a retirement fund. In the beginning the ratio was only $1.10 Canadian to buy a U.S. dollar. Our currency continually deteriorated against the American currency. In the early 1990s it ranged from $1.35 to $1.40 per U.S. dollar. Participation in my savings agenda at these rates was not logical or prudent. There was no support for this gap to widen any further, meaning any U.S. dollar purchases were likely to be at the peak of their value and vulnerable to speculators. Except for cashing it all in, my accumulated U.S. nest egg was without a purpose; retirement was still far from feasible.

Following successful negotiations with Jack, I suggested investing my savings with the firm in exchange for an ownership position. Furthermore, the firm would be granted a Right of First Refusal (an exclusive participation) on all U.S. prospects generated by RESULTS USA.

Motivated by my focus on Lake Valley, I further offered to barter my management services on new prospects for future considerations. My consulting hours would be logged but compensated only from project-generated future revenues.

Because of this, the participation goal for Nevada was more attainable as a result of my investment and the freeing up of monthly revenues otherwise allocated to management fees.

By the end of July 1992, our partnership negotiations were finalized and documented. RESULTS became a 29% owner in the firm's U.S. incorporated affiliate.

Utah was very active during that summer. Jack generated no less than five major workover AFEs. We selectively participated, depending on cost and degree of risk. Most were budgeted at twice the historical trends. Frequently arguments developed with Jack on assessing his operational costs versus our predecessor, Cracker. Jack considered this an apples and oranges comparison. It was an ominous omen and the wisdom of my judgement to promote him as successor Operator was openly questioned within the firm.

A new 13,000 foot well proposal, PEE-2, surprised us in August. Our 14.04% Working Interest translated into $320,000 U.S. in AFE costs. Technically this offset to PEE-1 was justified and a worthy investment. Oil prices were weak, however, and our business plan did not accommodate an expense of this magnitude at this early stage.

We actively marketed our interest, but the only logical and cooperative candidate was Jack. Days before PEE-2 spudded in October 1992, we assigned our Working Interest to him for a 1.404 % Gross Overriding Royalty.

This was the beginning of induced stress into my daily routine, a constant robbing of my energy. The days of sunning on my deck in peace seemed generations behind me.

The OH-1 Plug and Abandonment (P & A) program had ascended into a $93,000 U.S. headache. We had been expecting $35,000
to $40,000 based on an earlier 1992 AFE from Jack. Scrutiny of the
invoices was disturbing. Since Jack **now** supplied many of the services and equipment facilitating this workover, we hoped against hope
that we would not be torn in the USA like my predecessor employers.

Early in 1993, we elected to Quit Claim (assignment of total
asset interest without compensation) our 31% Working Interest in a
suspended and remote Salt Water Disposal (SWD) well, 'East #1'.
Jack had proposed a costly remedial AFE to improve and expand
water injection capability. The facility was under-utilized as it competed with new water disposal wells with more convenient road
access and lower operating costs. The severity of Utah winters made
these benefits crucial. Historically the East#1 had operated at a loss
and we were happy to rid ourselves of a P & A liability. We were to
discover later that new drilling and additional well purchases by
Jack in the vicinity soon reversed the balance sheet. We had no regrets; Jack's ability and determination to turn this operation around
was encouraging.

Our other SWD well was more strategically located 15 miles
to the west, where such facilities were scarce. Many of our producing wells were pipelined to this well, 'West #1', substantially reducing operating costs. Disposal by other Operators, including Jack with
several dozen non Joint Venture wells, contributed $30,000 to $40,000
U.S. monthly in fees.

At the same time that Jack rejuvenated the east side East#1
SWD well, he notified us of a disposal fee reduction at our west side
West#1 SWD well from $0.40 per barrel to $0.30 per barrel.

In the spring of 1993, we received another new well AFE. The
GEE-2 was a 10,000 foot offset to the very successful, decade old
GEE-1. Our 16 % Working Interest translated into $225,000 U.S. This
development location ranked highest in our property values. As a
west side well, Wasatch sands were encountered at shallower depths
than east side wells such as PEE-2. Therefore, the Drilling and Completion budget was 25% less. We could not persuade ourselves to
pass on this opportunity, so we obtained bank financing by mort-
gaging our personal assets.

Whatever Jack's reasoning, he did not proceed with this project.
It was one of the few times Jack's timidity or lack of perseverance
was regretted. At first we were annoyed at the administrative costs

the firm incurred in establishing the bank Line of Credit and the Loan approval. Before long, though, we realized how fortunate we were only to lose a few thousand dollars in appraisal and legal fees. Had this well proceeded, the personal consequences would have been disastrous. Not that they did not turn out that way anyway, but it could have been much worse.

Jack's West#1 SWD fee reduction was vehemently opposed during the summer of 1993. Our letters correctly addressed his extensive personal use of our Joint Venture disposal facility, an obvious conflict of interest, and the absence of a competing facility. As one of our best revenue producing wells, the integrity of our entire program was at risk.

In rebuttal, we were advised that other competing facilities could and would be used unless the disposal fee remained reduced by 25%. Secondly, $0.30 per barrel was the standard competitive rate. Thirdly, we had exaggerated his personal use of the West#1 SWD facilities.

Verification of all three assertions was aggressive but inconclusive. Discussions with the State Oil and Gas Board confirmed no competitive SWD facilities with *excess* capacity within a five mile radius. The State also verified that, to their knowledge, the field fees charged ranged from $0.40 to $0.60 per barrel. Finally we compiled a production spreadsheet for all wells operated by Jack. Results confirmed significant water volumes were disposed at our West#1 SWD well, either on a prolonged basis or intermittently for wells produced only a few days monthly to hold the lease.

In the fall of 1993, we began to recognize questionable charges on the monthly Joint Interest Billings (JIB), particularly for August and September. Jack had recently hired a new Accounting Manager, 'Katey', and we exchanged numerous calls, letters, and telecopied messages on operating costs. Inexperience was suspected, but we were advised she had a ten year accounting background with a major oil company that had been active in the Basin.

When it appeared our Operator was not responsive to our concerns, my patience grew thin and the correspondence turned nasty. Our working relationship deteriorated on a pace with Katey's responses. Regrettably my skills lacked prolonged patience for managing these type of issues.

One such dispute involved duplicate billings in succeeding months for $44,000 in service rig costs on the same well. Each invoice number and cost was slightly different. Based on the daily workover reports, one was obviously in error. Given that Jack owned the service rig, it should have been reversed without delay. Instead it lingered on for months before our balance was corrected, contributing to the friction between us.

Of the more obvious abuses, the JIBs indicated trucking costs to transport water **from** producing wells were charged to the West#1 SWD well. The regular hourly water hauling rate was $40 to $60, depending on truck size. Minimum billing was 1 1/2 hours. No one could argue that producing wells, not disposal wells, were responsible for the costs of hauling and disposing of formation water. No one except Katey, that is. I was a poor teacher, and failed to convince her of the obvious.

Fortunately Katey relented in the spirit of compromise and forwarded two months of back-up invoices for our disposal well and several producing wells that had curious sharp increases in water production and costs.

Particularly alarming was the disclosure that most water hauling costs charged **to** the West#1 SWD well came **from** non JV wells (in other words, Jack's wells).

Several of our JV producing wells were connected to the disposal facilities directly by pipeline but occasionally had water hauling costs billed **to** them. Coding errors are common in large operations, but we encouraged closer scrutiny by the truckers to limit future mistakes.

Truck Tickets from one of Jack's wells related to numerous charges for water shipments **from** our nearby JV wells to accommodate his well stimulation. When the water was recovered after the workover, it was returned **to** our JV wells. In each case the trucking costs were charged **to** the JV well. Because of this, the disposal volumes and fees doubled for our JV well. We stressed the need for Jack's water haulers to treat these entries with more care and understanding.

Finally, the issue that was most unsettling involved Water Truck Tickets that billed the West#1 SWD well for hauling 100 barrel loads of skimmed oil from the facility storage tanks to Jack's 100% owned wells. It must be assumed that no one scrutinized these two months of back-up before mailing, numbering over a hundred invoices. Being new to her employment, perhaps Katey did not realize that these shipments jeopardized our JV SWD operations financially and philosophically. This disclosure deserves elaboration, regardless of our environmental and regulatory concerns for transporting crude oil in trucks designed for water.

Our West#1 SWD facility had 4000 and 2000 barrel storage tanks. Produced water was stored and filtered so sediments would collect in the tank bottoms and any oil in solution would float to the top to be skimmed for Sales. Trucked and pipelined water deliveries averaged 2500 to 3000 barrels per day and it was common for up to 1% of this effluent to be oil. The rate for one of our JV wells, Cage 2-23, was 5% by Jack's admission due to an inadequate and inefficient wellsite Treater. By agreement, the skimmed oil was supposed to be routinely sold and allocated as production to our JV wells on a rotating basis. This precaution ensured taxes and royalties were paid and production properly accounted. Since the JV incurred all the operating and maintenance costs for the West#1 SWD facility, only JV wells were supposed to profit from these conservation measures. As an example, two months previous, repair of a leak in the bottom of the 4000 barrel tank had cost the JV in excess of $10,000.

Dialogue was exhausted and our differences of opinion remained. The rapidly escalating JIB costs had been a concern for many months. All this had been seen before and every effort was explored to limit the pain. It was time for the return of Bull Dog Bender.

Mac met with me in early November 1993 to discuss damage control strategy. Several letters were drafted to Katey and Jack requesting an audit schedule. Unfortunately, we did not receive much co-operation or response.

In mid-December we seized the initiative and provided Jack with a list of audit objectives and preferred February 1994 booking. We considered seeking a Court Order if authority was withheld.

Jack claimed to be booked until spring with MMS audits of his operations. Our inquiry to MMS in Denver revealed their intentions for only a routine late January, two day audit in Jack's office. In discussions with the MMS about our urgency to verify Jack's books, we proposed 'piggybacking' on the end of their audit. An offer to pay their costs and an assurance that our audit would not interfere with theirs (different objectives) failed to win their support. Examples of our concerns were supplied to the Denver office, but they refused to get involved. The most we could accomplish was to correct Jack's *misunderstanding* of MMS audit intentions and schedule.

We were shocked to receive Jack's notice by telecopier on December 28 advising that nearly half of our JV producing wells were being suspended indefinitely due to weather. Such action was unprecedented and had the immediate effect of devastating our Cash Flow at a time when oil and gas prices were at a seasonal high. We never quite understood this action, since few of Jack's wells were subjected to similar punishment.

Jack and I traded insults and insinuations for the first few months of 1994. Then silence prevailed, similar to the stand-off with Inc's Texas Panhandle Operator in 1986. At my request, the firm suspended payment of JIBs, beginning with the January 1994 Statement. This precaution only escalated the conflict.

In turn, Jack confiscated our revenues, which by this time were insufficient to cover costs anyway. We then requested the oil Purchaser place our revenues In Trust, preventing any access to these funds pending resolution of operational disputes.

In late April, in light of this mutually painful stalemate, Jack consented to an audit schedule of May 09-20, 1994. Mac and an assistant would review JV records from 1991 through 1993.

Jack was incensed with Mac's participation because of Mac's earlier audit of Cracker in 1991 on his behalf, claiming this now represented a deliberate conflict of interest. He insisted we use a local Salt Lake City auditor. We advised Jack that if this was his only choice, it was unacceptable to us. Our limited exposure with this Trustee during the Tripoli litigation in the mid 1980s was not favourable. We insisted on using Mac and prudently refrained from disclosing that I would be attending the audit as his assistant.

Jack did not hide his fear and apprehension of Mac's auditing skills, having witnessed his surgical strike on Cracker's books in 1991 with decisive effect.

When we showed up at Jack's office, the atmosphere was cold but cordial. We had been warned that a Sheriff would prevent our entry, however we were not contested. The lack of co-operation over the succeeding two weeks did not prevent us from performing our audit with surprising results. My U.S. Operations experience still had much room to grow. Mac also added new chapters to his auditing experience.

"Jack right off the top told us we would not get anything until the account was paid up. Neil had begun withholding JIB payments after uncovering

operational irregularities several months earlier. I knew he had no intention of releasing any more funds to Jack until his concerns were put to rest by the audit. Thus in our first challenge, we successfully negotiated with Jack to proceed with the audit but avoided addressing the account status.

During the audit we had another situation where we were denied seeing original documents. Rather than permit us access, Jack's staff supplied us with copies (sometimes) according to our list of requested documents. This inconvenience was in our favour. If we had to copy everything ourselves, we would have only been able to look at half of what we eventually got.

The surprising results to me were that what Neil had originally uncovered turned out to be a tip of an iceberg."

The audit itself was uneventful as we were pretty much ignored. We had eagerly looked forward to meeting with Katey, but we were disappointed when advised she had been fired in December. Departure and replacement had been well concealed; we had not noticed her absence.

We had to pay several visits to the State Oil and Gas Board (Board) to verify Rules and Applications of the HB110 Workover Tax Credit Policy. Jack's staff claimed ignorance and were unable to assist. The information retrieved from the Board verified significant tax benefits had been mistakenly allocated to Jack's wells. We calculated this error had cost Inc, and the firm, recoveries in six figures.

We changed motels frequently, not that we feared being traced or harassed. The weekend was utilized to tour the field operations. We benefited from discussions with current and past employees of Jack. The former, for the most part, were inconspicuous. Much was still learned in our conversations, particularly with Mac's tact to leech information. Past employees were most helpful in this regard.

Many of our audit concerns were visually observed and photographed.

An example was the West#1 SWD well, where oil was splashed over the top of the 4000 barrel tank and down the side. A sizeable quantity had accumulated within the dike surrounding the tank. There had been few oil sales reported for the past year, so we regarded this sign as odd. Disposal fees had declined to $10000 monthly, partly due to the suspension of so many wells. We reviewed the water disposal log at the facility office, and were surprised by the consistent daily deliveries indicated. Mac's confusion between past reports and the current inspection lingered.

West SWD#1 - right side of 400 barrel water *tank stained from oil splashing over the top and collecting in dike*

"We found out that a substantial amount of water was transported by pipeline directly to the SWD well pump for injection (including a few of Jack's wells). The injection meter was inoperative (had been broken for quite some time according to a pumper who happened by while we were inspecting the facilities). So there was no record of what volumes were actually going into the well."

The distance between our main sixteen well west side operations and the six well east side grouping was approximately thirty miles. It was fortunate we took the time to drive it.

An east side well, 'Earl Forester' #1, had Jack's service rig parked on the lease. Workover costs, now in six figures and half attributed to rig rentals, had been billed out for months. The well remained unproductive and was suspended on the day of our inspection. It was doubtful, given the general condition of the equipment, if any further, meaningful remedial action was possible. We planned to discuss our research with Jack, but he was involved in major acquisition negotiations and his schedule was apparently too hectic.

We were none too sorry when our audit was concluded Friday, May 20, 1994. Most of our days had been ten hours long for two weeks.

East side 'Forrester' well; Jack's idle service rig

A summary of our findings was prepared for discussion with Jack as he had requested an exit interview. Unfortunately he was unavailable that afternoon and we had no alternative but to leave a sealed envelope.

It referred to the following major challenges:

1) State and Tribal Tax Refunds due from selective JV new wells and workovers,   applicable to a maximum capital investment of $50,000 U.S. per well;
2) After Payout revenues due from Tribal 1-9 since December 1992; and
3) water hauling and disposal cost billing amendments.

Mac's audit assessment was particularly valuable to me; he was nearly speechless while compiling the summary. To imply we were hurt and annoyed at the findings was an understatement. In U.S. Operations, it seems the worst was always the next assignment. Mac was better qualified to elaborate.

"Most of what concerned Neil was in fact true and mostly much worse than he had suspected.

When an Operator owns Service Rigs and Tank trucks and employs in-house maintenance roustabouts, there is infinite room for 'errors' to occur.

We learned from the Truckers that it was common practise to skim oil from all wellsite water tanks. We knew from prior invoicing that this oil was usually hauled to Jack's 100% owned wells.

In addition to the Tax Refunds, Payout Status, and water hauling/disposal problems, we discovered that Jack's Service Rig, Truck, and Roustabout employees were capable of sustained periods where they worked 28 to 30 hours per day (sometimes on wells located on opposite sides of the field). Often there were no time sheets or descriptions of what these employees were actually doing.

What was mind numbing were areas where an operator could get away with things that could not be verified with a simple audit. The field trip that was conducted in the middle of our audit opened our eyes to problem areas we weren't able to discover initially. We changed our focus in the second half of the audit.

One example was charges to the Joint Venture Account for Service Rig hours when there was no apparent evidence that a rig ever went near the well.

Another example was the billing to the Joint Venture Account for 1 1/2 - 2 hours per well on a regular basis for 'cleaning out the sumps'. The sumps in fact were just 45 gallon drums buried in about a 3 foot deep hole in the ground. It should have taken a pump truck with a 4 inch hose about 2 minutes to clean out these 'sumps'.

One of our last auditing acts was to visit the Oil Purchaser to see what could be done to get the revenues sent directly to the Division Order owners. Jack had amended the Division Orders to allocate 100% of revenues to him. We were able to convince the in-house legal representative that both the Oil Purchaser and

"Sump" example

Jack had exceeded their legal authority. Subsequently they refused to release any funds, preferring to suspend 100% of the revenues until a Court Order directed them to do otherwise. We considered this a partial victory. It got Jack's attention real quick."

It took Mac about a month to prepare a comprehensive Audit Report and assemble supporting documents. A recovery claim for $450,000 U.S. was submitted to Jack in mid-summer, comprising twenty-seven audit queries.

By AAPL audit convention, Jack was obliged to respond within a reasonable time. When he did, we were disappointed he denied any wrong doing or responsibility. He indicated a willingness to settle several insignificant disputes amounting to a few thousand dollars. On the major disputes he was clearly unsettled and little or no progress on settlement developed.

While we expected compromise, Jack reacted by filing a Statement of Claim against the firm in September 1994. His law suit sought immediate payment of $70,000 U.S. for outstanding JIBs, plus Interest, Penalties, and Court Costs. Regrettably there was no reference to our Account imbalance resulting from amended audit claims exceeding $400,000 U.S.

The firm had to hire Salt Lake City counsel to file a Counter Claim within twenty-one days.

U.S. oil and gas operations in a fishbowl - The Doomsday Scenario!

Our operational revenues accumulated In Trust. As a Defendant, our legal costs accumulated daily. Once we filed our Counter Claim for audit recoveries, Plaintiff legal costs were added. Confrontation escalated. Both combatants entrenched behind their legal counsel.

Our only bright spot was the competent legal representation delivered by our Salt Lake City lawyer, 'Lonnie'. He performed his role with purpose and integrity. Our billings were always reasonable. The irony was, had we contracted Lonnie's services a year earlier, history might well have turned out very different for the firm. More about that in EPISODE 14.

In mid October we flew to Salt Lake City for a joint resolution meeting with Jack and his attorney (whom we also understood was a good friend and an investor in his operations). Lonnie chaired the discussions at his office and, on several occasions, refereed.

It was a classic "agree to disagree" attempt at settlement. Under Lonnie's guidance we continued to exchange correspondence, exploring all possible solutions and compromises.

Jack knew we were bleeding to death financially. Time was on his side and he played his poker hand to perfection.

The eventual outcome months later, mostly resulting from EPISODE 14 circumstances, was a travesty. All the firm's efforts and investments became worthless.

The firm turned over all its' Utah assets to Jack in exchange for withdrawing litigation. The revenues In Trust were applied to unpaid JIBs. The audit claims were forgiven.

What a waste and misfortune. I liked Jack for our common interests.

He had recently taken up flying and owned several aircraft; single and twin engine. His wings were earned in the busy airspace around Salt Lake City. Many of his logged hours were in the dangerous Wasatch Mountain terrain between Salt Lake and Vernal. He had proven himself.

He started a family late in life like me. His first son was born a year after mine. His devotion to family was admirable and genuine.

He was an astute investor, purchasing an historic 8000 square foot stone home in prestigious southeast Salt Lake City. It came complete with an elevator, indoor pool, and several acres of prime land. By sub-dividing, he recovered most of his multi- million dollar investment.

In the beginning we enjoyed each other's hospitality. He taught me to eat all kinds of food with hot sauce and to drink Russian Vodka straight while enjoying it.

I thought we trusted each other. I was a fool and Jack was not.

EPISODE 14:NEVADA-LOADED DICE, MARKED DECK

I
(Viva Las Valley)

Once comfortable (not necessarily satisfied) with the direction of the firm's existing U.S. properties, my attention returned to Nevada.

Contact was established with Donald at the beginning of August 1992. He explained the initial discovery well was delayed until 1993. Although the location had been licensed, the project still lacked an Operator and "sophisticated" investors. Since our last discussion, he had negotiated additional Freehold Leases that increased extent of the prospect from 16000 acres to nearly 40000.

My desire to solicit the firm's participation, once a thorough presentation had been finalized, was shared. The firm's expertise in reservoir simulation and completion design qualified it as a valuable sophisticated candidate. Donald readily accommodated my research needs by supplying logs and technical studies recently acquired for the offset wells.

For the first time it was intimated to Jack that a Nevada exploration project was being assembled that may interest him. My discussions were vague to protect confidentiality.

Jack had significant financial backers, as evidenced by his recent new well AFEs and property acquisitions. He had purchased a 12000 foot-rated drilling rig and already completed several deep Wasatch wells in the past year. Inc had an opportunity to participate in some of Jack's initial wells, but the bank's preoccupation with divestiture precluded involvement.

The results from these $2,000,000 U.S. drilling indoctrination were not particularly encouraging. Considering the weak and unstable energy prices during 1992, timing was not ideal and contributed to prolonged payout periods.

Jack and his drilling company all profited from valuable learning experiences and equipment shakedowns. Controlling Lost Circulation was an inherent drilling problem for Wasatch wells in the Uinta Basin. It had also been the major impediment to the Lake

Valley offset wells a decade earlier. Experience with improved remedies was a desirable talent for any prospective Lake Valley Operator.

At this early stage of our relationship, Jack's aggressive and 'work-aholic' attitude had attracted my attention and respect. This is not to say we did not have our differences on technical interpretations. Jack was appreciated, however, as a **'doer'** rather than a 'talker'.

In November 1992 the Nevada concept was finally ready for presentation to the firm. My greatest challenge was reducing a full filing drawer of research into a concise prospectus. In case the firm was not interested, since by agreement they had First Right of Refusal, my report format was structured for mass marketing. Many effective introductions already published on Nevada, particularly Railroad Valley, were utilized.

A brief history served as a lead into the specifics of Lake Valley.

In 1954 Shell Oil discovered the Eagle Springs Field, on the east side of Railroad Valley. Early seismic data indicated the presence of an anticline in the Miocene to recent valley fill, and Shell's discovery was drilled on this anomaly. In late 1976, Northwest Exploration Company drilled the discovery well of the Trap Spring Field on the west side of Railroad Valley. Currant Field, Bacon Flat Field and Grant Canyon Fields were discovered in 1979, 1981, and 1983, respectively, on similar features.

Eagle Springs, Trap Spring, and Currant fields are all productive from Lower Tertiary reservoirs. The Bacon Flat and Grant Canyon fields are productive from Paleozoic reservoirs. The trap at each field, however, was the same with an unconformity providing the top seal, and the main boundary fault of the graben being the ultimate lateral seal.

Most of these productive fields were very small in areal extent. Grant Canyon, of Nevada's famed Railroad Valley in northern Nye County, for example, took up less than 320 acres. Since its discovery, production totals over 21,000,000 barrels of oil, mostly from just two prolific wells. One of these wells, in fact, was for years consistently among the two or three most productive in the continental U.S., yielding over 4,000 barrels of oil per day. Many geologists believed that similar and even larger fields (possibly as much as 100,000,000 BO; e.g. Bortz 1989), awaited discovery in the Basin and Range.

The principal reservoir rock at Grant Canyon and other less known Nevada fields was intensely fractured, brecciated, and hydrothermally veined Devonian dolomite. Vuggy quartz veinlets and breccia cements account for most of the reservoir's oil-bearing secondary porosity. Common to all subsurface interpretations in these fields was the reservoir setting — fractured Paleozoic carbonate capping buried basement highs immediately beneath and sealed by clay-rich, Oligocene - to Miocene - age volcanic and sedimentary rocks. Gently folded mid-Paleozoic carbonate strata, including the Devonian Guilmette Formation (the principal reservoir rock), were in fault contact with locally metamorphosed siliciclastic and carbonate rocks of Cambrian through Ordovician age.

"The Nevada Basin and Range Province has all the ingredients needed for good oilfields. Veteran explorationists will see many similarities to other areas where they have been successful.
A prime ingredient is source rock, and Nevada has two good formations. One is Mississippian Chainman Shale. The other is the Devonian Pilot Shale.
Reservoirs more native to Nevada are the porous and fractured Tertiary clastic volcanic rocks from which many of the fields produce. To date, the seal for the majority of the producing oilfield traps is the valley fill material that covers nearly all Nevada's valleys." by **Willis H. Alderman, Western Oil World, October 1992**

"The Grant Canyon oil field is herein considered to be a type model for future oil and gas production from the Cenozoic basins of the eastern Great Basin. It is believed that low-cost gravity methods could define several Tertiary-covered buried hills in most of the Cenozoic-formed valleys (basins) in eastern Nevada with similar oil possibilities as that found in the Grant Canyon field.
The deeper structurally formed potential oil and gas traps can be evaluated with seismic work across the valleys and the mountain ranges. These deeper structural accumulations could have even larger reserves of oil and gas under the valleys and mountains than that found in the Grant Canyon field.
Source of the oil is the Mississippian Chainman Shale. Reservoir rocks are the Devonian Simonson carbonates which have 8 to 14 percent porosity. The type of drive causing the oil to flow is a hydrodynamic water movement connected to higher pressure sources. Water below the oil is reported to have artesian drive.
Low production costs for flowing oil fields, like the Grant Canyon, justify exploration work in all potential valleys (basins) in western North America." by **Floyd Moulton, Geological Consultant, Utah Geological Association Publication 16, 1987**

"Prolific oil production from unusual reservoirs has recently drawn exploration attention to Nevada. Fifty-eight wells have produced 24.4 million bbl of essentially

gas-free oil from highly fractured volcanic, carbonate, and sandstone reservoirs.
Oil columns range up to 1,700 ft, and a strong freshwater drive is generally
present. Producing depths range from 1,900 to 7,000 ft, and water production is
a common problem.
Virtually all production established to date in Railroad Valley occurs in fault-
bounded structures with oil trapped immediately below the Miocene (or base of
valley-fill) unconformity.
Reservoirs are typically highly fractured, vuggy dolomites and limestones of
Devonian or Pennsylvanian age." by **Ted Flanigan, Oil & Gas Journal, Oct 23, 1989**

The firm was genuinely interested, but required time to thoroughly evaluate the data and obtain additional information before committing.

Several days later Donald called to advise of a Lake Valley Joint Venture meeting and presentation in Salt Lake City on December 09, 1992 and extended an invitation. The timing was ideal, as meetings had already been scheduled with Jack that week to discuss 1993 workover budget and strategy.

Donald was enthusiastically informed that the firm was considering participation. Donald was most pleased, as he was very aware of the firm's technical reputation and skills. He was supportive of my solicitation efforts and offered to waive the promotional burdens on the initial well to encourage an affirmative decision by the firm.

The special guest for Donald's meeting was the Exploration Manager for a Billings, Montana oil company. It was very active in western Nevada and had expressed preliminary interest in the potential of Lake Valley and eastern Nevada. Donald hoped it would provide leadership as Operator and subscribe to the majority of the uncommitted Working Interest.

From my observations the five minor participants, comprising the current 50% Working Interest, viewed their role simply as investors. Their technical capabilities were suspect, based on apparent disinterest throughout the presentation. Future events proved this assessment accurate.

Geological and Geophysical presentations by area experts consumed most of the day. Their studies were thorough, professional, and educational. An armload of new technical reports, maps, and reservoir cross sections was collected. The meeting ended very optimistically.

One of the handouts was presented and authored by a distinguished Salt Lake City Geologist. His role was strictly a consultant to the project and no ownership or royalty participation was involved. He certainly qualified as an expert, having published numerous Technical Papers on the hydrocarbon potential of Nevada for more than a decade. Many of these were in the firm's library, but this day he provided a comprehensive SYNOPSIS of Lake Valley. The prize we were chasing was best defined by my notes accumulated throughout the day.

LOCATION : 58 miles east of the Grant Canyon field (Railroad Valley). Geological prospect setting - buried Palaeozoic structures within a single north-south fault feature. Strong parallel with Grant Canyon/Bacon Flat/Eagle Springs area of Railroad Valley.

WELL DEPTH / PAY: Drillsite location - apex of a buried Paleozoic structure. Designed to test potential oil accumulations at Tertiary/ Paleozoic unconformity and additional seismically defined internally folded structures. Target structure is higher than the two nearby deep tests with numerous live oil shows. Proposed total depth of 7,000 feet penetrates six oil reservoirs, ending 750 feet into Simonson. Potential pay:

Lower Tertiary Sheep Pass Limestone	Pennsylvanian Ely Limestone
Mississippian Scotty Wash Sandstone	Mississippian Joana Limestone
Devonian Guilmette Limestone	Devonian Simonson Limestone

TRAPS: Down-faulted mountain block structural traps. Three buried Paleozoic features in a single north-south fault trap trend covered by Tertiary sediments. Each sealed on top and laterally by younger, fine grained, Tertiary sediments. Internally structural folded reservoirs sealed by layered shales as per two Tenneco Oil Co. seismic lines.

SOURCE BEDS / RESERVOIR ROCK: Three major source rocks - organic rich Lower Tertiary, Mississippian Chainman, and Devonian Pilot Shales. Presence confirmed by seismic data tied into two nearby deep tests and proprietary gravity data. Live oil shows and seismic data indicate good reservoir potential in six potential payzones. Drillsite location expected to contain oil and gas that migrated through offset wells.

OIL GENERATION / MIGRATION: Brent #1 and Amoco DJ #1 live oil shows confirm hydrocarbon generation and migration. Major thrust between drillsite structure and DJ #1. Migrating oil and gas moved up thrust plane to southeast, then up section under top seal sediment or first top-sealed porous reservoirs.

BRENT #1: Total depth 9178'. Live oil shows from 4580' to 4860' in Scotty Wash and Chainman Shale. Gas and oil shows from 6215' to 6250' in Pilot Shale according to mud log. Mud log gas shows at 8430' and 8975' in Simonson.

AMOCO DJ #1: Total depth 12,750'. Mud log oil shows top of Ely at 4950'. Total of **42 separate oil shows** in samples and mud from 5815' to 6678'. Oil on mud pits at 5859'.

RESERVE POTENTIAL:

Zone	Est. Acres	Recoverable Bbls Oil
Sheep Pass	680	3,400,000
Ely	2000	40,000,000
Scotty Wash	2000	30,000,000
Joana, Guilmette, Simonson	1000 each	20,000,000 each

Based on Grant Canyon model, with 18 million barrels, 120 acres, 500 feet of pay, and 300 bbls/acre-foot. Also Blackburn model, with 6.4 million barrels, 160 acres, 200 feet of pay, and 200 bbls/acre-foot.

Before returning to Calgary, Jack was acquainted with the Prospect. I was pumped and he shared my enthusiasm. A complete package was promised once all the additional data had been duplicated.

The firm was equally impressed and elected before Christmas to commit for 15% Working Interest. A private Silent Partner, comprising four professionals with lengthy industry experience in Geology, Engineering, and Land, committed to an additional 5%. Their interest was buried in our total recorded Working Interest of 20%. We executed a formal Participation Agreement that assured us their financial contributions and technical input to supplement our capabilities.

My good news was relayed to Donald and he relayed his bad news to me. The Billings oil company had advised that they were fully committed in western Nevada. They passed on participating in Lake Valley. Donald was informed of my promising discussions with Jack. A positive decision was anticipated early in January.

New Year 1993 began with great optimism. Jack agreed to a 25% Working Interest position and Operatorship. One of his deep drilling rigs would be available by mid-April.

Donald, being the only lawyer in the Joint Venture, assumed responsibility for designing the Operating and Farm In Agreements and subscribing the remaining Working Interest to his parent company.

After numerous amendments to the drafts, all documents were executed and notarized by mid-March. In the interim, Donald had purchased additional acreage at the Bureau of Land Management (BLM) February lease auction. The Lake Valley Prospect now comprised nearly 70,000 acres. In accordance with our Agreements, participation in each well would earn a similar interest in a 14000 acre block. Five wells were planned over a two year period. As promised, Donald waived the promotional fees for the firm on the first well in exchange for technical services on the drilling and completion. It had been a long time coming for me.

As if we needed any further encouragement, a significant and strategic Bacon Flat Field discovery was announced. Extracts from the **March 1993 edition of Western Oil World, authored by Don Lyle**, drew the industry's attention.

"*Balcron Oil of Billings, Mont., drilled a well at a spot surrounded by dry holes and a watered out producer and found a 160-acre field that produces nearly 2000 bo/d.*"

"*Balcron moved 900 feet north and a little west of the Bacon Flat 1, the discovery well and only well in the field. That well watered out after producing 314,640 bo in seven years, says Eric Johnson, district geophysicist for Balcron, who developed the project with Bob Schalla, Balcron's exploration manager.*"

"*It tested at 225 bo/hour of clean 26 degree gravity oil from 5164 to 5240 feet through a two-inch flow line. Flowing tubing pressure was 60 psi and shut-in pressure was instantaneous at 340 psi.*"

"*We're convinced it's capable of higher flow rates, but we're not convinced it wouldn't cone or preferentially flow water through fractures, Johnson says.*"

"*He says the field has definite structural limits. A dry hole a quarter mile west reached Guilmette more than 1300 feet deeper with no oil shows. A dry hole a quarter mile north and a well to the south did not find Guilmette at all.*"

"*Clearly all these wells are off the fault block, and that means the field can't cover more than 160 acres, Johnson says.*"

The quotes in this section are clues to a mystery that beset our prospect. Before proceeding, review these one more time. For the remainder of this EPISODE you can challenge your detective skills by venturing a guess at who or what "shot JR".

II
(If It's April Fool, This Must Be Nevada)

I was absolutely convinced that Donald's call on April 01, 1993 was a classic April Fool joke. No amount of logic could explain it. His news caused pandemonium throughout the offices of the firm and our Silent Partner.

Donald advised that Jack had unfortunately resigned as Operator and withdrew from the Lake Valley Prospect. In what he considered to be overriding great news, a successor Operator had already committed in writing to participate. By assuming Jack's 25% Working Interest and other Interests held by Donald's firm and the parent of Donald's firm, the new Operator now exercised 51% Working Interest and control of the Prospect.

We later discovered that the new Operator also paid a significant cash contribution to Donald's firm.

My blood pressure was still recovering from this shock when Donald advised me the new Operator was none other than my old Texas nemesis, ACE Petroleum. ACE was an active and established player in eastern Nevada.

During the previous months, when the search for an experienced Operator captivated our strategy sessions, Donald was specifically requested to avoid the temptation to approach ACE. As support for my prejudice, my CRI (Texas) gas sales nightmare related in EPISODE 11 was shared.

In addition, the firm's President had an unpleasant experience with ACE recently when he was contracted as one of their Expert Witnesses.

ACE was defending against a law suit claiming they were unfairly draining the gas reserves of offsetting wells. ACE refused to pay full consulting fees when the Court ruled in favour of the

Plaintiff. The firm's President had spent a long time evaluating documents and preparing a presentation, including trips to Oklahoma and a week in Trial at his expense.

He had to settle for a portion of the $30,000 U.S. owed. Another Expert Witness, a small independent from Texas, had to do the same. He copied the firm some of his correspondence with ACE's Legal Department. It was no secret with Donald that we wanted to avoid this Red Flag at all costs.

During the next few weeks we were really **torn** on direction.

We were prepared for the technical risks of Lake Valley, but the last minute operator change was an unexpected crises.

Our finances and other active operations had been tailored to meet our participation in the first well. Depending on results, loan requirements for continuing to drill would be satisfied by a successful or encouraging outcome. We had already expensed around $30,000 U.S. for our share of new leases and recurring Lease Rentals. In February we participated with Donald in the acquisition of thousands of strategic acres offsetting the abandoned Amoco DJ #1. Mentally we had already passed the point of no return.

Our gut feeling and troubling operational events led us to consider backing out. **Never underestimate the worth of your gut feeling.**

After visiting with Jack on the phone, we could have and should have withdrawn as he had. With the first well scheduled to begin drilling in late April, Jack and Donald came to a disagreement over terms and conditions of the Operating Agreement and financial issues.

Jack indicated he was confronted with new obligations and was not prepared to adjust his commitment at the last minute. So he withdrew. Jack was no fool and we would have been wise to follow his lead.

ACE proposed numerous controversial changes to the Operating Agreement. Most of the next six weeks were consumed negotiating with Donald on these amendments. One that caused us great concern was the removal of Insurance Coverage for non operating, minority interests.

It was conventional for the Operator, who <u>has</u> to have full insurance anyway, to provide this protection under his blanket coverage and invoice the participants for their share. This way the Operator is assured of standard Joint Venture indemnification in the event of a well blow-out or personnel accident. The Working Interest Owners benefit from much lower premiums and the comfort that all parties have equal coverage. Jack's Agreement provided this, ACE's did not.

Through Donald's California connections, we finally arranged a one-well Policy. The gross cost was several thousand dollars and it had to be renewed for each succeeding well. All participants had to be convinced to subscribe, as drilling an exploratory well in naturally fractured reservoirs without 100% liability coverage was unthinkable.

Changes to other terms and conditions of the Operating Agreement were beyond our control to prevent. If any of the other minor Working Interests had supported us, we might have been more successful. By mid-May the revised Agreements had been executed and Notarized. Donald also insisted on changes to our Farm In Agreement. This now honoured our 20% Working Interest in only the 160 acre spacing unit around the first well. In all subsequent acreage, it was reduced to 10%.

Spud Date was contractually postponed until July 01, 1993. ACE Petroleum had located some additional old Tenneco seismic that ran through the section containing our Licensed location. We agreed it was prudent to acquire and reprocess the tapes to corroborate existing seismic and gravity studies. We committed to ACE's $50,000 U.S. AFE for this purpose.

The last week of June saw me off to Salt Lake City for a multi-purpose mission.

One day was spent with Jack on Utah operations and also to discuss, in confidence, the circumstances surrounding his withdrawal from Lake Valley. His admissions were most troubling and revealing.

On the Saturday, our Utah JV field operations were toured.

The next day, Donald and I drove to Lake Valley to physically observe the terrain and drilling location. As it was a six hour drive, we left at sunrise. We had lots of time to get to know one another. My elation came from learning Donald had served in the U.S. Air Force flying transports. When he left the Service, he became a lawyer and began building his oil and gas exploration firm. He seemed much younger and I was impressed with all that he had accomplished. Much of the ride was boring, creating plenty of time to discuss flying.

One comment stayed with me and troubled me. He affirmed this was the first time he had ever physically inspected a prospect before it was drilled. In Canadian operations, this is standard procedure for drilling or acquisitions.

Highway 93, looking south from the north end of Lake Valley, June 1993

Centre of Lake Valley, near "Well to Hell" location (Highway 93 on right, heading south), June 1993

Lake Valley, as the name implies, is a large flat desert expanse, perhaps fifteen miles wide and forty-five miles long. It is bounded by mountain ranges on the east and west sides. Highway 93, which begins at the TransCanada Highway intersection one half hour west of Banff, runs straight north-south through the Valley on its way to Las Vegas several hours south.

My prime purpose for inspecting the lease was to determine why ACE had moved the well location from the Licensed co-ordinates, which were exactly centred in a fault bound structure defined by previous seismic and gravity studies commissioned by Donald's firm. Moving out from the centre by any distance troubled me.

We could not drive all the way in as we had only an economy rental car that was too low to the ground for the desert brush.

We had to walk nearly an hour in a very dry heat to find the staked site. It was our understanding that ACE moved the location a few hundred feet to avoid a ravine. We found no such impediment; you could see the Valley floor for miles in a squatting position. A note was made to seek verification.

Brent #1 wellhead marker, looking east. Less than a mile east, prior to the mountains in the background, lies the "Well to Hell", June 1993

"You can step out a quarter of a mile and go up 500 ft (in the same formation) and it's a whole new world, says Kurt Burris, president of Cardinal Drilling Co. in Billings, whose two rigs have drilled more Nevada wells than all other companies combined." by **Don Lyle, Western Oil World, April 1990**

Lease road and power lines near "Well to Hell" lease, facing east, June 1993

Near "Well to Hell" lease, facing west, June 1993

Since the 1976 discovery of the Trap Spring Field, all subsequent fields had been found utilizing surface and subsurface geology and detailed seismic shooting. Along basin margins like our prospect, where employable seismic data are more difficult to obtain, it is critical to co-ordinate surface and subsurface geology with the seismic and gravity data.

We returned that evening by a different route, through Ely and Wendover. The latter was on the Nevada/Utah border, two hours (120 miles) west of Salt Lake City on Interstate 80.

It was a favourite destination during many of my Utah assignments over the years. Despite being in the middle of a desert, it ranks as another paradise for historians, gamblers, and tourists.

In the last years of World War II, the U.S. Air Force's 509th Composite Bomb Group trained here. This elite unit eventually dropped the atomic bombs that destroyed Hiroshima and Nagasaki in August 1945.

Although the base was deserted and derelict, it remained an undisturbed monument to the atomic era. Hundreds of wooden barracks, supply shops, and hangars, long since shorn of paint by the desert sun, wind, and salt, still stood in methodical rows. Most windows were broken or missing. The odd door or window sash creaked in the wind. Roads and runways, as in the past, were still neatly laid out. One runway has been maintained for local public and limited commercial use.

As far as the eye could see stretched history. There was no museum, no guided tour. None was needed. All one had to do was stand anywhere in this huge unsecured complex and breath the air.

Wendover, facing northwest, June 1993 (World War II barracks - foreground; main town and Casinos - centre; divided highway to Ely/Reno dissects two "busty" hills - left)

Wendover World War II hangars, facing west, June 1993

Wendover World War II ammunition bunkers beyond main east-west runway in centre, facing southwest from hangars, June 1993

Service road dividing air base hangars from barracks and townsite, June 1993

Wendover's population was only a few thousand, but several large casinos swell this number with transient gamblers daily. During my visits many commercial air charters were observed at the air base. My gambling luck in Wendover was always positive and entertaining.

Nearby to the north was the famous Bonneyville Salt Flats. During the 20th Century, many land speed records were established on this seemingly endless dry, flat lake bed of salt.

In my first introduction to the Salt Flats, I felt totally lost after driving for half an hour. Only one main entry ramp led down a steep bank to the lake bed. Far out from shore, without the benefit of roads or markers, 360 degrees of salt desert was a frightening realization. There were no distinguishing features to navigate back to the entrance.

It was early afternoon and the temperature exceeded 100 degrees F. My fear was overheating; car and driver. Water and food had been neglected and my gas supply was low. After driving for miles, a collection of vehicles and spectator bleachers could be distinguished on the horizon. My speed was slow to conserve fuel.

Suddenly an approaching car came into view. Assuming the driver knew the way out, all haste was made to follow. Unfortunately my car lacked the speed and contact was lost after a few minutes. With an educated guess and lucky judgement, the exit ramp loomed soon after.

Despite years of preaching planning and strategy before venturing into new U.S. territory, no precautions had been taken. It was a fear like no other, but my conscience told me it was deserved. My own adage had been ignored, **Expect the Unexpected**.

The next day, June 30, we flew to Denver for a Prospect presentation by ACE Petroleum. It was amazing how many senior management and technical personnel were assigned to this project; approximately ten if my memory serves me correctly. Thinking overkill could not be helped, unless this acquisition had been targeted for some time and was more significant than ACE had been admitting.

We later discovered that the available compressor was in Vernal, Utah. It was only ordered on the day it was needed. Loading and twelve hours of trucking delivered it when it was too late. The compressor sat on the site unused, under rental, for another month.

When it came time for the Senior Geophysicist's presentation, an answer why the well position had been moved was solicited. Apparently ACE believed Donald's Location was in a depression and, to be safe, it was moved *slightly west* to intersect with two recently acquired seismic lines.

We learned later in Examination for Discovery that the two recently acquired Tenneco seismic lines intersected 1880 feet west of the old location staked by Donald's firm. This was the distance ACE moved the well. There was little room for error, given the narrow width of our seismic and gravity defined elliptical structure and the severe formation dips known to exist in Nevada's graben valleys. Also reprocessing the old Tenneco seismic tapes had not been possible, therefore precluding interpretation that would have justified the moving of the location by such a distance.

"Grant Canyon oil field is a high mass 0.5 mi across that has been buried on all four sides by Tertiary clays. The flanking faults define the feature as a high remnant horst block, generally circular in form." **by Floyd C. Moulton, Utah Geological Association Publication 16, 1987**

III
(Well To Hell)

The well spudded two weeks behind schedule, near the middle of July. We were informed the delay was due to the unavailability of the Contractor rig which was used by ACE on its Nevada programs. This Operator was decidedly different for many astonishing reasons.

Drilling commenced on an $800,000 U.S. exploratory well with six unknown, unproved participants, representing 49% of the ownership, without Cash Calling at least the Dry Hole costs.

Our commitment was set aside and we waited patiently for an invoice. I know of no other similar experience, whether for a workover, drilling, lease acquisition, or even a seismic program, where the Operator neglected to solicit 100% of the AFE funds in advance. This was a first for me in U.S. operations, or Canadian operations for that matter. It was astounding.

We later received the first invoice summary roughly two months after this operation terminated. Included were costs for reprocessing the Tenneco seismic, which was never carried out, and recompletion costs which we had elected non-consent.

Our Silent Partner supplied the services of an experienced consulting Geologist, 'David', to monitor daily mud log and drilling sample descriptions. Prior to encountering Lost Circulation, David had strongly questioned whether the Mud Log was operational. There were no signs of elevated gas levels (in fact, no detectable background gas levels at all) despite having encountered several targeted reservoirs. In his 15 years of experience this was unprecedented, except when the equipment was malfunctioning. ACE, through Donald, replied that they had contracted the best mud logging outfit in Nevada. There were no equipment problems and everything was proceeding normally.

We learned later that the gas detector was inadvertently left unconnected until after intermediate casing was set, eliminating approximately 3300 feet and four of the prospective reservoirs from the benefits of hydrocarbon detection.

At mid point, just beyond 3000 feet and at a targeted Tertiary/ Paleozoic unconformity, severe Lost Circulation was encountered near the end of the second week. The Operator's solution to control the loss of drilling mud was to mix and squeeze several hundred sacks of cement into the formation. Despite budgeting for liberal amounts of Lost Circulation Material (LCM) in the Drilling Prognosis, there was only a limited supply on hand. More than 2000 barrels of drilling mud were lost into this zone.

Although we received daily reports by telecopier, this action occurred over a weekend and we learned of the remedy after the fact. This zone was therefore eliminated as prospective pay. The Operator's actions precluded testing of a potentially prospective zone.

"Weathered volcanics appear to be susceptible to mud and cement damage: Air drilling and open-hole completion have yielded good results in these reservoirs. Nevada's sandstone reservoirs may benefit from similar careful handling.
The two producing wells at Kate Spring held other examples of some challenges in Nevada well completion. The problems at Kate Spring are rooted in lost circulation..... .
In the north portion of Trap Spring field, wells drilled with air-foam through the reservoir recover about 50% more oil on average than wells drilled with conventional mud.
Drilling and completing a successful wildcat in Nevada requires both conventional and unusual considerations. Completion may be jeopardized by failure to gather critical information about a zone when it is first encountered. A conservative approach is indicated. Recognize and evaluate pay when it is first penetrated and aim to complete a producer in the first reservoir drilled." by **Ted Flanigan, Oct 23, 1989 Oil & Gas Journal**

Several hundred feet beyond the Lost Circulation zone, drilling was suspended for logging, followed by cementing of the intermediate casing. We preferred to drill on to Total Depth (TD) of 6000 feet and then log the entire well before incurring the cost of casing. We were, however, just as anxious to evaluate the potential in the first 3300 feet which contained four promising reservoirs and several drill reports where the **bit dropped several feet**.

We had arranged with ACE to wire our logs via satellite transmission on the day they were run so we could have them digitized immediately for computer simulation . The entire suite of logs disappeared for eleven crucial days and only showed up the

day before the entire drilling operation reached TD. Their discovery resulted from our investigative efforts. ACE's Exploration Manager was unaware that all logs had remained in the Logging Company's Field office waiting on distribution instructions from the Operator.

The geologic horizons penetrated after the Lost Circulation, as interpreted from chip samples by ACE's highly experienced mud logger, were incompatible with the Drilling Prognosis. The geologic sequence, predicted by seismic, simply was not present. In fact, besides a new Ordovician facies (general appearance or composition of one part of a stratigraphic rock body as contrasted with other parts), several expected zones of interest were encountered in the wrong sequence or depth.

We later discovered that by moving the well 1880 feet from the centre of the seismic target, the Lost Circulation zone represented the depth at which the wellbore drilled out of the predicted reservoir.

Instead of drilling through Devonian Simonson reservoir from 5000 to 6000 feet, the wellbore encountered igneous (Granite) rock at 5200 feet. Operations were suspended soon after.

No seismic interpretations for the targeted structure predicted the presence of Granite. Clearly this was nowhere land compared to the AFE, but interpretative minds would have surmized that the signs were not all bad. Most carbonate-hosted Nevada oil fields, like Grant Canyon and Blackburn, were spatially associated with igneous intrusions. These intrusions were once the potent magmatic heat sources favourable for natural hydrothermal rock rupture.

"The wells drilled east of the Grant Canyon field encountered an intrusive rock emplaced with Devonian and Mississippian formations below the Tertiary sediments. The intrusive granite rock is very dense and not responsive to seismic energy, thus not allowing the reflective display print to show the Tertiary sediment-filled low east of the field now defined by well control." by **Floyd C. Moulton, Geological Consultant, Utah Geological Association Publication 16, 1987**

Since we had seen several interesting gas kicks, hydrocarbon shows in the mud logs, and deviated hole and cavings from 4200 to 4900 feet in the Devonian Guilmette, we were keen to evaluate the logs for this lower portion of the hole.

Prompt satellite transmission delivery had been ensured this time by communicating directly with the Logging Company. There were convincing signs of natural fracturing in several thick porous sands. David and I worked until midnight, on the Friday the logs arrived, with a petrophysical expert from Schlumberger's Calgary office. This brainstorming created more enthusiasm. We stayed up most of the night designing a three part Drill Stem Test (DST) program.

"A thin section taken from a core at 4,059 ft in the Guilmette pay section in the Grant Canyon Unit 4 is a crystalline dolomite with open fractures lined with quartz. The core from Grant Canyon Unit 1 demonstrates the heavy fracturing. It appears that fractured dolomite connecting vugular porosity accounts for most of the effective pay." by **Veal, Duey, Bortz, and Foster, Oil & Gas Journal, Apr 04, 1988**

"Oil appears to be contained predominantly in fracture porosity rather than in rock matrix." by **Ted Flanigan, Oil & Gas Journal, Oct 23, 1989**

We received a Plug and Abandonment (P&A) Notice from ACE Petroleum by telecopier the Friday morning that logging was in progress. Several Working Interest participants had visited drilling operations regularly. Since they had not witnessed oil flowing to the pits, they verbally agreed with ACE's P&A proposal. They departed the lease early Friday morning, hours before log prints were available for study.

We documented our opposition to this P&A Notice, since logging was still in progress and no DSTs had yet been discussed or conducted.

It was mid-afternoon the next day, Saturday, before we could track down someone of authority at ACE to discuss a DST program. With Donald's invaluable assistance, we participated in a three way conference call to share our interpretations based upon conventional log evaluations and our scientific modelling which we had worked all night to complete.

ACE's Manager insisted that 'no cores would be cut and no DST s would be conducted. The well was obviously dry as no oil had flowed on the pits while drilling. Operations were in progress to plug the well back to the 3000 foot interval of the intermediate casing string'.

"Oil shows in samples tend to be subtle because oil tends to occur only in fractures and not in rock matrix. Furthermore, little gas is present so mud-gas detection is difficult. Wireline logs are only marginally useful because of the fresh formation water and secondary porosity. For these reasons drillstem testing appears to be the best single open-hole evaluation method.
Well performance is quite variable. Completion methods can clearly affect productivity, but it appears that proximity to major fracture zones or fracture zone intersections is the primary control on individual well performance." by **Ted Flanigan, Oil & Gas Journal, Oct 23, 1989**
Kicks on gas detectors generally occur only after oil has been reversed into the mud system during drill-stem testing." by **Veal, Duey, Bortz, and Foster, Oil & Gas Journal, Apr 04, 1988**

Before ACE went ahead with the P&A, a $100,000 workover AFE was distributed to attempt a recompletion of the cement squeezed Lost Circulation zone. We declined to participate, but were invoiced anyway.

The program design lacked a credible methodology for overcoming the effects of a formation damaged by severe cement and drilling fluid invasion. Without massive acid stimulation (none was proposed), we viewed the program strictly as a waste of money. It proceeded at a cost of $100,000 and accomplished nothing.

It was quite a ride. The rig had experienced an inordinate number of drill pipe breaks (minimum of six) during the five weeks of drilling operations. Several occurred while penetrating prospective reservoirs and/or fractured intervals. We held our breath and prayed we did not have a blowout, or worse - an environmental disaster. There was no desire to test the solvency of our Insurance Broker.

When we raised the question of recurring equipment failures during a conference call, we were advised that drilling string had previously been used in a sour gas environment and the pipe

had not been inspected for several wells. In my experience, more than one break during a job is cause for concern. That we escaped without incident was the only silver lining in this big black cloud.

Since this was the first of a five well, two year program, it was obvious changes would have to be implemented. Following the predictably unsuccessful recompletion effort, the well was abandoned. We were convinced of a discovery, even though many of the primary reservoirs remained untested. Despite spending $900,000 U.S., there was precious little technical data to apply to the next well.

The only ace in our hand was the failure of ACE to Cash Call the well costs. In late August 1993 we advised the Operator that when we were billed for our share of the well costs, payment would be advanced only after a JV meeting was convened to address their performance in the first well. A comprehensive critique of the well's history was included.

Months went by without any interaction with ACE, although we tried many times through Donald. He did his best to act as intermediary and resolve our dispute so drilling could proceed. Of course it was not his personal financing on the line. In late November 1993, without warning, ACE filed a Statement of Claim against the firm for full payment of well costs.

We learned later the reason for the prolonged silence. In October, ACE's Houston head office had fired the Manager of Exploration and Production in charge of its Denver office. He had direct responsibility for managing the Lake Valley Prospect. The subsequent law suit for $180,000 U.S., plus Court costs, included the $20,000 U.S. for the completion program that we had waived and elected to go penalty. This had been alluded to during the previous months as invoice summaries were updated. Unfortunately no one at ACE took notice or responded. Although our exclusion was supported with documentation, ACE refused to amend their Statement of Claim.

The battle of the well was over; the battle of the Courts was about to begin.

IV
(Chuck's Chop)

There was no recollection from my career, nor is there expectation of repeating during the remainder of my lifetime, such a spectacle in crisis management and lack of accountability as this first Lake Valley well. Unless there was some other hidden motive, we could not ascertain any logical explanation for conducting exploratory operations in such a haphazard manner.

Throughout September 1993 we met almost daily with our Silent Partner to determine a strategy for uncovering the discovery that had been ignored in the first well. It was imperative to prevent the same disaster in succeeding wells. Our calls and correspondence to ACE went unanswered and we were politely advised by Donald not to expect any change.

The second well contractually had to be spudded before year end 1993 to earn in the next 14,000 acre block - with a working relationship made in Hell!

Mac was involved to address the advantages of auditing as a means of disclosing areas of weakness and mismanagement in the drilling operations. We realized, regardless of our objectives, that results would not be attainable in time to influence conduct on the next well.

We considered legal action but shuddered at the thought.

In my numerous U.S. oilpatch legal actions, the Canadian side had yet to prevail.

The firm had no previous litigation involvement. Their closest exposure was the attempt to collect an Expert Witness consulting fee debt from our current opponent.

The compromise was to hire a lawyer to co-ordinate a JV meeting. The purpose was to remit the *applicable* well costs we owed in exchange for an open forum to discuss the management of the first well and recommend amendments. We naively believed ACE would accept accountability and reduce well costs to the JV accordingly.

The firm's President was due in Denver the end of the September on business.

In a judgement now regretted on a daily basis, Chuck was tracked down at a law firm different from the Firm's days. Our predicament and uncertainty was briefly explained.

He disclosed he was already representing a client embroiled in litigation with ACE. Our desire for a solution that avoided litigation was emphasized. We were in the process of screening choices of assistance.

Would he entertain a dinner meeting with our President in Denver, at our expense, to explore the scope of his services and whether a conflict of interest existed with his current case?

He consented to the informal meeting at no obligation or expense to the firm.

Based on this dinner discussion and Chuck's recommendations, all subsequent Lake Valley strategy was managed by Chuck as our legal representative.

During October and November, through a series of phone calls, letters, and FAXs to the Denver Regional and Houston Corporate offices, Chuck presented our proposal for a JV meeting to air concerns before commencing the second well. In other words, both sides would be assured of the opportunity to express their position before the participants. The attendance of Counsel would be optional, if so desired by ACE.

No reply of any kind was received by Chuck or the firm prior to the serving of a law suit by ACE against the firm on 24 November 1993.

It all really ended before it started. We were cautioned about Chuck's excessive billings. One of Chuck's clients had terminated his account and association for this reason.

Our first billing statement grouped several months of services. It was prior to litigation and therefore was not large. As in past experience, however, each and every phone call, whether one minute or an answering machine, was invoiced at a minimum quarter hour. Chuck's rate was now up to almost $200 per hour. We could accommodate this arrangement, but it was irritating.

Also, duplicating his dinner discussions with Parry in 1991, Chuck had invoiced us two and one half hours for the date that he had dinner discussions with the firm's President.

Before calling Chuck, it was verified that dinner had lasted about an hour and a half. Our President had gone to Chuck's office at the end of the day as scheduled. He waited in the Reception area for twenty to thirty minutes while Chuck attended to other obligations.

In my discussion with Chuck about the billing, he advised that several hours were spent in discussion at his office prior to dinner.

He was entitled to invoice that consulting time, despite contradicting our verbal agreement.

Our President had been on an international assignment and unavailable for many weeks. Unbeknownst to Chuck, he had just returned that day and was privy to our conversation. When it came to integrity, he was the only person I know who respects and practises it more than me.

Red Flag! We discussed this uncomfortable situation, and its parallel from 1991, with our Silent Partner participants. Despite having represented us for several months, our **gut feeling** was to terminate Chuck immediately. We were seriously taking steps to that effect when ACE filed their law suit and our world turned upside down in a panic.

We took the precaution of soliciting time and cost estimates from Chuck to defend our position and bring the case to Trial. If it was worth fighting for, then we would seek damages from ACE for their conduct and interference with the recovery of significant natural resources.

Chuck's letter stated we should expect to spend a year and $100,000 U.S. or more to get to Trial. Based on our estimate of potential reserves attributable to the first well, it was not a difficult choice to file a Counter Claim and Statement of Defence.

We did have an option. We could have, should have, settled ACE's law suit, turned over our interests and acreage to them or Donald, and used these lessons for future survival. **Life goes on but not forever.** Because we chose the easy route, our journey was one of constant pain and misery.

Almost all available time and energy, including weekends, for the next three months were consumed addressing a virtual avalanche of legal documents: Response to Claim, Interrogatories and Answers to Interrogatories, Supplementary Interrogatories and Answers, and so on.

On March 28, 1994 we flew to Denver for an all day strategy session with Chuck and our expert witness in reservoir evaluation. Chuck introduced us to his firm's Senior Partner, Tom, who would be assisting him from now on. He also advised the inclusion of a third lawyer from Salt Lake City, since our Statement of Defence had to be filed in the same District Court that ACE (or Donald) chose to commence litigation. Since Chuck also had us contract the services of a drilling expert, we now had five high priced consultants billing us in U.S. dollars.

Although our monthly costs were averaging $15,000 U.S., little progress was being achieved getting to Trial. ACE 's co-operation was almost non-existent, requiring legal threats and actions such as Motions To Compel. They were astute poker players.

The resistance from ACE was so orchestrated that we had to get a Court Order to access their files. Chuck's law firm and ACE were in the same Denver office tower; ACE had all the technical files sent to Houston.

We had to duplicate our efforts with the Court, grinding away precious time and finances that ACE could readily afford. They had an internal Legal Department. The Lead Counsel was none other than the same attorney who refused to honour Trial and consulting fees to our firm's President years before.

June 21-24, 1994 was spent at ACE's Headquarters in Houston with Tom. The seismic data we had insisted on reviewing had been sent back to Denver just before our arrival. Tom read the riot act to their Lead Counsel.

At our departure, we dropped by her office to pay my respects. She was stretched out in her chair, feet up on her desk, discussing personal matters with someone on the phone. It was my decision not to disturb her.

What we were able to discover in their files solidified our position. Unfortunately it required several more Motions To Compel before we gained access to the controversial records.

At the beginning of August we received a most disturbing letter from Chuck. It necessitated an urgent meeting with our Silent Partner investors.

Chuck's letter stated that our chances of being successful in our law suit were very limited. The ability of ACE to continually stall proceedings meant expenses would escalate. It was in the firm's best interest to consider withdrawing our action and settling. The effect was similar to a karate chop from a trained assailant on an unsuspecting spectator.

Such wisdom after $140,000 U.S. in fees and eight months of sacrifice.

In a follow-up call, he advised us his budget for Depositions, conservatively numbered at thirteen but not yet scheduled, was an additional $75,000 to $100,000 U.S. Trial was perhaps still a year away.

In mid-August, in a conference call with Chuck and Tom, and involving our Silent Partner investors, we fired Chuck from the case. We offered Lead Counsel to Tom and he accepted.

Immediately we noticed a reassuring change of attitude and a quicker pace. Chuck was non repentant, since he continued to address events of the case, which meant he was logging hours and influencing events.

On September 01, 1994 a private phone discussion was held with Tom regarding Chuck. He was aware our reservoir Expert Witness from Denver would be spending the second week of September in our office, at his request, reviewing files. Tom considered it timely for a joint meeting to discuss strategy and deal with our concerns involving Chuck's performance.

Tom assured me there would be no invoicing of his time, except a few mutual hours with our Expert Witness. Since it was a public relations trip at his insistence, travel costs and hours would be adsorbed by the law firm. As the senior partner, he had that authority.

In confidence, and in private, we elaborated on eleven issues of controversy over Chuck's performance and billing habits, like billing us for dates that correlated to Saturdays and Sundays. We would no longer tolerate any involvement by Chuck.

Tom was sympathetic with many of our concerns and agreed to a substantial reversal in our next billing statement. He assured us that Chuck was removed from the case.

The President drove him to the airport to use every minute of consultation effectively. Tom's parting comments was to this effect — "if I were in your shoes I would do whatever it takes to settle; you should never have considered litigation in the first place".

A few weeks later Tom's invoice for August arrived without any reversals.

Chuck always sent his invoice by Federal Express, then billed it to our account.

Tom's September Billing Statement arrived before the end of the month, as he was scheduled to be back east and out of contact for an extended period.

His time and expenses during his Calgary stay were logged and billed. There were numerous entries for Chuck's time. Their hourly rate was increased from $195 U.S. to $235 U.S. without any warning or explanation.

Once we recognized the futility of being torn by everyone in the U.S. oilpatch, we called ACE immediately to schedule a private settlement meeting.

In early October we flew to Denver to share our Lake Valley discovery secrets.

The President and I each had prepared an hour presentation. At least a dozen ACE senior and middle management attended, including their Lead Counsel from Houston. Her only comment at the conclusion was *'we didn't do anything wrong, you still owe us all the money'*.

Instead of a settlement, ACE demanded more compensation. The new balance was now $220,000 U.S. There was no compromise; no accountability; no integrity. That is why **I am** sharing this EPISODE.

Despite avoiding direct reference to any individual or corporate identity, time may reveal this company's true values, particularly now that it has an Alberta presence. No wonder the oil industry in our two countries is so different.

Subsequent settlement discussions went nowhere. ACE's attorney *demanded personal guarantees and liabilities from the Officers and Directors of the firm*, which was incorporated in Utah. Another requirement was the cancellation of my (RESULTS USA) Lake Valley GORR agreement with Donald. The firm was also expected to turn over its acreage to ACE.

Meanwhile Tom's October Billing Statement for $17,000 U.S. showed up. We could not even remember talking to him that month. Numerous entries from Chuck were queried and we were told they were hours he neglected to invoice earlier in the year.

In addition to my initial investment in 1992, another $23,000 had been contributed during 1993. My services had been excluded from the work force for two and one half years in exchange for consulting fees averaging less than $2000 per month.

This time the hard way was chosen. It was contrary to my character, but I quit.

In late November my partner was advised that I considered the U.S. affiliate insolvent. The war was lost by having to defend two fronts simultaneously; Nevada and Utah were both buried in litigation with no end in sight. Because personal liability could not be accepted as demanded by ACE, and because I had no more blood or sacrifice to give, we parted ways. Declaring bankruptcy was not a viable or acceptable option for my partner. He had other business interests to protect from the negative publicity that would be generated by bankruptcy.

My partner left the back door open, as a chivalrous gesture between comrades. In return for a symbolic one dollar cheque (American, in case you were wondering), my interests in all the U.S. assets (and liabilities) were assigned to the firm and the door was shut on U.S. operations. My training had cost me over $100,000 U.S. and temporarily my self-esteem.

V
(Field Of Dreams)

Was Lake Valley worth it?

In capable hands, who knows!

An American based investment banking/research firm circulated a lengthy newsletter in March 1994. Several North American speculative mineral and energy prospects were extolled, particularly Nevada's attributes. The report's special emphasis on Nevada was of significant interest to me. Its author had been an observer at the June 30, 1993 Denver presentation on Lake Valley. In reviewing this material, one wondered what message was intended eight months into the Lake Valley controversy.

Permission was denied to quote portions of this material. As a stock holder in one of the Canadian diamond firms written up in the report, however, a copy was retained for reference. The following is my attempt to paraphrase the report's content regarding the potentially vast undeveloped natural resources of Nevada.

Gold exploration and production created enviable wealth for the State of Nevada during the 19th Century. Energy exploitation of the energy resources in the Basin and Range provinces, particularly in the valleys of eastern Nevada, could become Nature's successor storehouse of riches before the end of the 20th Century. The discovery of the Grant Canyon Field in 1983 established the State as a potential source for world class petroleum reserves unparalleled in American history.

Weakened by declining energy prices in the mid-1980s, the petroleum industry was forced to re-examine the prospectus of North America. Major energy companies withdrew from exploring areas like Nevada in order to concentrate their efforts in the international arena. Financially troubled intermediates like Cage were forced to farmout prospects, such as their lucrative eastern Nevada acreage, due to budget constraints. This opened the door for junior independents like Donald's firm.

Industry experts expressed their opinion that the quantity and quality of Nevada's reservoir rock met or exceeded those of other areas in the continental United States, excluding Alaska. Based on Grant Canyon's performance, recoverable oil reserves in the hundreds of millions of barrels were possible for Nevada's targeted, unexplored structures. The prospects were complex and their interpretation required state-of-the-art technology and analytical methods; largely missing to date.

Advances in petrophysical (well logging) and completion equipment, combined with more sophisticated expertise, lessened the possibility of missing prospective zones in exploratory wells. Junior oil companies therefore became more aggressive. My firm's involvement was solicited in order to capitalize on its unique applications of reservoir simulation technology to evaluate old hunting grounds like Lake Valley. In our opinion, applying this expertise in a compatible environment had the potential to uncover numerous eastern Nevada structures competitive with Grant Canyon, Lake Valley included. Repeating; in a compatible environment.

The 1993 Bacon Flat discovery, referred to previously in this episode, was indicative of the potential rewards available to well managed, technically specialized, and innovative exploration teams.

Having said that, the expectation of discovering 100 million barrel oil fields while applying outdated technology and techniques was wishful thinking in the extreme. For publicly traded participants, it was in the shareholder's best interests to ensure that geochemical, geophysical, and reservoir data from each venture was conceptualized, captured, and analysed using the latest technology. Otherwise, one may as well have been dreaming.

Lake Valley was reconciled in my mind by imagining a manned Space Shuttle Mission in place of our first well. Considering the outcome, public scrutiny would have been much more efficient in judging management performance than was the legal system.

Welcome to our field of dreams.

Entrance to Bonneyville Salt Flats, stretching beyond horizon on right

The Great Salt Lake, 35 miles west of Salt Lake City, June 1993

EPISODE 15: CALGARY - MAGICAL MYSTERY TOUR

I
(Full Circle)

It all ended for me on the fifth of October 1995.

Life had been so much simpler during the year. Litigation, operator disputes, audits, suspended revenues, covert conduct, suspicious phone calls, threats, wasted energy - in other words, U.S. Operations - were behind me. I was still searching for a purpose, a direction, but was aided in the knowledge and conviction of the purpose and direction that was not sought!

A week earlier an unsolicited phone call had been received from an engineer employed with a large Canadian energy company, 'Company'. She had been assigned to a U.S. drilling project in Nevada and had heard of my background through the grapevine. Their group was unfamiliar with oil and gas operations south of the border. It was their first operated venture in the United States.

As a freelance consultant, it was imperative to lend consideration to any and all assignments. At the time I was gainfully involved in marketing the non core petroleum assets of a Calgary-based Junior. My arrangement was very flexible and accommodated other projects.

The purpose of the phone call was to invite me to an informal review of the Company's activities and plans. Being unsure if I could or would help, one half hour of consultation was offered without charging a fee. In return neither party would be committed to any contractual obligation.

The meeting began at 10:40 and terminated at 11:30. Four representatives of the Company attended, including their Manager of Petroleum Engineering, 'Kyle'.

They admitted to being in virgin territory and solicited my theory for rules of engagement. The Company's Senior Management had been promoted to drill an exploration prospect in Nevada. The Promoter, from Salt Lake City, served as Contract Operator and the Company provided the investment. Drilling was in progress and completion expected within a few weeks. Little was known about the promoter beyond the name.

My gravest U.S. operational concerns were shared, based on personal experiences during the previous fifteen years. Specific examples were related for each controversy, relying on spontaneous memory rather than prepared text.

My audience listened in disbelief and uneasiness.

At the conclusion the Petroleum Engineering Manager was asked to "summarize the Company's U.S. oil and gas operations strategy". He held up a blank sheet of white paper. My only comment was that it might be too late for assistance. Without guidance, they could be stripped naked before knowing it.

Kyle agreed and requested my attendance at the Operations Management Group meeting at 10:00 on October 17, 1995.

My instructions were to prepare a presentation elaborating on the differences between U.S. and Canadian oil and gas operations. Concentrating on the provocative topics of our informal meeting, my delivery would attempt to overcome their deficiencies in U.S. operational strategy and provide background on their Promoter.

We agreed my consulting fee of $65.00 per hour would apply. My FEE SCHEDULE was supplied to Kyle for execution prior to providing my services.

This assignment was a distraction from my marketing services, from which a break was welcomed. Recognizing the timing was crucial, my goal was to share my painful learning experiences genuinely and constructively.

To ensure my presentation was effective, several reliable sources in my Utah network were contacted. The Promoter's background was researched and confidential references solicited. Copies of their latest Annual Report and News Releases were obtained.

There were Red Flags everywhere and it was worrysome. The father was the President and the son was the Corporate Counsel. Track record was not encouraging.

My diaries and technical references were researched. Trusted associates were visited and a summary prepared of precautionary measures and recommendations. A list of Calgary-based industry Professionals of all disciplines with U.S. oil and gas experience was compiled for the Company's future referral.

My presentation was designed to accommodate a one and one half hour allocation in the itinerary. Although there was no plan to log more than three hours, between fifteen and twenty hours were contributed to the cause to ensure the delivery was diligent and comprehensive.

A two page handout was prepared, listing STRATEGY REC-OMMENDATIONS, SUGGESTED SITUATIONS TO AVOID, and OPERATING COMMITTEE GUIDELINES. The purpose was to simplify and generalize provocative areas of concern that otherwise would be too time consuming to debate.

An early arrival enabled me to establish a comfort zone within the meeting environment.

Ten copies of my handout were distributed, a lucky guess but exactly accurate.

My presentation went overtime by ten minutes, since it started equally behind schedule. All topics were discussed and all queries addressed, thanks to the foresight of the handout.

In conclusion, my Rules Of Engagement adages for Canadians conducting U.S. Operations were emphasized. Fate served me well when they were respected but tortured without mercy when they were ignored: 1) **Expect The Unexpected**; and 2) **Verify, Verify, and Verify**.

It was hoped my presentation would help prevent the disasters endured during my fifteen years of U.S. experience.

It was a relief to return to my marketing services with enthusiasm, comfortable in the knowledge that I was no longer a prisoner of U.S. Operations, merely an observer.

Several weeks later my invoice for $195 was submitted, representing three hours consulting services at $65.00 Cdn. per hour.

My fee allotted two hours for the October 17, 1995 meeting (including transit time to and from the Company's offices). The third hour represented preparation of the two page handout, presentation research and interviews, and long distance phone and courier expenses to procure an identity for the Company's Promoter. I felt generous.

Here is the response received from the Company's Petroleum Engineering Manager:

"RE: United States Oil & Gas Operations
Please revise your invoice dated 95-11-03 to show 1.5 hours at $65.00 per hour.
Our records show that your presentation to the Operations Management

Group on October 17 was 1.5 hours in duration (copy of agenda attached). In addition, we did not commission or authorize your handout or reference check calls; as such these are for your account."

Bearing in mind that my client ranked in the top ten largest Canadian integrated energy companies, this reply was interesting. While millions of dollars were targeted for Nevada wildcat exploration, the energies of a senior technical contributor were channelled into saving his employer $97.50. After fifteen years of U.S. Operations, my travels had taken me in a full circle.

My Rules Of Engagement had obviously made an impression; however it was assumed my beneficiary could and would distinguish Friend from Foe. This was not Canadian esprit de corps and we were not in the U.S. oilpatch yet. It would have been humorous if not so tragic.

Focus! Focus! Focus! From my experience in the U.S. theatre of Operations, Operators and Promoters would be only too happy to relinquish one hundred dollars, on an intellectual misunderstanding, while juggling hundreds of thousands under the guise of contractual protection. It happened all the time and to protest invited litigation.

My initial **gut feeling** had opposed U.S. involvement, even on a casual basis. Kyle reinforced my faith in **gut feelings**. It was painful to recognize similar symptoms of naiveté and ignorance that prevailed during my first ventures into U.S. Operations.

Although there were plenty of other reasons for writing this collection of episodes, this experience was proof of the value my message could serve the well-being of others. I am indebted to this Company for this positive revelation.

To my knowledge, almost every Canadian energy firm venturing south of the border since 1980 experienced grief, to some degree. It is no secret that the fundamental Canadian tradition is to look for balance and fairness in everything. Because of this, if a genuine source of adulation for the privilege of investing in the U.S. oilpatch is discovered, it is my solemn pledge that a sequel will include a rebuttal to this book.

II
(Ultimately Nothing Matters, And So What If It Did ?)

To all the individuals and corporate entities in this book, who contributed to my pain and sometimes my gain, and recognize themselves, I have one message. It is borrowed from an inspirational book called *The Joy Of Not Knowing It All*. Regardless of the past, one can choose to create a rewarding future with determination and presence of mind. As a survivor of TORN IN THE USA , I subscribe to the prophecy:

Ultimately Nothing Matters, And So What If It Did ?

WHERE ARE THEY NOW?

Alphabetical listing and brief personal history of Canadian reviewers and/ or input contributors.

Atkinson,T.;
P. Geol.

Manager of Acquisitions, Ulster Petroleums Ltd.
Born Sault Ste. Marie, Ontario 1955-03-30.
Eighteen years oil industry experience.

Baird, H.J. (Hank);
P. Eng., P. Geol.

Independent Petroleum Engineering Consultant.
Born Castor, Alberta 1951-09-06.
Twenty-three years oil industry experience.

Bender, Thomas M. M. (Mac);
CMA

Consulting Joint Venture Auditor, Bender Management Ltd.
Born Calgary, Alberta 1941-04-15.
Thirty-five years oil industry experience, eighteen in Joint Venture auditing.

Boddy, Wayne;
P. Eng.

Consultant, Calgary.

Bowens, Richard;
Ph. D.

Resides in Calgary.

Brown, Kathy;

Support Staff, Calgary insurance agency.
Born and raised in Calgary.
Twenty-four years researching Civil War history.

Chinneck, Charles G.;
P. Eng.

Retired Petroleum Engineer.
Born Edmonton, Alberta 1928-09-23.
Resides in Calgary.

Cox, Bob;

Senior Landman, Poco Petroleums Ltd.
Born Kimberly, British Columbia 1941-05-30.
Twenty-nine years oil industry experience.

Cooke, Michael S. P.;
B.A. (Economics), MBA

President & CEO, Brooke Capital Corporation, President & CEO, Canadaian Conquest Exploration Inc.
Born Karuizawa, Japan 1949-07-08.
Twenty-two years corporate banking and oil industry experience.

Dearlove, Frank;

Resides in Calgary.

Freeman, Geoffrey W.;
P. Eng.

Industrial Minerals Consultant, Newfoundland.
Born St. John's, Newfoundland 1952-06-24.

Gorkoff, T. H. (Tom);
P. Eng.

Resides in Calgary.

Harrison, W. R. (Bill);

Resides in Calgary.

Hecht, John S.   Controller, Grad & Walker Energy Corporation.
Born Lacombe, Alberta 1956-01-20.
Twenty years oil and gas industry experience.

Kwan, Daisy   Accounting Manager, junior oil and gas company, Calgary.

Layton, David B.;
B. SC   Owner/Operator of Wildrose Charters and Sailing School, Calgary,
Owner/Operator of Straight Talk Safety and Environmental Training.
Born and raised Calgarian.
Early retirement from Shell in 1994.

Leeson, Neil V.;
P. Eng.   Consulting Petroleum Engineer, RESULTS USA.
Born Halifax, Nova Scotia 1949-09-19.
Twenty years oil industry experience.

MacGregor, Ken R.;
P. Eng.   President & CEO, Panorama Resources Ltd.
Born Ottawa, Ontario 1941-05-19.
Thirty years private and public oil industry experience.

Malo, Tim L.;   Lawyer, Sole-Practitioner, Calgary.
Born Calgary, Alberta 1954-10-13.
Twenty years oil industry experience.

Mitton, Rodney D.;
B. Comm., CA   Partner in a venture capital enterprise, Calgary.
Born and raised in Moose Jaw, Saskatchewan.
Eighteen years oil industry experience

Nixon, Richard J.;   President, Cord Oil & Gas Management Limited,
President, In House Software Limited.

Olson, Dennis J.;
P. Eng.   Resides in Calgary.

Studer, Ned;
CMA   Treasurer, Startech Energy Inc.
Born Brooks, Alberta 1948-08-03.
Thirty years oil industry experience.

Seaton, Thomas J.;   President of executive search firm, T. J. Seaton Management Inc.
Born Poznan, Poland 1950-08-29.

Thiessen, Neil;
P. Geol.   Vice President Exploration, Merit Energy Ltd.
Born in Saskatchewan.
Twenty-four years oil industry experience.

Williamson, Art;
P. Eng.   Vice President Operations, Anderson Exploration Ltd.
Born Fargo, North Dakota 1940-08-18.
Thirty-two years oil and gas operations experience.

GLOSSARY

On this and the following pages is a compilation of terms used in my book. Critical definitions were defined within the preceding episodes as they occurred, therefore some duplication exists.

AAPL: American Association of Petroleum Landmen

Acidize (Acid Treatment): Treatment of oil-bearing formations by chemical reaction with acid to increase production. Acid is injected into the formation under pressure, etching the rock and bringing about an enlargement of the pore spaces and passages through which the reservoir fluids flow. After time under pressure, it is pumped out. Well is then swabbed and put back into production. Chemical inhibitors and additives are combined to serve various purposes, such as corrosion prevention.

Acre-foot (Acre-ft): Unit of volume used in reservoir analysis equivalent to the volume necessary to cover one acre to a depth of one foot

Aeration (Aerate): Technique of injecting air or gas into a drilling fluid (mud) to reduce the density of the fluid.

AFE: Abbreviation for Authority For Expenditure. Estimate of the cost of an operation as prepared by the Operator and submitted to the non - operators for approval prior to commencement of the operation.

Affidavit: A sworn statement in writing made under oath or on affirmation before an authorized magistrate or officer.

Air Drilling: Method of rotary drilling that uses air as the circulation medium. Penetration rate is increased appreciably over conventional mud drilling but is inefficient when penetrating water bearing formations.

Amine: Various compounds derived from ammonia, valuable in sweetening natural gas to remove acid components.

Annual Report: Representation, to the public and shareholders, of a company's yearly progress and highlights of activity, including financial summaries.

API: American Petroleum Institute. Leading standardizing organization on oil-field drilling and production equipment. Also an oil field expression, indicating a job is being done properly by code.

API Gravity: Measure of the gravity of liquid petroleum products, derived from specific gravity, and expressed in degrees. A specific gravity of 1.0 is equivalent to 10^0 API.

Appellate Brief: Formal request to a Court to review the judgement of another tribunal.

Aquifer: A rock that contains water. In a water-drive reservoir, it is that portion of the reservoir that contains the water.

Artificial Lift: Any method to raise oil to the surface through a well after reservoir pressure has declined to the point at which the well no longer produces by natural energy. Sucker-rod pumps, hydraulic (triplex) pumps, submersible pumps, and gas lift (Plunger Lift) are examples.

ATC: Abbreviation for Air Traffic Control

Audit: Formal and methodical examination and review of books in order to verify an account status.

Barrel (bbl or BBL): Unit of measure of volume for petroleum products. One bbl equals 42 U.S. gallons (gals), 35 imperial gals, or 0.1589873 M^3.

Barrels Per Day (BPD, bpd, B/D, b/d): Measure of the oil, water, or condensate rate of the flow of a well per day.

Basin: Synclinal structure in the subsurface, formerly the bed of an ancient sea. Good prospects for exploration as they are composed of sedimentary rock and provide traps for hydrocarbons.

BCF (bcf): Abbreviation for billions cubic feet of gas.

BLM: Abbreviation for the Bureau of Land Management, a federal agency responsible for monitoring and managing energy resources.

Blow-out: Uncontrolled flow of downhole gas, oil, or other well fluids to atmosphere. A well blows out when formation pressure exceeds the pressure being applied to it by the column of drilling fluid and measures are not taken to rectify this situation.

Bottom-hole: Descriptive of the lowest or deepest part of a well.

Breach Of Contract: Failure without legal excuse to perform any promise which forms the whole or part of agreed upon terms of a contract.

Bridge Plug: Downhole tool (composed primarily of slips, a mandrel, and a rubber sealing element) that is run and set in casing to isolate a lower zone while testing an upper section.

British Thermal Unit (BTU): Measure of heat energy based on the amount of heat required to raise the temperature of one pound of water one degree Fahrenheit.

BS&W: Abbreviation for basic sediment and water (water and other extraneous material) present in crude oil. Must be kept quite low before pipelines will accept the oil for delivery to refinery, usually maximum 5 percent.

Breccia: Rock made up of highly angular coarse fragments. May be sedimentary or formed by crushing or grinding along faults.

Build-up Test: Test in which the well is shut in for a prescribed period of time and a bottom-hole pressure bomb run in the well to record increases or decreases in pressure. From this data and the knowledge of nearby well pressures, effective drainage radius or presence of permeability barriers may be ascertained.

Cable-Tool Drilling: Percussion method of drilling whereby a heavy bit makes hole by a pounding action. Largely replaced by rotary drilling.

Carbonate Rock: Sedimentary rock that is primarily composed of calcium carbonate (limestone) or calcium magnesium carbonate (dolomite).

Carried Interest: Agreement between tow or more partners in the working interest whereby one party (carried interest) does not share in the working interest revenue until a certain amount of money has been recovered by the other party (carrying party). Normally the carrying party advances all of the development costs of the carried party.

Cased Hole: Wellbore in which casing has been run.

Cash Call: Managing Partner's request for each participant's share of anticipated costs of a capital project in advance of the work commencing. In the event of cost overruns, a Supplemental Cash Call is submitted for payment after the fact.

Cash Flow: Measure of corporate worth that consists of net income after taxes.

Casing: Steel pipe placed in a well to prevent the wall of the hole from caving during drilling and to provide a means of extracting production.

Casinghead Gas: Gas produced in association with oil.

Casing Point: Depth at which decision is made to set casing and complete the well.

Cavernous Formation: Rock formation that contains large, open spaces, usually the result of dissolving by formation waters that may, or may not, still be present.

Caving: The collapse of the walls of the wellbore.

Cement Bond: Adherence of casing to cement and cement to formation. Good bond is desirable prior to completion.

Cement Bond Log: An acoustic survey or sonic logging method that records the quality of hardness of cement in the annulus between the casing and formation. Well bonded casing shows a fast transit time of an acoustic signal.

Cement Casing: To fill the annulus between casing and hole with cement to prevent fluid migration between permeable zones; also to support the casing.

Cenozoic: Geologic era during the Tertiary/Quaternary period lasting 66.4 million years, beginning with the present. Includes Miocene and Oligocene stages referred to in Episode 14.

Clastic Rocks: Consolidated sedimentary rock composed of the cemented fragments broken from pre-existing rocks of any origin by chemical or mechanical weathering (conglomerate, sandstone, shale).

Closing (Deal Closed): Time at which a transaction is finally consummated. Seller conveys title and buyer fully pays the purchase price.

Commercial Production: Production of a sufficient quantity of oil or gas to justify keeping the well in production.

Common Carrier (Gas): An individual or corporation undertaking to transport gas, owned by others, to a buyer for compensation.

Condensate: Also known as distillate. Normally in the vapor phase in gas reservoirs of great depth and high pressure. Condenses as reservoir pressure is reduced to produce a light hydrocarbon liquid.

Conglomerate: Sedimentary rock composed of pebbles of various sizes held together by cementing material.

Contempt of Court: Any act which is calculated to embarrass, hinder, or obstruct Court in administration of justice or which is calculated to lessen its authority or dignity.

Controller: Chief accounting officer of a corporation with financial authority.

Core: Cylindrical sample taken from the formation for purposes of examination by a special coring device.

Core Analysis: Study of a core in a laboratory to determine the following formation properties: porosity, permeability, fluid content, angle of dip, geological age, lithology, and probable productivity.

CPA: Abbreviation for Certified Public Accountant.

Cross Section: Profile portraying an interpretation of a vertical section of the earth explored by geophysical and/or geological methods.

Crown Land: Land owned by government (Federal or Provincial in Canada).

Cuttings: Fragments of rock dislodged by the bit, brought to the surface in the drilling mud, washed and dried, then given to the geologist for study.

Daily Drilling Report: Record made each day of all important occurrences on a working rig.

D&A: Abbreviation for dry and abandoned; used in drilling reports.

Darcy: Unit of measure of permeability. The ease with which rock transmits fluids. The permeability of reservoir rocks is usually of such small magnitude that it must be measured in millidarcies (1/1000 darcy).

Defendant: Person required to make answer in a legal action or suit.

Degrees API: Unit of measurement of the American Petroleum Institute that indicates the weight, or gravity, of oil.

Deposition: Testimony taken down in writing under oath.

Depositional Environment: Conditions under which a series of rocks were laid down, such as wind-borne, river-borne, ocean-borne, deltaic where river entered the sea), and interdeltaic (between river deltas).

Desk and Derrick Club: Organization of secretaries, clerks, etc., (usually women) employed in the oil industry, whose purpose is partly educational and partly social.

Development Well (Exploitation Well): A well drilled in proven territory in a field for the purpose of completing the desired pattern of production.

Deviation: Inclination of the wellbore from the vertical. The angle of deviation or drift is the angle in degrees, taken at one or several points, that shows the deviation from the vertical as revealed by a deviation survey.

Discovery Well: First oil or gas well drilled in a new field that reveals the actual presence of a petroleum-bearing reservoir.

Disposal Well: Well drilled or used for disposal of brines or other fluids to prevent contamination of the surface by such wastes.

Division Order: Instructions, signed by all interests, to the oil and gas purchaser showing how the purchase price is to be divided. All money due the working interest is normally paid to the Operator who, in turn, apportions it in accordance with the interests held.

Docket (Agenda): A list of legal causes to be tried; a formal abridged record of the proceedings in a legal action; a register of such records.

Dolomite: Type of sedimentary rock similar to limestone but rich in magnesium carbonate. Often found as a reservoir rock for petroleum.

Drainage: Migration of oil or gas in a reservoir toward a wellbore due to the pressure reduction caused by the well's penetration of the reservoir.

Drainage Radius: Area of a reservoir in which a single well serves as a point for drainage of reservoir fluids.

Drilling Break: Sudden increase in the rate of penetration by the drill bit, possibly indicating penetration of a high pressure zone and high risk of blowouts.

Drilling Mud: A suspension, generally aqueous, used in rotary drilling and pumped down the drill pipe to seal off porous zones and to counter-balance the pressure of oil and gas. Consists of various substances in a finely divided state, among which bentonite and barite are common.

Drilling Prognosis: A forecast of expected rock formations to be encountered, the depths at which the drill bit will penetrate each formation, and any potential hazards such as lost circulation, presence of water, or difficult drilling conditions.

Drill Pipe: In rotary drilling, the heavy, seamless tubing used to rotate the bit and circulate the drilling fluid. Usually come in 30 foot lengths.

Drill Stem Test (DST): A test taken by means of a special testing tool to determine whether or not oil or gas in commercial quantities has been encountered in the well bore. The tool incorporates a packer, valves and/ or ports that may be opened or closed from the surface, and a pressure recording device. It is lowered to bottom on a string of drill pipe and the packer set, isolating the formation to be tested. A port is opened to allow the trapped pressure below the packer to bleed off into the drill pipe, gradually exposing the formation to atmospheric pressure and allowing the well to produce to surface, where well fluids may be sampled and inspected. From the record of pressure readings, a number of facts about the formation may be inferred. This test is universally used to yield useful information and permit continuation of drilling after completion of the DST to explore other possible pay zones.

Drilling Spacing Unit: A unit of the size required or permitted by legislation for the drilling of a well.

Dry Hole Costs: Costs for any well that does not produce oil or gas in commercial quantities.

Dual Completion: A single well from which two separate formations may be produced at the same time. Most common method of segregating production from each zone is by running a tubing string with a packer inside the production casing, with the second zone produced through the annulus.

Election At Casing Point: The decision, after q well has been drilled and tested, to go ahead and set casing and attempt a completion of the well.

Electric Log (Electric Well Log): Record of a well or borehole by lowering electrodes in the hole and measuring various electrical properties of the geological formations traversed to provide identification and determination of the nature and amount of fluids contained and location in terms of depth.

Epoch: Division of geologic time; when capitalized it becomes a formal division of geologic time corresponding to a series of rock and a subdivision of a period.

ERCB: Abbreviation of Energy Resources Conservation Board of Alberta.

Examination for Discovery (Deposition): Testimony of a witness, taken in writing, under oath or affirmation, before some judicial officer in answer to questions or interrogatories.

Expert Witness: One who testifies in Court on a specific topic for which he/she has acquired special skill or knowledge.

Exploration Well: Well drilled in an area where no oil or gas production exists. About one wildcat in nine proves productive, but not necessarily profitable.

Extrusive Rocks: Applied to those igneous rocks derived from magmas or magmatic materials poured out or ejected at the earth's surface.

Facies: General appearance or nature of one part of a rock body as contrasted with other parts.

Farm In: Agreement identical to a farmout agreement, with the operator as the earning party.

Farm-In: To accept a farmout.

Farmout: An agreement whereby the owner of a lease agrees to dispose of a portion of the lease to another party, in return for that other party performing certain acts, such as drilling of a well, under specifically set forth terms and conditions

Fault: Geological term denoting a break in the subsurface strata; a fracture or fracture zone along which there has been displacement of the sides relative to one another parallel to the fracture. Usually results in sealing of an oil bearing formation against a non-porous section and facilitates the accumulation of oil at this point.

Fault Trap (Block): Subsurface hydrocarbon trap in which an impermeable rock layer has been moved opposite the reservoir bed along a fault.

Fiduciary: To hold in trust; one who holds in trust; a trustee.

Fish: Any object left in the wellbore during drilling or workover operations that must be recovered before work can proceed.

Fishing: Operations on the rig for the purpose of retrieving from the well bore sections of pipe, casing, or other items which may have been inadvertently dropped in the hole.

Fishing Tool: Tool designed for the specific purpose of recovering broken or lost equipment from the well.

Flow Meter: Device to measure the amount of fluid or gas moving through pipe. Barton is a brand name.

Foam Drilling (Foam Fracturing): Drilling (Fracturing) technique that uses compressed air or gas, to which a foaming agent has been added, as a circulation medium .

Formation: Bed or deposit composed substantially of the same kinds of rocks throughout; a lithologic unit. In hydrocarbon areas each formation is given a name., sometimes based on the fossils found in the formation.

Formation Damage (Skin): Reduction of permeability in a reservoir rock arising from the invasion of drilling fluid and treating fluids into the formation adjacent to the wellbore. When quantified, it is often referred to as 'skin'.

Formation Fracturing: Method of stimulating production by increasing the permeability of the producing formation. Under high hydraulic pressure, a fluid (such as acid, water, diesel, crude oil, liquefied petroleum gas, or kerosene) is pumped down through tubing or drill pipe and forced out below a packer into a formation. Pressure causes cracks to open and the fluid penetrates through the cracks. Sand grains, walnut shells, or similar materials (propping agents or proppants) are carried in suspension by the fluid into the cracks. When pressure is released at the surface, fluids return to the wellbore. Cracks partially close on the proppant, leaving channels for gas and fluids to flow around them to the well.

Formation Water (Connate Water): Water originally in place in the pore spaces of a formation from the time the formation was laid down.

Fracture: Crack or crevice in the formation, either induced or inherent.

Freehold Land: Land not owned by the Crown (Government).

Gas Chart: Chronological well record (usually seven day periods) of gas rates and pressures inscribed by coloured pens on circular graph paper fastened to a rotating clock. Later integrated with the orifice size in the flow meter to provide a continuous readout of numerical values.

Gas-Cut Mud: Drilling mud characterized by fluffy texture and reduced density due to the retention of entrained gas from the formation traversed by drilling.

Gas-Oil Ratio (GOR): Measure of the volume of gas produced with the oil.

Gas Show: Gas that appears in the drilling-fluid returns, indicating the presence of a gas zone.

Gathering Line: A pipeline, usually small diameter, used to gather oil and gas from the producing field to a point on a main pipeline.

Gathering System: Pipelines and other equipment required to transport oil, gas, and/or water from the wells to a central point (battery) where the accessory equipment required to deliver a clean and saleable product, to a market or pipeline, is located. Includes separators, compressors, treaters, storage tanks, dehydrators, and associated equipment.

Geochemical: Relative and absolute abundance of elements and atomic species in the earth which are governed by principles for the distribution and migration of the individual elements.

Geologist: Scientist whose duties consist of procurement and interpretation of data pertaining to the strata of the earth's crust

Geology: Science that relates to the study of the structure, origin, history, and development of the earth and its inhabitants as revealed in the study of rocks, structures, and fossils.

Good Faith: Honesty of intention, not taking unconscionable advantage of another and freedom from knowledge of circumstances which would require investigation.

Graben: Geologic term for a block of the earth's crust, generally long compared to its width, that has moved downward between two faults.

Granite: Igneous rock composed primarily of feldspar, quartz, and mica. It does not contain petroleum.

Gravity Drainage: Movement of fluids in the reservoir toward the wellbore due to the force of gravity. In the absence of water drive or gas drive, it is an important source of energy to produce hydrocarbons.

Gross Overriding Royalty (GORR): Portion of proceeds from the sale of oil and/or gas that is paid to a lessor and is free of all development and operating expenses.

Horizontal Separator: see separator

Horst: Geological term referring to a block of the earth's crust that has been raised upward between two faults (opposite of a graben).

Hydraulic Pumping (Triplex): Method of pumping oil from wells using a downhole pump without sucker rods. Consists essentially of two reciprocating pumps coupled together and located in the well. One functions as an engine and serves to drive the other pump - the production pump. Surface power is supplied by a standard, engine- driven pump. The engine end is operated by heated formation water (power water) under pressure, the water being drawn from a power water tank by a triplex plunger pump. Either a single string of tubing or two parallel strings may be utilized. With a single string, power water is pumped down the tubing to the pump, which is seated in the string, and the mixture of power water and produced fluid is returned through the casing-tubing annulus. With two parallel strings, one string supplies power water to the pump, while the other returns exhaust and produced fluid to surface. It is efficient for lifting large volumes at depths greater than 10000 feet.

Hydrothermal: An adjective applied to heated or hot aqueous-rich solutions, to the processes in which they are concerned, and to the rocks, ore deposits, and alteration products produced by them.

Igneous Rock: A rock mass formed by the solidification of molten material injected into the earth's crust or extended out on its surface, such as granite.

In-kind: The taking by an owner of his share of gas or liquids for separate marketing or disposition, rather than permitting his share to be disposed of jointly with gas or liquids belonging to other owners.

Intrusive Rocks: Igneous rocks which have solidified from magmas that have been injected into older rocks at depth without reaching the surface.

Infill Well: Well drilled between known producing wells to better exploit the reservoir.

Initial Potential (IP): Initial production recorded after testing operations and recovery of load oil. Approximates closely the maximum productivity at completion without subsequent reservoir damage.

Intermediate Casing String: The string of casing set in a well after the surface casing. Its purpose is to keep the hole from caving and to afford a strong string of pipe to which blow-out preventers can be attached.

Intrusive Rock: An igneous rock , while in the molten state, has penetrated into or between other rocks and has solidified.

Invaded Zone: Area within a permeable rock around a wellbore into which filtrate (usually water) from the drilling mud has passed, with the consequent partial or total displacement of fluids originally present in the zone.

Isopach Map: Geological map of subsurface strata showing the varying thickness of a formation underlying an area. Widely used in reserve calculations, secondary recovery planning, and general exploitation work.

Joint Interest (Venture) Billings (JIB): Statement (usually monthly) of operational costs incurred by the Operator on oil and gas properties and proportioned to all JOA parties.

Joint Operating (Venture) Agreement (JOA): Contract between two or more parties which governs the relationship of those parties as it relates to a specific, identifiable, tract of land.

Kick: Entry of gas, oil, or water into the wellbore. Occurs because pressure exerted by the column of drilling fluid is not great enough to overcome the pressure exerted by the fluids in the drilled formation. If not addressed promptly to kill the well, a blow-out will occur.

Landman: Person in the petroleum industry who negotiates with land owners for oil and gas leases, option, minerals and royalties, and with other producers for joint operations relative to production in a field.

Lease: Legal document executed between the landowner or lessor and another party as lessee that grants the right to exploit the premises for minerals. Also refers to a place where producing wells and batteries are located.

Lease Rentals: Annual rental paid by the lessor by the lessee in lieu of oil or gas production during the life of the lease.

Lessee: Recipient of an oil and gas lease.

Lessor: Conveyor of an oil and gas lease.

Letter Agreement: Instrument which is evidence of a manifestation of mutual assent on the part of two or more persons as to the substance of a Contract.

Liquefied Natural Gas (LNG): A liquid composed chiefly of natural gas (mostly methane). Must be put under low temperature and high pressure in order to liquefy it for transportation where a pipeline is not feasible.

Liquefied Petroleum Gas (LNG): A mixture of heavier, gaseous, paraffinic hydrocarbons (mostly butane and propane). Easily liquefied at moderate pressures and may be transported as liquids but converted to gases on release of pressure.

Lithology: Expresses the individual character of rocks in terms of mineral composition, structure, etc. or refers to the study of rocks.

Load Oil: Crude or refined oil used in fracturing a formation to stimulate a well, as distinguished from the oil that is normally produced by the well.

Log: A systematic recording of data. Many different logs are run in wells being drilled in order to obtain various characteristics of formations.

Lost Circulation (Lost Returns): Loss of quantities of whole mud to a formation, usually cavernous, fissured, or coarsely permeable beds, evidenced by the complete or partial failure of the mud to return to the surface as it is being circulated in the hole. An abnormal condition when drilling a well, and usually every attempt is made to regain circulation. It can lead to a blow-out and, in general, reduces efficiency of the drilling operation.

LSD: Abbreviation for Legal Subdivision. One of sixteen subdivisions of a 640 acre section of land.

Magmatic: Of, pertaining to, or derived from magma (hot, fluid matter within the earth's crust, which is capable of intrusion or extrusion and produces igneous rocks by cooling).

Marginal Well: A well approaching depletion of desired natural resource to the extent that any profit from its continued production is doubtful.

Mineral Right: Ownership of the minerals under a given surface with the right to mine and remove them. It may be separated from the surface ownership.

Mcf (MCF): Abbreviation for 1000 cubic feet of gas produced, transmitted, or consumed in a given period of time.

Mechanical Cutter: A fishing tool, containing metal-cutting knives, lowered into the inside (or over the outside) of a length of pipe stuck in the hole, in order to cut the pipe. The severed portion then can be brought back to surface.

Metamorphic Rock: Rock derived from pre-existing rocks by mineralogical, chemical, and structural alterations due to processes operating within the earth's crust. The change is sufficient to produce a new rock. Marble is an example.

MMcf (MMCF) or **MMscf** (MMSCF): Abbreviation for 1,000,000 cubic feet;

measurement of large quantities of gas. ('S' refers to standard conditions of 600 F and 14.7 psi)

MMS: Abbreviation for Minerals Management Service, a Federal natural resource monitoring and conservation agency in the U.S.

Motion for Delay: Motion to obstruct, put off, postpone, defer.

Motion for Mistrial: Motion to declare an erroneous, invalid, or nugatory trial, either before or during trial.

Motion (Argument) **to Dismiss:** Motion requiring a complaint be dismissed because it does not state a claim for which the law provides a remedy, or is in some other way legally insufficient.

Mud: The liquid that is circulated through the wellbore during rotary drilling and workover operations to bring cuttings to the surface, cool and lubricate the bit and drill stem, protect against blowouts by holding back subsurface pressures, and depositing a mud cake on the wall of the borehole to prevent loss of fluids to the formation..

Mud Analysis: Examination and testing of the drilling mud to determine its physical and chemical properties.

Mud Engineer: A specialist in drilling fluids who has knowledge of chemistry, engineering, and the behavior of drilling fluids.

Mud Log: Record of information derived from examination of drilling fluid and drill-bit cuttings

Mud Logging: Recording information derived from examination and analysis of mud circulated out of the hole and drill-bit cuttings. A portion of the mud is diverted through a gas-detecting device and examined further under ultraviolet light for the purpose of detecting the presence of oil or gas., usually in a portable laboratory set up at the well.

Mud Pit (Settling Pit): Pit near the drilling rig into which mud flows and heavy solids are given the opportunity to settle out.

Natural Gas Liquids: Liquid hydrocarbon mixtures which are gaseous in the reservoir but are recoverable by condensation or absorption. natural gasoline, condensate, and liquefied petroleum gases fall in this category.

NEB: Abbreviation for National Energy Board, a Federal natural resource monitoring and conservation agency in Canada.

Net Present Value: Present value of all future returns discounted back to time zero at the average opportunity rate of the company.

Net Production: Amount of oil produced by a well or lease, exclusive of its BS & W content. A company's net production is also called working interest oil.

Non Associated Gas: Under initial reservoir conditions, the gas is in a single phase. If there are hydrocarbons vaporized in the gas which are recoverable on the surface, the reservoir is called gas-condensate.

Non-operator: Party having an interest in a lease who allows another participant to conduct the development and operation of the property in the mutual interest of all participants.

Notary Public: Individual empowered by statute to administer oaths and take affidavits, affirmations, and declarations requiring his signature and notarial seal.

Offset Well: Well drilled on tract of land adjacent to another well in the same pool.

Oilpatch: A colloquial expression for an oilfield. If one goes to an oilfield, then one goes to the oilpatch.

Oil Trap: Reservoir rock containing petroleum that is trapped or enclosed by an impermeable rock in such manner that migration and escape of the contained hydrocarbons is prevented.

Oil-Water Contact: Point or plane where the bottom of an oil sand contacts the top of a water sand in a reservoir. Sometimes termed the oil-water interface.

Open Hole: Any wellbore in which casing has not been set.

Open Hole Completion: Method of preparing a well for production in which no production casing or liner is set opposite the producing formation. Reservoir fluids flow unrestricted into the open wellbore.

Operator: Person or company, whether proprietor or lessee, actually operating a well or lease.

Overburden: Strata of rock that lie above the stratum of interest.

Overburden Pressure: Pressure exerted by the overburden on the formation of interest.

Overriding Royalty (ORR): An interest which is carved out of the lessee's working interest. It entitles its owner to a fraction of the production, subject only to the deduction s specified in the agreement between the parties.

Overthrust: A thrust fault with low dip and large net slip, generally measured in miles.

P & A: Abbreviation for plugged and abandoned.; placing cement plugs in a dry hole to abandon it.

P & NG Rights: Abbreviation for Petroleum and Natural Gas Rights

Packer: Downhole equipment consisting essentially of a sealing device, a holding or setting device, and an inside passage for fluids. Used to block the flow of fluids through the annular space between the tubing and the wall of the wellbore by sealing off the space between them. Classified according to their configuration, use, and method of setting and whether they are retrievable (removed when necessary) or permanent (must be milled or drilled out and thus destroyed).

Paleozoic (Palaeozoic): Geologic era during the (in order of youngest to oldest) Permian, Pennsylvanian, Mississippian, Devonian, Silurian, Ordovician, and Cambrian periods and lasting 325 million years, beginning 245 million years ago. Includes most of the stages referred to in Episode 14.

Pay Sand (Pay Zone): The producing, or drilling objective, formation.

Payout: That point in time when the revenue from a well exceeds the costs to drill and operate that well; i.e. when the well begins to show a profit.

Perf: Abbreviation for perforated interval or the operation 'perforated'.

Perforate: To pierce the casing wall and cement for the purpose of providing holes through which formation fluids may enter. Accomplished by lowering into the well a perforating gun, or perforator, that fires bullets or shaped charges electrically from the surface.

Permeability: Measure of the ease with which fluids can flow through a porous rock. The ability of fluid to flow within the interconnected pore network of a porous medium.

Petrophysics: Study of the properties of rocks and their relationship to the fluids they contain in both the static and flowing states. Includes properties such as porosity, permeability, fluid saturation, electrical conductivity of both rock and fluid, pore structure , and radioactivity.

Plaintiff: The party who commences a personal action or lawsuit to obtain a remedy for injury to his/her rights.

Plan of Reorganization: Act or process of organizing again or anew. Under Chapter 11, it involves preparation of a plan of reorganization by a bankruptcy trustee and submission thereof to the Court. After a hearing, the Court determines the feasibility of such plan, followed by approval if it finds such plan feasible and proper.

Plug Back: To place cement in or near the bottom of a well for the purposes of excluding bottom water, side-tracking, or producing from a formation already drilled through. Also can be accomplished by means of a mechanical plug set by wire line, tubing, or drill pipe.

Porosity: The ratio of the aggregate volume of interstices in a rock or soil to its total volume, stated as a percentage.

Primary Term: Specified number of years granted to a lessee to perform all acts necessary and incident to the ultimate objective of locating and removing hydrocarbons and minerals. Remains in force as long thereafter as production is obtained from the property.

Production: That phase of the petroleum industry that has to do with bringing the well fluids to the surface and separating them, followed by storing, gauging, and preparing the product for market.

Pumper: Oil company employee or contractor who attends to producing wells for the purpose of ensuring steady production, preparing reports, testing, gauging, etc.

Pumping Unit: Machine that imparts the reciprocating motion to a string of sucker rods extending to a positive-displacement pump at the bottom of the well. Usually a beam arrangement driven by a crank attached to a speed reducer.

Quitclaim (Quit Claim): Legal deed to convey, release or relinquish a legal claim to other party.

Rathole: A hole of a diameter smaller than the main hole that is drilled in the bottom of the main hole.

Raw Gas: An unrefined gas as it exists from the reservoir, prior to entering the refinery or processing operation.

Receiver Manager (Trustee): Someone who holds the legal title to property, or a portion thereof, in trust for the benefit of another. With the title go specified powers and duties relating to the property, called fiduciary responsibilities.

Recovery Factor: The percentage of oil or gas in place in the reservoir that ultimately can be withdrawn by primary and/or secondary techniques.

Reef: Type of reservoir trap composed of rock (usually limestone) formed from the bodies of marine plants and animals.

Reserve Report: A report of proven and probable hydrocarbon assets compiled from rigorous application of established and proven engineering methods. The accuracy of the reserve figures is in direct proportion to the amount and quality of data available.

Reserves: The unproduced but recoverable oil or gas in place in a formation that has been proved by production.

Reservoir: A subsurface, porous, and permeable rock body in which oil and/or gas is stored; primarily limestone, sandstone, dolomites, or combinations.

Reverse Circulation: Return of drilling fluid through the drill stem, or tubing, to the surface after being pumped down the annulus in reaction to special problems, such as hole caving (versus normal circulation down the drill stem and upward through the annular space surrounding the drill stem).

Right Of First Refusal: Right to meet terms of any offer or proposed contract before it is executed; i.e. first opportunity to purchase when it becomes available.

Rope Socket: Device for securing the end of a steel cable into a connecting piece, such as a clovis, hook, or chain.

Rotary Drilling: Drilling method where a hole is drilled by a rotating bit to which a downward force is applied. Bit is fastened to and rotated by the drill stem, which also provides a passageway through which the drilling fluid is circulated. Drill pipe joints are added as drilling deepens.

Roustabout: A labourer who assists the foreman in general duties around wells and property of the producing company.

Royalty: That part of oil, gas, or minerals paid by the lessee (producer) to the lessor (conveyor of lease) or to one who has acquired possession of the royalty rights. Based on a certain percentage of the gross production from the property.

Run Ticket: A record of oil (water) transferred from the producer's storage tank to the pipeline or refinery (disposal well). Basic legal instrument by which the lease (disposal well) operator is paid for oil produced and sold (water injected).

Sack (Sax or Sx): Volume measure. Cement is sold in sacks (bags) of 94 pounds or 1 ft3 .

Saltwater Disposal: Method and system for disposal of salt water produced with crude oil. typical system consists of collection centers (or pipelines) to gather the water from several wells, central treating facility where water is conditioned to remove scale or corrosion forming agents, and a disposal well to inject the treated water into a suitable formation.

Salvage Value: Resale value of tangible equipment used on a lease.

Sample Log: Graphic representation of the rock formations penetrated by drilling that is prepared by the geologist from samples and cores.

Samples: Well cuttings obtained at definite footage intervals during drilling. From examination, the geologist determines rock type, formation being drilled, formation tops, and indications of oil and/or gas content.

Sandstone: A detrital, sedimentary rock consisting of individual grains of sand (mostly quartz) cemented together by silica, calcium carbonate, iron oxide, etc. Common rock for petroleum and water accumulations.

Sediment: Matter that settles to the bottom of a liquid or tank bottoms. Buried layers of sedimentary rock are often referred to as sediments.

Sedimentary Basin: Geological depressed area with thick sediments in the interior and thinner sediments at the edges.

Sedimentary Rock: Rock composed of materials transported to their present position by wind or water. Examples are sandstone, shale, and limestone.

Seismic: A geophysical exploration method based on measurement of wave fronts propagated by dynamite explosions.

Separator: An item of production equipment used to isolate the liquid components of the well stream from the gaseous components. May be horizontal or vertical, cylindrical or spherical vessels. separation is accomplished principally by gravity, the heavier liquids falling to the bottom and gas rising to the top. Gas leaves from the top of the separator, oil from the bottom. A float valve or other liquid-level control regulates the level of oil in the bottom of the separator.

Severance Tax: Paid on production from privately owned and State-controlled acreage in most States and based on standard rates that differ according to the type of hydrocarbons.

Shale: A fine-grained sedimentary rock composed of silt and clay-sized particles. Ranges in composition from pure clays to calcareous or siliceous clays. It is the most frequently occurring sedimentary rock.

Shut-in Well: A well, usually a gas well, which is shut-in for lack of market or is waiting on a pipeline connection.

Skin: Amount of formation damage (pressure drop) caused by the invasion of foreign substances into the exposed section adjacent to the wellbore during drilling and completion operations. Expressed in dimensionless units, a positive value denoting formation damage and a negative value indicating improvement.

Solution Gas: Lighter hydrocarbons that exist as a liquid under reservoir conditions but that change to a gas when the reservoir is produced.

Sonde: Logging tool device that senses and transmits formation data.

Sour Gas: A natural gas containing objectionable amounts of hydrogen sulphide.

Source Rock: Geological formation in which oil, gas, and/or other minerals originate.

Specific Gravity: Ratio of the mass of a body to the mass of an equal volume of water at a specified temperature.

Spot Market, Gas: Market for gas sellers or brokers to accommodate buyers, often on a one time basis, whose normal supply has been interrupted or inadequate.

Spud: To commence actual drilling operations to begin the hole.

Squeeze Cementing: Forcing of cement slurry by pressure to specified points in a well for the purpose of obtaining seals at the point of squeeze to isolate a formation, seal off water or permeable zone, and repair casing leaks.

STB: Abbreviation for stock tank barrel stored at atmospheric surface conditions in a stock tank. Lacks much of the dissolved gas at reservoir temperature and pressure conditions.

Statement of Claim: Original or initial pleading by which an action for relief is commenced under codes or Rules of Civil Procedure

Stimulation: Any of several processes (acidizing, formation fracturing,) to enlarge old channels or create new ones in the producing formation of a well.

Storage Tank: Tank for storing and gauging oil pending transfer to a pipeline or buyer.

Structural Trap: Hydrocarbon trap in which the trap is formed because of deformation (folding or faulting) of the rock layer that contains the hydrocarbons.

Structure: Geologic term that refers to the rock formation of interest.

Stuck Pipe: Drill pipe, drill collars, casing, or tubing that has inadvertently become immobile in the hole.

Stuffing Box: A packing gland screwed in the top of the wellhead through which the polished rod operates on a pumping well. It prevents the escape of oil, diverting it into a side outlet to which is connected the flow line leading to the oil and gas separator or field storage tank.

Subterfuge: Deception by artifice or stratagem in order to conceal, escape, or evade.

Suspended Well: Any oil or gas well that has been identified as productive but is yet to be developed or is waiting on improved economics for resumption.

Swab: To operate a swab on a wireline to bring well fluids to the surface when the well does not flow naturally. Temporary operation to determine whether or not the well can be made to flow. If not, a pumping unit must be installed as a permanent lifting device to lift oil to surface.

Take or Pay (TOP) **Contract:** An agreement in which a buyer of gas agrees to pay for the purchase of a minimum quantity over a period of time regardless of whether or not the buyer actually 'takes' the purchased gas.

Tank Battery: Group of production tanks located at a point in the field for the storage of crude oil.

Thief Sand: A formation that takes in drilling fluid or produced hydrocarbons as the fluid is circulated in the well.

Thrust Fault: A reverse fault that is characterized by a low angle of inclination with reference to a horizontal plane.

Total Depth: The maximum depth reached in a well.

Trap: Layers of buried rock strata that are arranged such that petroleum is allowed to accumulate.

Transporter: Carrier, without ownership, of gas or oil for a fee to an end user.

Treater: Vessel in which oil is treated for the removal of BS&W, either by addition of heat, electricity, chemicals, or all three.

Trip Gas: Accumulation of gas, usually a negligible amount, that enters the hole while a trip is being made.

Tubing: Small-diameter pipe that is run into a well to serve as a conduit for the passage of oil and gas to the surface.

Turnkey Contract: Drilling contract that calls for the payment of a stipulated amount to the drilling contractor on completion of the well. The contractor furnishes all the equipment and labour and controls the entire drilling operation independent of any supervision by the operator (owner).

Unconformity: A surface of erosion that separates younger strata from older rocks.

Undeveloped Acreage: Unproved acreage that is possibly productive but not considered proved as there are usually no nearby wells. The only indications of possible oil or gas are taken from regional geological studies and/or general geophysical surveys.

Undivided Interest: A fraction interest in minerals that, when conveyed, gives the new owner that fractional interest in the described tract.

Unsecured Creditor: A debtor who is owed a debt that is not backed by pledged collateral or security agreement.

Valley Fill: Valley underlain by unconsolidated rock waste derived from the erosion of the bordering mountains.

Voir Dire: Preliminary examination to determine the competency of a witness or juror.

Vug: Cavity in a rock, often with a mineral lining of different composition from that of the surrounding rock.

Vugular Porosity: Secondary rock porosity formed by the dissolving of more soluble portions of the rock in waters containing carbonic or other acids.

Watered Out: Descriptive of a well that has gone to water.

Water Encroachment: Movement of water into a producing formation as it is depleted of oil and gas as the result of production.

Wellbore (Borehole): Hole drilled by the bit. May be open (no cased), cased, or both.

Well Permit: Authorization, usually by a government conservation agency, to drill a well. Sometimes required for well deepening or remedial work.

Well Servicing: Descriptive of the work and business of well repair and maintenance.

Wellhead: Equipment used to maintain surface control of a well. It is formed of the casinghead and tubing head. The Christmas tree is affixed to the top of the tubing head.

Wildcat: Well drilled in an area where no oil or gas production exists.

Wire Line (Cable): Rope composed of iron or steel wires twisted into strands that are in turn twisted around a central core of hemp or other fibre to create a rope of great strength having some flexibility.

Withholding Tax: A deduction from oil or gas sale proceeds, to be remitted by the Operator, in the Owner's name, to the taxing authority.

WOR: Abbreviation for water-oil ratio.

Working Interest (Operating Interest) (Leasehold Interest): Interest in an oil and gas lease that includes responsibility for all drilling, development, and operating costs. In revenue calculations, the portion of oil production remaining after deduction of royalty interest.

Workover (Work Over): To perform one or more of a variety of remedial operations on a producing well with the intent of restoring or increasing production.

BIBLIOGRAPHY AND RECOMMENDED READING

A Courthouse At Appomattox; Neil V. Leeson (unpublished, April 1995)

A Type Model For Future Oil And Gas Fields In The Cenozoic Basins Of The Eastern Great Basin; Floyd C. Moulton, Utah Geological Publication 16 (Utah Geological Survey, 1987)

Bacon Flat Well Pays Off For Balcron; Don Lyle, Western Oil World (Hart Publications, March 1993)

Basin and Range May Hold More Big Oil Fields; Henry K. Veal, Herbert D. Duey, Louis C. Bortz, and Norman H. Foster, Oil & Gas Journal (PennWell Publishing Co., April 04, 1988)

Borehole Evaluation and Completion: Carbonate, Volcanic, Clastic Reservoirs of Nevada;
Ted Flanigan, Oil & Gas Journal (PennWell Publishing Co., October 23, 1989)

Civil War Handbook; William H. Price (L.B. Prince Co., Inc, 1961)

FERC Pressing U.S. Gas Pipeline On Take Or pay Affiliates' Roles, Abandonments; Patrick Crow, Oil & Gas Journal (February 15, 1988)

Field Trip Highlights Tremendous Petroleum Potential For Operators In Nevada's Basin And Range Regions; Willis H. Alderman, Western Oil World (Hart Publications, October 1992)

George C. Marshall Museum; (free public brochure, 03/88)

Great Smoky Mountains; (free public brochure - U.S. Department of the Interior National Park Service, 1994)

KRI Resource Nuggets; Lawrance W. McGary, March 1994

Lee Chapel and Museum; (free public brochure)

Lexington, Virginia Historical Facts; (free public brochure)

National Air and Space Museum, Smithsonian Institution; (free public brochure, 04/81)

Nevada Has Faults But The Pay Is Good; Don Lyle, Western Oil World (Hart Publications, April 1990)

Newfound Gap Road Auto Tour; Ed Goldstein (GSMNHA Publishers, 1993 : Phone 423-436-0120)

Official Guide to the Smithsonian; (CBS Publications, 1976)

Smokies Guide; (GSMNHA Publishers, Summer 1996 : Phone 423-436-0120)

Target Ploesti; Leroy W. Newby (Kensington Publishing Corp, 1983)

The 1982 World's Fair Official Guide Book; (Exposition Publishers, 1982)

The Joy Of Not Knowing It All; Ernie J. Zelinski (Visions International Publishing, 1995)

Tour Book - Illinois, Indiana, Ohio; (American Automobile Association, 1995)

Tour Book - Kentucky and Tennessee; (American Automobile Association, 1995)

Tour Book - Mid-Atlantic Area; (American Automobile Association, 1995)

U.S. Air Force Museum, Wright-Patterson AFB, OH; (free public brochure)

Virginia Military Institute Visitor Guide; (free public brochure)

Washington, D.C. Sightseeing Guide; (free public brochure)

Wright Patterson Air Force Base Legacy; (free public brochure, 1981)

PEOPLE, PLACES, EVENTS, and VENUES INDEX

NOTES: (1)Only full names are tabulated. After initial introduction, reference was mostly on a first name basis and therefore excluded from further indexing. (2) Contributors are listed alphabetically Last Name first; all other individuals appear First Name first. (3)Due to frequent use of acronyms and nicknames in referring to oil company and well names, all are excluded to avoid confusion; geographical locations, however, are factual and are indexed.

PHOTO INDEX